Trucking Business and Freight Broker Startup 2023

Blueprint to Successfully Launch & Grow Your Own Trucking and Freight Brokerage Company Using Expert Secrets to Get Up and Running as Fast as Possible

Alexander Sutton

As a way of saying thank you for your purchase, I wanted to offer you access to this amazing book for free: Entrepreneurial Drive

Access the course here: https://tinyurl.com/4fpf6u2n

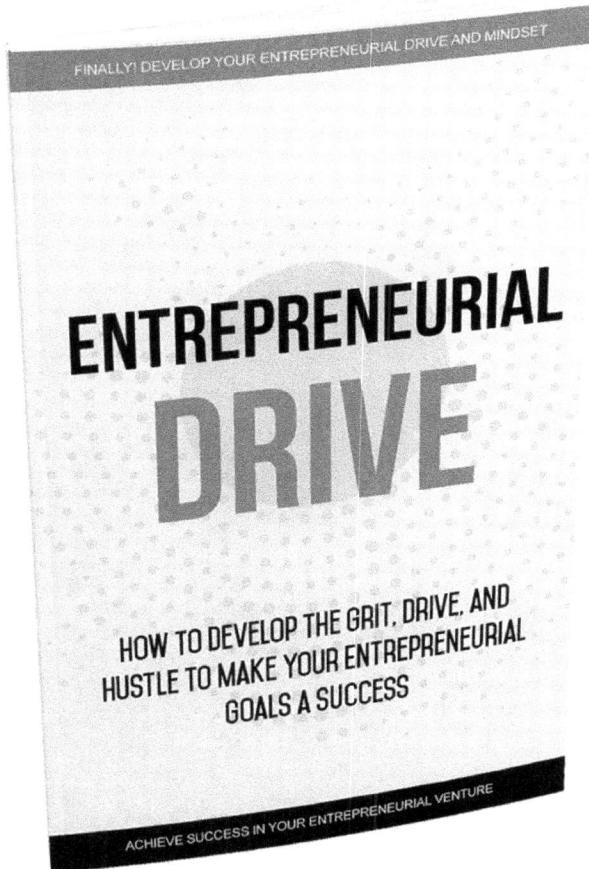

This guide takes you through the characteristics of a gritty person, the habits that gritty people develop, and shows you what you need to do to build your grit to leave your old life and become a successful entrepreneur and turn your dreams into reality.

Contents

Introduction - Trucking Business Startup 2023

Have you ever asked yourself, "How do eCommerce businesses like Amazon, Zara Alibaba, and Hello Fresh move their products from their premises to customers' doorsteps so quickly?" The answer, of course, is with trucks. More people in the country are buying products online in the U.S today than ever before, which is good news for the trucking industry.

Statistics by the American Trucking Associations (ATA) show that in 2020, trucks transported freight weighing 10.23 billion tons. Data also shows a massive shortage of drivers in the U.S. It is estimated that the trucking industry will need 100,000 drivers soon, and subsequently, companies are desperately searching for drivers to meet the demand.

It is inconceivable that an industry with more than 7 million truck drivers can have a shortage of drivers, but that shows you how fast this industry is growing. Therefore, what better time for you to invest in it than now?

Trucking companies help businesses meet their logistics goals. Logistics is the general process of controlling how resources are obtained, stored, and moved to their destination. This function is an important part of any business, whether online or offline. Every business, especially those in the manufacturing industry, should be concerned with how its products are moved along the supply chain.

A new business may not own enough trucks to transport its products to customers all over the country. It will need to hire truckers to deliver goods on its behalf. Timely deliveries by truckers can make customers happy, and they may, in turn, become loyal to the brand. That is why every trucking business worth its salt strives to be efficient and reliable. This is the only way to ensure a steady flow of clients for your trucking business and, consequently, profits.

Indeed, the trucking industry is necessary for maintaining the efficiency of many homes and businesses. For example, ATMs would run out of money without this industry, gas fuel would no longer be available to consumers within two days, manufacturing would stop within hours, and there would be a food shortage of epic proportions within three days. It is essentially recession-proof.

There are also many personal reasons you may want to start a trucking business this instant. You may be bored with your current job, or you want to be your own boss, or you want to stop doing a 9-5 job, or maybe you want to improve your lifestyle.

The good thing about starting this kind of business is that it is easy to start and expand. You will not have to invest much money upfront before generating profits when working in this industry. You can begin as an owner-operator trucking company. You can then scale your business when your profit margin and clientele increase. You will own a fleet of trucks and hire people to drive them when you scale it.

As of February 2021, The U.S Department of Transportation reported that 91.5% of trucking companies own six or fewer trucks. This statistic means that you can still survive in the market even with a few trucks. Hence, no need to worry that you do not have enough capital to buy a large fleet of trucks when you are starting. The industry has also benefited immensely from innovations that make it easy to operate the business.

This book will give you a step-by-step guide that you need to follow when starting a trucking business. If you already know how to drive a commercial truck and have the necessary driving license, writing a business plan is the first thing you need to do. The next step will be to register the business, select a business entity, and create a business name. You will also need to get the permits, licenses, and insurance required. Afterward, you will choose a truck and then get funding.

If you have never worked in the trucking industry before, you will have to know the different types of trucks and ensure that they are always in tip-top shape. Sounds exciting, right? Learning the workings of a big machine like a truck and using it every day to ensure that you reach your destination on time definitely sounds more interesting than being holed up in an office somewhere all day. Besides that, every trip will be like an adventure; you will meet and interact with different people every day, and perhaps some of them could become lifelong friends. You will also visit many other places you might have never seen if you were in a different industry.

Going by this long list of things to do and skills to acquire, you may have realized that starting this kind of business is not something you can accomplish in a day. It requires planning and willingness to learn all the nitty-gritty about the company and the industry as a whole. Once you have established your business, you will also need to know about the changes in the industry so that you can adjust accordingly and survive the competition in the industry.

If you are reading this book, you are already setting yourself up for success. This is because it contains information that has been written after years of experience. We have also identified the best strategies and the most important information that you'll need for this business to be successful.

This book is for you:

- If you are a truck driver and do not want to continue working for someone else.

- If you work an office job and would like to get a share of this billion-dollar industry.

- If you already own a trucking business and would like to learn both how to scale it up and about the best technologies that you need to use as a business owner in this industry.

When you are done reading this book, you will learn a lot to help you become an exceptional trucking business owner. Some of the things that you will learn include:

- Types of trucking businesses.

- How to price your services.

- The types of license and insurance you need to obtain when starting a trucking business.

- The mistakes you and your drivers need to avoid to ensure your business does not go bankrupt.

- How to buy the best trucks that are reliable and affordable.

- How to raise capital to start your business.

If done right, owning a trucking business can help you become financially independent and give you the freedom and time to do the things you love, like traveling or surfing. Anybody can start this business and become successful as long as they have the right information at their disposal. Read on to discover how you can become a part of this fast-growing industry and say goodbye to your financial woes.

Why Should You Invest In The Trucking Industry?

F irst thing's first: let us define what a trucking business is. A trucking business is essentially a transportation business that you operate using a truck. In other words, it involves transporting freight on land. It comprises any company that brings goods, cargo, or people from one place to another.

Some trucks are more suitable for transporting cargo, whereas others are ideal for carrying groups of people. You should ensure that you buy the appropriate truck for the kind of business you want to operate.

Trucks utilize shipping routes to transport goods all over the U.S to carry shipments for different industries. Shipping using trucks enables you to transport small or big shipments and cargo that need special conditions. Shipping with trucks also can be quite affordable, especially if the goods are being picked from a big port like New York City or Los Angeles.

There are many reasons why this is the right time to start a trucking business. These are some of the reasons why it makes sense to do so:

Shortage of drivers

Now is a great time to invest in this industry because of the increasing rates, higher freight demand, and driver shortage. The grim statistics in this industry show that the average age of a truck driver is 55 years. For years now, trucking companies have found it hard to attract young drivers into the industry. Experts cite the age limit for joining this industry as a driver as the greatest obstacle to many young people working. You must be 21 years old to become a truck driver in the U.S. The few available drivers have made the prices of hiring a truck go up, and the increasing number of people ordering things online is pushing the demand for trucks to go through the roof. Therefore, there is no better time to own a carrier truck than now.

Set your own working hours

Investing in this business will allow you to create your own schedule, since you will no longer have to answer to an employer. This freedom may not be possible when you are just starting, but it could become a reality after you have gained financial independence. Who doesn't want to make money while vacationing or in their sleep? This is one of the businesses that will allow you to do that.

Networking

Becoming an owner-operator trucker will allow you to meet many business owners in different industries and interact with them. Just be friendly and genuine with them, and in no time, you will create long-lasting relationships with them that you can leverage in the future. For example, they can help you develop ideas for other businesses, which means more money for you.

Ability to travel

Starting a trucking business will enable you to travel across state lines frequently, which means that you will get to travel to far-flung states as well as those close to your home. You could travel to Texas, Michigan, Wisconsin, California, and Georgia. With time, you will know all the routes like the back of your hand. There is no greater feeling than waking up in one state, eating your lunch in another state, sleeping in yet another state, and getting to enjoy the best sights that they have to offer.

Advertise for companies by putting banners on your truck

Some companies will approach you and ask you to stick their brands on your vehicle and pay you for that. This marketing strategy is an interesting way of making your truck generate money for you in more ways than one.

Rent it out

Sometimes, you might be unable to find freights. During such periods, don't let your truck stay idle. The best thing for you is to rent it out to big trucking companies and earn about $800 a month. This way, you will be earning passive income by virtue of owning a truck.

Build your business credit

Owning a trucking business will help you build your business credit. Open an LLC and ensure that you keep up with all your tax payments.

Legacy

Another great thing about owning a trucking business is having something to live on for your children. Hopefully, they can also pass it on to the next generation. Some of the big companies we know today have been passed down from generation to generation, including Ford and FedEx. Therefore, you need to put your heart into the business and think of it as building something long-term.

You will never run out of business

During the pandemic, trucks were allowed to operate, since they were considered one of the essential businesses in the country. This privilege means that if there is another epidemic in the future, your trucking business will not be rendered bankrupt due to a lack of clients.

Leverage

If you have a successful trucking business, you can easily use it as collateral to get a loan from a bank. You can do this as long as you have verified bank statements or tax records, among other things. You can then use the money the lenders give you to expand your business or invest it into stock or real estate.

Charity

You can use your profits to donate to charitable causes that interest you. This way, your business will not just benefit you and your family, but also your community as a whole.

How exactly does the trucking industry operate? If you are new to the world of trucking companies, this is something you might not have a clear answer to when starting. Here is a simple explanation for that.

An Overview of the Trucking Industry

Trucking services transport goods safely and on time to their destinations. Nevertheless, trucking takes many forms that help large businesses and consumers. Though trucking services vary, they are grouped into their specialties.

Door-to-Door

These services are present all across the country. Most of the time, these services take place at the manufacturer's location or the point of origin. When a person buys something online or via a catalog, a trucking company will go to the place where the item is located at the time of the sale and transport the product to a consumer's doorstep. Small trucks are usually used for this type of trucking service.

These items are often collected from a warehouse and taken to a port, where the products are then transported abroad and delivered to the consumer by another company.

Business-to-Business

This type of transportation happens the same way as the door-to-door kind, but the shipment sizes are usually much bigger, and the truck used for the shipment may be bigger too. The trucking company uses tractor-trailers when transporting many goods from point A to B. Most of the products shipped in this industry include:

- Electronics

- Furniture

- Manufactured goods

- Industrial supplies and parts

- Dried goods that don't require refrigeration

Specialized or Heavy Haul

These services are mainly seen with businesses and government agencies. These products are either too big to fit into normal trucks, or they are so heavy that they exceed the maximum limits that the regular truck can carry. These include items like:

- Transformers

-

Planes

- Generators

- Modular homes

- Boats

Many heavy haul goods are transported daily. Custom quotes are issued before they are shipped, plus considerably lengthy wait durations in which the right equipment is bought or assembled. Based on the size and weight of the item, shipping can take a long time, and the company should allocate the right amount of time for time-sensitive shipments.

Temperature Controlled Shipments

Some shipments need to be carried while using temperature-controlled equipment. These items generally need to have a specific temperature to retain their present quality. There is usually a backup system ready so that if the existing cooling system develops a problem, another will start functioning automatically so that the products remain fresh. This service is common with food manufacturers such as meat and ice cream or farming. These services need special trucks, and numerous trucking companies provide them.

Factors that Determine Trucking Companies' Rates

There are several factors that trucking companies use to set their prices. These include:

- Specialty care

- Speed of shipping

- Type of freight

- Mileage

Clients must provide all the information about a shipment and any special needs that they might have during the quoting process. Faster shipping is more expensive compared to slower shipping. Heavy loads and specialty shipments must be priced per shipment.

Next, let us look at how much money you should be prepared to spend when starting this kind of business.

How Much Money Do You Need to Start a Trucking Business?

Like any other business, a trucking business will require you to spend money on several things before getting your truck on the road and earning money. These are some of the highest costs you need to incur when you start this type of business.

In the beginning, you will need between $6,000 and $15,000, excluding your machine. This amount will cater to formation documentation and registration. These cost between $900 and $1,500. IRP plates could cost between $500 and $3,000 for each truck. A permit and Heavy Vehicle Use Tax could cost you somewhere between $100 and $600 for each truck. You may also need extra tax, which is state-specific and would be about $500 for each car.

Drivers are paid 30.3 cents for every mile they cover with a truck or roughly $32,000 yearly on average. A normal large-scale trucking company may require capital of as much as $5 million. Therefore, these circumstances would only favor small trucking businesses that can begin operating quickly and only need a little capital. When starting your trucking company, it would be best to start with one truck to keep your costs as low as possible.

Variable and Fixed Costs

Your costs for starting this kind of business will be categorized into variable and fixed costs. Some of your variable costs may include fines, repairs, and fuel expenditures. On the other hand, fixed costs would comprise insurance, taxes, annual permits, regular maintenance, and the price of buying a truck. Cumulatively, these expenses will make up about 60% to 70% of your operating costs.

Getting a US DOT Number

Before you begin running your business, you will need a US DOT number. The US DOT or MC will cost $300.

Business Registration

If you are a new business owner, you must register your company. The business registration cost may differ depending on the state you are registering in. The average cost of registering a business will be roughly $500.

Unified Carrier Registration (UCR)

The UCR payment for two automotives is $69. The fee for three to five cars is $206. To learn more about the registration fee, check out the UCR site.

Purchasing Vehicles: Used Versus New

The machine you buy should be in great condition. Buying a truck for a high price is worthwhile in the long term because your maintenance expenses will be minimal. Nevertheless, a used truck can also suffice, provided that it has a clean maintenance record and its files have the correct information. A good and roadworthy second-hand vehicle also has the benefit of having reduced annual insurance premiums, which many new businesses find attractive.

Pick a rig that is at most five years old and a diesel engine that has covered fewer than 600,000 miles. You may spend more dollars on these specifications, but this will result in about 8-10 years of stress-free driving without costly repairs.

A major mistake that most new truckers make is buying a cheap truck to save money, only for them to regret it later when the vehicle develops a fault numerous times and needs repairs regularly.

Purchasing a truck can cost you as little as $15,000 and as much as $175,000. Anticipate paying a deposit of between $1000 and $10,000, depending on your selected unit.

Getting Insurance

An insurance policy is one of the most necessary yearly fixed expenses. The insurer takes into account various factors to calculate your total insurance expenses.

Some of the factors they consider are your truck's location, items carried, and the age of your unit. Based on the state of your vehicle, the yearly insurance cost will be as much as $10,000 for each truck. This amount can vary depending on the driver's experience, vehicle's condition, model year, and the kind of coverage. Installing an electronic logging device that FMCSA has registered may also lower insurance premiums.

CDL License Endorsements

You or the drivers operating your truck are required to add various endorsements on the CDL so that they can handle specialized trucks or dangerous cargoes. These are some of the endorsements you can acquire:

- **H-HAZMAT** - This endorsement will enable you to carry dangerous products such as flammable or combustible fluids, explosives, gases, and other things that can cause harm. Getting these endorsements costs roughly $100 and an extra $87 for TSA screening.

- **P-Passenger transport vehicle operator** - This endorsement will allow you to carry more than 16 passengers with the driver included. This endorsement's average fee is $14. Drivers are expected to take both a skill test and a 20-question test.

- **X-transporting Hazmat in a tanker** - This endorsement will enable you to handle trucks transporting hazardous or waste materials in placarded quantities, requiring both H & N endorsements. The regular cost for this endorsement is $14. The driver is also expected to take a hazmat test with 20 questions and a tanker test of 30 questions.

Besides these expenses explained above, you also need to spare $5,000 for attaining customers and marketing. These marketing strategies may take the form of business cards, advertisements, social media presence, and creating a website.

It would be best if you also consider purchasing an ELD solution that can help you lower the variable costs. For example, you can lower fuel wastage by improving driver safety and minimizing idling. You can also lower possible liabilities by keeping track of driver behavior. Additionally, you can lower administrative work by automating various processes such as truck maintenance and IFTA reporting.

Which steps should you follow when starting a trucking company?

The following steps will help you have a clear picture of what you need to do from when you get your driving license to when you get your first customer. These steps can be applied by an owner-operator or a fleet owner regardless of their size and the amount of capital they have when starting their trucking business.

Steps to Follow When Starting a Trucking Company

The U.S. depends on the trucking industry to ensure that people are fed, the economy continues functioning, and supplies are transported to the areas needed. Even though the industry experiences constant fluctuations, trucking services are always in demand.

There are several steps that you must follow to begin a trucking company. These include:

1. Select a niche

2. Be clear about your services

3. Draft a business plan

4. Seek the services of a skilled business attorney

5. Pick the legal structure of your business

6. Prepare for bookkeeping and accounting

7. Evaluate your finances

8. Create your brand identity

9. Comply with the authorities

10. Do the calculations

11. Create an online presence

12. Market your company

Step 1: Select a Niche

There are many different kinds of freight that you can transport, but you can choose to stick with one kind of freight and offer better services than your competitors, and clients will prefer you to carry their loads for them.

Just like doctors specialize in specific diseases or conditions, you can apply the same thing in the trucking business. When you specialize, clients will believe that you offer the best possibility to handle their problems.

Customers desire to have some assurance that their commodities will be delivered in perfect conditions to be sold. If they know that you deal specifically with their freight, they will have more confidence that you will do the job efficiently.

These are some of the popular niches found in the trucking industry.

- Over the road (OTR), regional or local drivers

- Less than truckload (LTL) drivers

- Tanker drivers

- Flatbed drivers

- Refrigerated freight drivers

- Freight hauler

- Dry van driver

The type of niche that you choose might be the area where you have the most experience or a transport gap that requires filling your local market.

However, if you are finding it hard to find an appropriate niche, you can use these strategies to determine the best niche for you:

- Find any special kinds of commodities that come from your area or state.

- Have you assisted friends to move their commodities on an unofficial basis? Ask yourself if other people have the same needs.

- Does your personal background in the trucking industry and experience give you unique knowledge not common in the trucking industry?

Remember, regardless of the niche that you settle on, do not try to be the right trucker for every customer.

Additionally, advertising by targeting the businesses that require your type of skills will give you the best outcome.

You could be an experienced truck driver, however, you may require specific training to be the best trucker in your chosen niche. Therefore, hone your skills, even though you are already an experienced trucker.

Step 2: Be Clear About Your Services

Once you have identified your niche, think about the kind of services you intend to offer. The services will determine the kind of equipment you should purchase, the amount of trucking insurance that you will have to pay, and many other elements of your business.

This is the stage where you will need to select a trucking business model. After identifying the business model you want, the next step will be to write a business plan.

Step 3: Draft a Business Plan

This is an important step that you should not ignore. You can keep it simple and ensure that you include all the necessary information. It is important because it will prompt you to think about things keenly and steer clear of any blunders.

Writing a business plan will act as a training ground for you to practice evaluating your finances and examining your competition. You do not need to write a long business plan; a one-page long document would suffice.

Step 4: Seek the Services of a Qualified Business Attorney

Enlisting the services of an experienced business attorney can enable you to avoid expensive legal blunders and safeguard your business when necessary.

The government bodies that control the trucking industry (the Federal Motor Carrier Safety Administration or MFSA and the Department of Transportation or DOT) have stringent regulations, and they expect companies in the industry to adhere to the rules religiously. Hiring an attorney who only deals with transportation safety compliance can be very helpful for your company.

The attorney can give you valuable advice about the best practices, and they will also be well versed with the legal information if you break any of the FMCSA or DOT rules. A great lawyer will also assist you to share ownership interests with investors or partners in a manner that will give you versatility in the future and protect every party.

Step 5: Pick the Legal Structure of Your Business/Your Legal Business Model

Before beginning your trucking business, you should decide on the kind of entity you are required to register. The legal business structure you choose for your business impacts everything, including your liability, how you file taxes, and whether you should observe any other requirements at the national, state, or local levels.

When you are new to this industry, choosing a business structure might seem like an arduous task. Therefore, it is advisable to take your time before deciding which one is best for you.

For instance, a partnership or sole proprietorship could be affordable and fast in the short term. However, it might leave your business exposed to more risks, bring about negative tax treatment, and cause issues for you in the long run.

An LLC (Limited Liability Company) business structure is a better option for most trucking companies, and for larger trucking companies, a corporation is a perfect choice; more so if they have investors.

Take enough time to read about and familiarize yourself with the different business structures and determine which one helps you achieve your goals best.

Note that if you do business under a different name other than your legal business name, most states need you to register your business with the county clerk or secretary of state in the country where you are based.

Step 6: Be Prepared to do Bookkeeping and Accounting

To monitor your finances when beginning a trucking business, you need to do bookkeeping and accounting; failing to do so will mean you will not know the business's cash flow. It will also be crucial when you are filing taxes. Business accounting is how your business collects, interprets, organizes, and presents information about its finances. On the other hand, bookkeeping involves recording, organizing, storing, and retrieving financial data. Accountants can assess the financial state of a business and give financial advice to the business owner to enable them to make wise decisions.

Bookkeeping and accounting are usually used interchangeably. However, there is a slight difference between the two. The main difference between the two words is that bookkeeping entails recording and categorizing financial facts, while accounting involves utilizing the information by analyzing, strategizing, and doing tax planning. Essentially, bookkeepers are tasked with ensuring that the bank account of the business is balanced, making simple reports, and helping with ensuring that your financial records are in order at all times.

An accountant, on the other hand, will give you important advice about taxes and file federal and state taxes for you. Without the help of an accountant, you run the risk of violating tax laws or underpaying. The accountant can also help you evaluate your finances and tell you whether you need funds to get your trucking business off the ground.

You need the services of both professionals because each plays a vital role in the success of your business.

Step 7: Evaluate Your Finances

When you start this kind of business, it is important to be aware of the amount of money you need to put into your project. You will need money to pay for insurance, driver's wages, and leasing or buying trucks and trailers.

You need to know if the money you have is enough. If it is inadequate, you may need to seek financing for your business. We will discuss the financial options available to you in detail later on in the book.

If you are not aware of the numbers, you will have a difficult time growing a lucrative business that can operate for years to come. Your cash flow will influence most of your decisions.

As a new business, it will be prudent to only spend money on the most important things and try to save as much money as possible to ensure that your business survives. Having an accountant and a bookkeeper will help you monitor your finances and know what your cash flow is especially for the purpose of filing taxes.

Step 8: Create a Brand Identity

We all know the brand identities of big companies such as Coca-Cola, Apple, Pepsi, and McDonalds. Brand identities are great for making a business memorable and building its credibility. Fortunately, you do not need to have a big company to care about a brand identity. Even with a small trucking business, brand identity is crucial. Thus, you must take it seriously. Businesses will entrust you with goods worth hundreds or thousands of dollars. If your business has a weak brand, it might be difficult for you to find customers. To create a strong brand identity, you need to ask yourself certain questions, which are:

1. What values influence the way you conduct business?

2. What is the most crucial aspect of your customer's experience?

3. How can your clients benefit from your company that is unique from your competitors'?

4. Who will require your services?

5. What personality or identity do you want your business to portray?

The answers to these questions will determine which branding decisions you will make once your business starts operating, such as the name of the company, website design, and company logo. Other branding elements of a trucking company include business cards, a company website, and truck decals or wraps. There is stiff competition in the trucking industry, and it is only the companies with a clear and genuine brand that prosper and survive in the market.

Step 9: Comply with the Authorities

This industry is governed by numerous laws and needs unique licenses, insurance, and permits. Jumping through these hurdles successfully will increase your odds of succeeding in this industry.

We will discuss the permits and licenses in detail later on in the book.

Step 10: Do the Calculations

There are many expenses that you are likely to incur once you start operating your trucking business, such as startup costs and recurring costs. You also need to set prices: consider the prices of the competition, the cost of operating the business, and the profits you intend to make.

Step 11: Develop an Online Presence

Create a well-designed and professional website.

Step 12: Market Your Company

Marketing is one of the most important functions of a business. Basically, a business's survival depends on the effectiveness of its marketing efforts. Use all the possible marketing avenues available to you, such as mailing lists, business cards, and clients' referrals.

Types of Trucking Companies

These are the five models recognized by CDL, which is the biggest online community of truck drivers in America:

For-hire truckload carriers

This is the most common trucking business model for most startups. The trucking companies in this category carry freights belonging to other companies, thus, they neither produce nor manufacture anything. Therefore, for-hire trucks that use this business model assist companies that require supply chain management and logistic support by selling their fleet space to them. This business model relies on other companies' freight demand.

However, it is not as simple as it sounds. When you choose this model, you still have to decide the type of freight you will haul, whether you will require special equipment to carry it, and decide whether you will operate nationally, regionally, or locally, and whether your drivers will be employees or contractors.

The major disadvantage of using this business model is that freight contracts turn over and other trucking companies are invited to bid. Therefore, as a trucking business owner, there is no guarantee that you will always win a contract with a particular company. Thus, most of the time, you will need to look for different customers to ensure that you do not run out of work when one customer's freight diminishes.

Inter-modal trucking

These kinds of companies transport shipping containers to or from shipping ports or rail yards. It is the ideal model for companies that are situated close to a big cargo port or train hub.

Most companies would be happy to ship freight using rail since it is easier and faster than trucks. However, the disadvantage of using rail to transport freight is that clients are still expected to move their commodities to the rail depot as well as ensuring that the freight is collected again and taken to the final client.

This process requires many hands to handle the freight: two trucks and their drivers and the people operating the rail. The goods are transported by rail for a big percentage of the journey. Since many hands are needed, this model provides good business for truck drivers located nearby.

Private fleets

These kinds of fleets offer the products they transport, and their own drivers, trailers, and trucks. This is perfect for someone who is starting a company that will manufacture a product that already has a ready market. Examples of companies in the market that have private fleets are Frito-Lay, UPS, and FedEx.

Household movers

Just like the name suggests, these kinds of movers assist people to move. Sometimes they offer additional services, such as loading and unloading items into the truck and even helping customers pack their belongings. You have to decide if you will offer these services and plan for infrastructure, permits, and licenses.

Most clients who need to have their household things transported are usually single individuals. People who like to keep fit love working for trucking companies that specialize in moving services. The main disadvantage of working in this niche is that there will be a higher risk of injuries for your employees because of the physical nature of the job. Additionally, it is impossible to anticipate the state of the house that you will be moving on a given day. Therefore, sometimes you will end up working in a filthy house or packing up another person's dirty belongings.

Less than truckload carriers

LTL or less than truckload carriers transport goods that are a fraction of a truckload. This indicates that you can carry tiny quantities of commodities from many varying sources on one trip. Such carriers might ship between 10 and 30 different items to different clients and work locally, regionally, and globally. This type of trucker comes in handy whenever there is something that is too huge to be sent via the postal service. Such a company will normally use either doubles or 53' trailers to transport small items that require business or home delivery within America.

An LTL company can make its dispatch and drivers schedule these products' delivery to the homes of customers, or it can request the customer to go and collect the goods from its local distribution center.

LTL or less than truckload is one of the most preferred trucking firm types. It is one of the most affordable ways of transporting cargo and most shippers like it.

Summary

There are many plausible reasons why you would want to start a trucking company, including charity, to create a legacy, for networking purposes, and to become your own boss, among others. Some of the common goods that you will be hauling include electronics, food that does not need refrigerators, and furniture. The goods you carry will depend on the niche you are in.

In the next chapter, we will look at how to write a business plan, the different types of business structures, and their pros and cons.

Getting Prepared

When you are planning to start a trucking company, there are four types of business structures that you can choose from depending on your preferences. These are:

- LLC

- Sole proprietorships

- Corporations

- Partnerships

In most states, you don't need to have a business entity when starting this kind of business. If you skip this step, the state assumes that your business is a sole proprietorship, meaning that you and your business are synonymous. Creating a business entity can prevent you from getting stressed and save you time and money.

Registering your trucking business under the state is an excellent idea for two main reasons; it will protect your assets and help you take advantage of specific tax savings. The biggest gain when setting up your business is that it becomes completely separated from your personal properties. If you are a sole proprietor, your truck, house, and vehicle will be part and parcel of the business, and lenders can seize it in the event of bankruptcy.

Sole Proprietorships

This business structure is a company or business operated by one person for their benefit. It is the most basic type of business structure. Proprietorships have no separate existence from their owners. The liabilities connected with the business are also the individual liabilities of the business owner, and the business ends when the owner dies. The proprietor bears the risk of the business that lenders can seize even his or her assets to repay the business debts without caring to know if they are used in the business or for personal use.

Single proprietors encompass retailers, service providers, and professional people doing business for their personal gains. Even though a sole proprietorship is not a different legal entity from the owner, it is a different entity in accounting. The financial undertakings of the business, such as receipt of payments, are done separately from the owner's financial dealings, such as rent or mortgage payments.

Pros:

- **It is simple** – this is the most popular type of business organization in the U.S. since it is the easiest and most affordable to start.

- **Little legal restriction** – it does not have charter limitations on operations, and there are not many reports that need to be filed with various government bodies.

- **Easy to discontinue** – the business can be dissolved whenever the owner feels like doing it.

- **The owner is the actual boss** – they have to make all decisions, enjoy all the profits, suffer all the losses, and be responsible for debts.

Cons:

- **Raising capital is difficult** – This is an issue because one person's assets are less than those of a group of partners.

- **A short life of a business** – If the proprietor is removed from the business in an unexpected, untimely and unplanned manner, the business may have repercussions for the creditors.

- **Unlimited liability** – The proprietors are liable for all the business liabilities. All their assets are tied to the business, and lenders can use the assets to settle the business' debts at any time.

Partnerships

This business structure is an agreement implied or expressed between two or more people who come together to do a business together and earn profits. Every partner gives property, money, skill, or labor, and every partner also shares in the loss and profit of the business, and each one has unlimited personal liability for the business's debts.

Limited partnerships restrict the personal liability of each partner for the business' debts based on the amount they have contributed. Partners should file a certificate of limited partnership with the state.

Pros:

- **It is easier to raise capital compared to a sole proprietorship.**

- **There are more resources for creative activity, support, and decision making.**

Cons:

- **Unlimited liability**

- **Shared authority** – being forced to share the authority for making decisions among the different partners can slow down the decision-making process and regularly cause disagreements.

Corporation

This business structure is a legal entity that operates under the law. Its charter limits the scope of its name and operations. Articles of incorporation should be filed with the state to create a corporation. Stockholders are shielded from liability, and the stockholders who the corporations also employ can enjoy some benefits like health insurance. These benefits are tax-free. The main disadvantage of this business structure is that a C Corporation has double taxation because both profits and dividends are taxed.

S-Corporation or Small Business Corporation

S corporations are distinct closed corporations made to give small corporations a tax advantage if IRS Code requirements are fulfilled. There are limitations on the number of members that a corporation should have. The owners waive and report corporate taxes on their federal income tax returns, which helps them avoid the double taxation of ordinary corporations.

Pros:

- **Stockholders have unlimited liability** – Just like in a partnership, liability for stockholders is limited to the money invested in the business. Additionally, creditors may not confiscate assets owned by individuals. However, nowadays, creditors usually ask the stockholders to give personal guarantees before issuing a business loan.

- **It is easy to expand the business** – There is the ease of raising capital through selling stock legally.

- **It is easy to transfer ownership** – If there is a buyer available, stockholders can sell their stock at will.

- **Long life** – the business can exist for an extended period since it is legal. Younger family members can inherit shares in the corporation.

Cons:

- **There is the risk of double taxation unless the corporation elects S-corporation**

- **The corporate charter limits operation to the issuing state unless permission from different states is obtained.**

- **Government regulation** – The corporation should acquire the corporate charter from the state, and it must observe all record-keeping and state regulations related to corporations.

Limited Liability Corporation (LLC)

Most small trucking businesses and owner-operators prefer to register as an LLC. An LLC is similar to a corporation, making the authorities deem your assets and business property separate. However, it takes less effort to manage than a corporation, particularly for small businesses.

An LLC operates as a combination between a corporation and a sole proprietorship. Owners must be members, which may be challenging to transfer, whereas, for a corporation, it is easy to transfer. Nevertheless, there are not many regulations to follow like in a corporation.

When registering as a limited liability corporation, you are expected to produce the articles of organization of your business. This document contains information such as when you began your business, the members, the purpose of the company, etc.

Pros:

- **It gives the business owner more flexibility for personalizing the business structure.**

- **Member liability is limited** – In most states, an LLC could have just one member (it has the advantages of a sole proprietorship, but it limits liability)

Con:

- **It needs a detailed operating agreement due to the high ability of flexibility or variability.**

Business Legal Structure Versus Business Tax Structure

The main difference between these two is that the state is responsible for preparing a business structure, whereas the IRS handles the tax structure at the national level. When your business is established, you need to separately register your tax structure with the IRS to receive your EIN – Employer Identification Number.

It is worth noting that the IRS does not acknowledge LLCs. Therefore, you may be viewed as a C-corporation, S-corporation, partnership, or sole proprietor for tax reasons. You can still enjoy all the benefits of having an LLC. However, the tax process varies.

Most of the small trucking companies register as an S-corporation under the IRS. It can be prudent to hire a professional to help you because you will be required to file additional paperwork to register a business like that.

When you choose an S-corporation status, you stand to benefit, because you will save on payroll taxes or FICA taxes (Federal Insurance Contributions Act) and dodge double taxation.

One of the most important steps you need to take when starting a trucking business is writing a business plan. Here are the sections that a business plan contains, what to include in each area, and why.

Writing a Business Plan

A good number of truckers do not bother to write a business plan. However, it is essential to create one because it acts as a roadmap that will guide you to the ultimate goal of any business, which is making profits. It will also come in handy when you approach partners, investors, or lenders to fund your trucking business. A business plan is usually the first thing they want to see before making any decision about your offer or request.

Here are the steps you need to follow to create a comprehensive and effective business plan.

You first need to ensure that you have registered your business and chosen a business structure from the list we mentioned earlier. You can choose to register in your state or a different one.

After registering your business, the next step will be to conduct extensive research to ensure that you have all the necessary information to write a good business plan. Learn the industry's basics and critical business information such as return on investment, profit and loss, cash flow, and other relevant information. Also, do these things if you have not done them yet:

1. Find out the assets you have and what their value is. Your truck will be an asset if you buy it. If not, it could be a liability.

2. How much will you spend on business operations? Add up your expected average fuel expenses, miles driven, and miles per gallon. Maintenance and operation prices enable you to know how much you will charge your clients to profit.

3. Find out how to manage project management and costs and expenses to know your profit margin.

4. Find out the charges in various freight lanes.

5. Outline your operating procedures for various types of freight and where they will be collected and transported to.

6. Comprehend contract market versus spot market rates.

7. Figure out if you will include fuel surcharges in the rates you are charging and the advantages and disadvantages of doing this.

All these steps are crucial if you are looking for financing. Lenders will be interested in finding out both how you intend to make profits and your backup plan in the event that things go awry.

Apart from being a blueprint for operating your business, this document shows potential partners, investors, and financial institutions that you are a trustworthy person to work with. You will be selling these individuals yourself, your company, and the fact that financing your plan, and you, is the right thing to do.

There are two key things to have in your plan. These are industry knowledge and general business knowledge.

When writing the industry knowledge, mention any skills you possess in the trucking industry and any areas in which you intend to specialize. Your investors will be happy to learn that you are an exceptional driver.

Show that you have the necessary skills and expertise needed to begin a trucking company. You are not merely a truck driver. Rather, you are an expert who can operate a successful trucking business, and you know what is needed to run a business, make profits in the trucking industry, and succeed as a business. Ensure that you explain how you will distinguish yourself from your business rivals. Resist using common buzz words such as reliable, on-time, faster, and friendlier.

Remember that people buy from someone because of the reasons why an owner goes into business and not just because they are in business. There is probably a purpose other than generating profits that made you start this business. Ensure that it is clear in everything that you say and do. That will make you stand out and help you get investors and other financial supporters charged up, with a bit of luck.

General business knowledge means that your business plan should demonstrate that you are aware that sometimes in business, things do not work out as expected and that you have a contingency plan in place for such situations. It should show that you understand how to track cash flow, loss, profit, and expenses, build a client base and ensure that your business operates efficiently. It should also demonstrate that you are generally financially adept and know about corporate structure and taxes.

Before people invest in your business, they will invest in you and your personality. Most importantly, you should be a part of your own business plan.

How to Write a Business Plan

Apart from including yourself in your business plan, you should also differentiate your strategy from the other firms in the industry. Investors expect to see a certain order and format in your business plan. Remember that the business plan is not just for financial institutions and investors but also for you. So, make sure that you can understand it and check it when you need to. Here are the essential sections and what to include in each one:

Executive Summary

This is a short summary of your company as well as yourself. It should explain why you are starting a trucking company, show who you are, and what distinguishes you from your competitors. This means that you must include the most important information about your business, such as the mission statement, management, history, location, and a description of your legal structure. Take this section very seriously, because it is your first opportunity to make a good first impression, and there will be no other chance to do that. Put some effort and thought into writing it. Think about hiring an experienced editor or writer to assist you to write an excellent executive summary and give it final editing after writing all the crucial information that should be in your business plan. If you want to get the best results, you may write it last after you have completed the other sections of the business plan.

Company Description

This is the section that resembles the "About Us" page on a website. It should offer more details about you, your business knowledge, and your experience. If there is more than one business owner, give more information about them and the management team. Lastly, restate what distinguishes you from other trucking businesses. Also, use this section to explain who your perfect client is and how you intend to find them and create a customer base. After reading this section, the reader should have answers to questions like:

- Will you focus on a certain freight area?

- Will you focus on a specific logistic arm, cargo type, or region?

- Do you have a special partnership opportunity that has contacts?

- Who will your employees be? What attributes do they have that will make them important members of your team?

- Who will be working together with you?

Operational Plan

The operational plan explains the business's "how" and "what." What are the important positions in your company? How will you deal with dispatch and routing? Will you combine the roles of operating the business and operating a route? Will you have other drivers?

Also, explain how you will employ technology to maximize profits in your business. For example, describe how you intend to use small business software to do mileage tracking and accounting tasks. Automating your accounting process will help you save money and time. You can also mention that you will use Freight Factoring services to help you receive payment fast instead of waiting for days or months for the load broker to settle a payment. You can even get advances and broker credit checks from these companies, and all you have to do is apply. Another technology you may mention in this business plan section is load boards. This entails searching online to find dependable brokers and profitable loads fast and planning the best routes for the highest profits.

Indeed, trucking has become a technologically advanced industry. It is important to demonstrate how to capitalize on advanced routing and other strategies to make your business as lucrative as possible. Utilizing technology can also help your business stand out from your competitors.

Services

Here, you will need to add information about the services you will provide to your clients. In this section, you need to bring out two key things. The first is the customer outlook. Describe the problems that your customers are dealing with that you will be solving. If you are going to be supplying a product in a location where it is scarce, explain how doing that is profitable, which will show why your services have a high demand.

The second thing you will write here should demonstrate that you understand profitability and the market. Include details like the materials you transport, the industries you will be offering your services to, and pricing. If you break down the pricing, explain why you have priced your services in that manner.

Market Analysis

The trucking market is congested. You need to explain the specific need you will be meeting and show how well you comprehend it. Discuss your target market, its size, your competition, and the clients' needs that you will fulfill. Knowing your target market will show the people who want to invest in your business that you have researched industry trends and positioned yourself for success. Showing a deep understanding of your competitors demonstrates your capability to outdo them.

You should also be aware of the market share you hope to seize and how you plan to achieve that goal. Focus on profit and loss forecasts and how you arrived at those findings. Lastly, illustrate that you know government rules and how they impact your business.

Therefore, the main things that you must deal with in this section are:

- **Competitor analysis** – This part is all about the competition. Who are your business rivals? Who are their clients? What are their weaknesses and strengths? How will you meet a need they are not currently focusing on, and how will you do it efficiently?

- **Pricing and profit margins** – Which pricing structure are you using? How are your prices different from your competitors? What margins must you have to make a profit?

- **Industry rules** – If you neglect your taxes, your trucking company is bound to fail. Therefore, it is prudent that you understand all the state and federal laws that affect your business and have a compliance plan in place. List the different licenses and permits you will require, and then explain how you will ensure that your company acquires them.

Management and Employees

Your business plan must contain information about your hiring method if you intend to have extra office help or employees. Give details about your recruitment process and how you will onboard new staff. Owner-operators and brokers need to observe the compliance requirements of the brokers and shippers that whom they do business with.

Ensure that you learn and comprehend the safety records, regulatory compliance, and basic industry standards before hiring more carriers. If you recruit a carrier who does not comply with the regulations or one who has a bad safety record, you could be jeopardizing the whole company before it even starts operating.

Hiring experienced drivers with a good performance record will help you develop your business to increase your operation and start doing more freight lanes. It will also help to have a plan for retaining your employees and preventing a high turnover rate, because the market is very competitive, and there is a high demand for good drivers.

If human resource management and paperwork handling are not things that you enjoy doing or you don't know how to do them well, then you can consider hiring an H.R. manager and other professionals to help you with the work. Talk about how you intend to hire people in management positions when your business gets bigger.

Sales and Marketing Tactics

In a market with too many firms, the biggest problem that businesses have to deal with is standing out from their competitors. Describe your marketing strategies. Give details of making your business known to new customers and creating a loyal customer base. You should also explain how you will make sales which involve going out of your business premises and getting new clients. You can utilize services such as brokers or hire salespersons to call prospective clients for you. No matter the method you plan to use, you must have a sales strategy and explain it in this section.

Financial Projections

The general rule for the number of years you need to forecast your finances is five years. As the industry changes, you will need to change your plan accordingly, but you need to demonstrate to your investors that you have a strategy. Coming up with a plan beforehand is also important because it will give you a roadmap to guide you. You can also assess future possibilities depending on your business plan.

Funding Request

This step is a section where you will show your partners or investors the amount of money you need. You will attain this figure by deducting the money you already have from the full projected cost. Outline your assets and everything that you are investing in the business. Investors are happy to see that you have invested your own money or property before investing theirs in your business. You can use a profit and loss statement or a cash flow statement to help explain your financial situation.

Conclusion

Just like any other business plan, you need to know your industry, demonstrate that you know it, and offer a great financial strategy for operating a successful business. Keep in mind that a business plan is not only meant for investors. Rather, it will be a blueprint from now to the place you will be in five years and further. If you want assistance writing a business plan, you can check out the Small Business Administration's online guides. Other groups for small businesses provide valuable, free information to help you draft a business plan.

Further Preparations

Once you have written a business plan, you need to create a business name, email, and open a business bank account.

The Name

The business name for your company should be remarkable, represent your company well, and should also not belong to another trucking business. Also, ensure that you understand your target market well and know the exact emotions you would like your company to stimulate.

You have many options for a trucking company name, such as a dependable name like Faithful Road Shipping or Safe and Sound Shipping, a funny name like Just Run Trucking or No BS Shipping, or even a catchy name like Warren's Wheels, Tamra's Trucking, or Arrow Trucking.

Coming up with a business name can be both exciting and challenging. Fortunately for you, if you have a hard time coming up with a business name for your trucking business, you can use an online name generator.

You may also search online for a name that tickles your fancy. There are many sites where you can find lists of possible names that you can use for your business.

Advantages of a Business Email

Brand Awareness – A business email is a great way of promoting brand awareness, because most professional emails allow you to have a domain name with your company name. For example, Gmail's professional email domain is @yourcompany.

Build Trust – Such an email will also help you build trust with your customers because they will be sure that they are communicating with the right person when they see the email address.

Create Employees' Accounts and a Group Mailing List – A business email will also allow you to give your employees a professional email address later on when you bring them on board to help you run your business. You can also make a group mailing list, among other amazing features.

Stay Organized – Having a separate business email from your personal one will also help you be organized in your business and separate your work from your personal life.

Benefits of Having a Separate Business Account – Some truckers do not see the need to have a separate business account from their personal one. This practice requires a lot of discipline, because there is the risk that you may pay yourself too much money or overspend money that you should have spent on the business. Also, if your business is sued and your business and personal accounts are combined, your personal assets are in danger. These are the benefits of having a business bank account for your trucking business:

Relationship With a Lender – By opening a business bank account, you will be starting and fostering a banking relationship that can give you a loan or a line of credit at a future date. Most lenders prefer to look at the banking history of your business and not your personal accounts.

Protect Your Assets – If your business structure is a limited liability company or a corporation, having a separate bank account is important because it will help protect your properties by clearly separating your business and personal finances.

Tax Filing – Makes tax filing and accounting easier. This is because you can easily trace all the transactions and receipts.

Besides opening a business bank account, opening a credit card for your business is also prudent. When you figure out and master how to create business credit, you will be able to obtain credit cards and other financing in the name of your business instead of yours. You will also get higher lines of credit, better interest rates, and more.

Bank Accounts

A trucker's life is not easy. You end up spending many hours on the road, numerous days behind the wheel, and you cannot drive your rig on local roads to access a bank branch when you require their services such as depositing or withdrawing money. Discovering that your current bank does not have a local branch makes you as a driver feel frustrated, because they will force you to pay exorbitant ATM charges. Sometimes, your bank might even flag your account for fraud due to the regular travel to different states.

Therefore, finding a bank that understands your needs as a trucker would be a godsend. However, finding such a bank is not an easy feat. Since it is not possible for you to be in your home town for many days, mostly, you will be spending just a few days in a year there. This means that you need to look for a business banking provider with numerous branches all over the country. The bank should also understand the unique needs of people working in the trucking industry, especially drivers. These include reliable customer service, top-notch mobile banking, and longer branch hours.

Depending on your preference, there are a few such banks for drivers to choose from. Here are the best banks for a truck driver and the factors to consider when evaluating a savings account or business checking.

Factors to Consider When Choosing the Best Bank for a Truck Driver

Convenience

Truckers have certain needs, such as a place to find a hot shower when they stop to fill up their trucks and fast access to groceries and food, as well as the ability to get back on the road quickly, because wasting time means wasting money. Therefore, the last thing you want to deal with is an inconvenient bank. An ideal bank should not be located too far from your truck stop, since you do not want to waste too much time searching for a bank with reasonable ATM fees whenever you want to withdraw money.

A bank with many locations would be perfect for you. You will want to look for a bank with many branches along your regular routes. Hence, opening a bank account with a big national bank is the most suitable option for you. You might realize that an online bank or local credit union can be a great choice for you if you don't mind dealing with customer support online instead of going straight to a teller. Some banks will even refund you for a specific amount of ATM charges monthly which helps them compensate for not having a physical location.

An Understanding Bank

Truckers should be on the lookout for a bank that knows what being out on the road for extended periods entails. This need necessitates choosing a bank with world-class customer service available over the phone, online, and in person. You do not want to find yourself working with a financial institution that is rigid about the working hours. Since your work does not follow the 9-5 rule, you need to find a bank with a customer hotline that operates for many hours.

Some of the most popular banks are working hard to improve their online customer service experience. Banks that only operate online are famous for this because they have to be available on the internet to make it possible for them to answer customers' questions.

Helps With Savings

Finally, the ideal banks for truckers assist them in saving for their personal or business goals. Managing your money properly when on the road always seems like a daunting task to many truckers. You need to purchase food, laundry, and other expenditures to make your life comfortable and bearable. Being conscious about your budget is crucial when you are a truck driver, and everything you buy is highly-priced. Therefore, you need to find a bank that gives you rewards for being their customer, which can be in the form of savings accounts with the best APYs, money market accounts, and checking accounts that yield high returns.

If you have drivers, they will need to have a personal bank account that is truck driver-friendly. They would prefer banks that give them a savings account or a checking account and, if possible, both. A truck driver's work expenses and personal finances are hard to separate because being on the road for days on end means they have to pay for their bills at home and account for their expenses on the road. Therefore, they will require a bank that will make it hassle-free to manage their money on the road and at home.

These are the best banks for truckers who require personal accounts:

- **TAB bank (Transportation Alliance Bank)** – They offer banking services customized for truckers. You will earn interest on your checking account balance of 0.10 % APY.

- **Simple checking account** – It is an online-based bank that allows you to deposit using your mobile device, withdraw money from their ATMs for free, write physical checks and make direct deposits. You also get to earn an interest of 2.02% APY if you maintain a balance of at least $2,000 in your account.

- **GoBank** – Perfect for easy access to ATMs. It has ATMs in many Walmart stores all over the country. You can also deposit, pay bills, and do electronic transfers online, as well as enjoy all the other advantages of using a modern online bank.

The Best Banks for Business Checking

Owning a trucking business is a great thing because you will make more money than you can when working for someone else. Establishing your business is not an easy task, and neither is finding a good business bank account. However, you do not have to look far because I have listed them for you below:

TAB Business Checking

TAB provides a business checking account that offers customized services for trucking companies, startups, and small businesses. The bank assists trucking businesses in acquiring loans for asset financing and other investments, minimizing paperwork, monitoring cash flow, and managing fuel costs. Their business checking accounts offer a 1.75% refund on fuel bought using the business account and online bill pay and mobile banking. Receiving rebates on fuel expenses is amazing, because it means you will be saving money and using it for something else.

There are two types of TAB business checking accounts, namely: Analyzed business checking and business checking. Business checking is the bank's basic checking account, since it offers 100 free credits or debits each month, longer customer service hours, 0.25% interest on your balance, and telephone banking support. Analyzed business checking has more features, because it gives you a committed relationship manager and unlimited withdrawals and deposits.

Axos Bank (Online Based)

This bank was previously called Bank of Internet USA, and it is the oldest online bank in the U.S. It has been around for 19 years. It leverages its experience to provide a feature-packed, stress-free, and active business checking account that functions well for independent contractors and small businesses with their personal business entities.

This bank allows you access to ATMs all over the nation for free via its banking partners, 60 free remote deposits and 50 free items every month, and an interest of 0.8% APY on the balance in your account. You can also use paper checks with this bank, which is a service that is not common with most online banks. There is also a $10 maintenance fee every month on this account that is waived as long as you maintain a balance of $5,000 every day.

Axos is a great option for you if you spend many hours on the road and don't mind doing all your business banking activities online. The company offers web and phone support for customers who may have issues or questions about their accounts. Therefore, you can enjoy the convenience, and you will not waste time queuing in a brick and mortar bank.

Chase Bank

Chase business banking is also another great option for you because they have experience providing services to many small and big companies. The bank has more than 16,000 ATMs and over 4500 branches all over the country, which means that you have a high probability of being close to a Chase spot regardless of where your schedule takes you.

Chase Bank has three different business checking accounts: Chase Business Platinum Checking, Chase Performance Business Checking, and Chase Business Complete Banking. The latter is a great choice for small businesses, because it has little account balance and monthly service requirements to have fees scrapped off. It also provides unlimited online deposits, plus $500 cash deposits per month for free.

On the other hand, Performance Business Checking is ideal for medium-sized companies that require more services from a bank. You will get $20,000 cash deposits and 250 transactions every month for free, plus two domestic wire transfers. You will only need to have a balance of $35,000 for the monthly fee of $30 to be waived.

Finally, Business Platinum Checking provides a business checking account for big companies with complex monetary needs. You will be given $25,000 cash deposits and 500 transactions for free each month, and you need to maintain a monthly deposit of $100,000 to have the 95% fee scraped off.

Summary

The best bank for you as a trucking business owner or owner-operator is the bank that offers features that function for you, flexibility, and financial help. Whether you want a physical bank that you can access along your route or an online one, the choice is up to you. Decide what is best for you and choose the right bank that meets your needs best.

In the next chapter, you will learn about the various licenses and permits you need to operate in this industry.

Comply With Regulations

As you know, no business can survive if it avoids paying taxes, and the same applies to a trucking business. You need to have several licenses and permits before you start operating in the U.S. This chapter will delve into that and tell you how to qualify for each of them and where to get them.

Like most industries in the U.S., the trucking industry is heavily regulated to ensure that the public is protected from exploitation and gets the best services possible. It is also regulated so intensely because driving a commercial vehicle requires one to have greater skills, knowledge, and experience. The Department of Transportation is the government agency that regulates this industry.

Driving a vehicle with two or three trailers, a truck hauling hazardous materials, a passenger vehicle, or a truck with a tank is a huge responsibility. Therefore, the authorities are doing all they can to ensure that nothing is left to chance. Both the federal government and states regulate it. These are the government requirements that you need to comply with to operate legally in the U.S.

Commercial Driver's License

This requirement comes as no surprise to you; you and all your drivers should have a valid CDL to operate heavy trucks. If you get this license yourself, you will be able to drive a truck and learn firsthand about the trucking industry. Most trucking business owners started as drivers, and it will help you run the business better if you understand what being behind the wheel feels like. Acquiring a license requires a rigorous background check, a driving test, a written permit exam, and CDL training. To qualify for a CDL, you need to be not less than 18 years old. You have to be at least 21 years old to drive a truck from one state to another. Every state has unique testing standards for this kind of license. To know your state's requirements, get a CDL manual from the Department of Motor Vehicles office near you.

Get a Motor Carrier Authority Number and Federal DOT

These numbers are needed for your trucking company to carry cargo in the U.S. The purpose of a DOT number is to monitor how your company is complying with regulations and its safety record. The Motor Carrier number (MC) or the operating authority, as it is popularly known, indicates the type of trucking business you run and the types of cargo you are allowed to carry. You can get the two numbers by simply registering your business with the FMCSA-Federal Motor Carrier Safety Administration. You need to fill out the Safety Certification application and Motor Carrier Identification Report (MCS-250) to get these numbers. After applying, you will be given the USDOT and MC numbers. However, the FMCSA must still review your request for authority. The review comprises a compulsory dispute period whereby your application is displayed on the Federal Register for ten days. This duration is meant to give the public time to contest your request for authority.

You should be aware that to apply for the DOT registration, you should register as a business in your state first. You will do this process through the office of the Secretary of State.

Fill Out Your Unified Carrier Registration (UCR)

The UCR system was made through the 2005's Unified Carrier Registration Act. The lawmakers made it to do verification of active insurance coverage in every state where a motor carrier does business. You should use your company's MC and USDOT numbers to register.

The UCR Act replaced the old method of registering and picking fees from the vehicle operators involved in cross-state transportation. It is also referred to as the single state registration system. To get more information about your UCR, go to the website of the Department of Transportation of your state.

Acquire an International Registration Plan (IRP)

An IRP license plate given by your company's home state gives your truck a chance to operate in every state and many Canadian provinces. You need to pay a renewal fee for the plate every year. To find out more about this plate, you can go to the Department of Transportation website of your company's home state.

Know Heavy Use Tax Regulations

Any truck that weighs 55,000 pounds or more has to pay the Federal Heavy Highway Vehicle Use Tax. When you want to pay taxes for your heavy trucks, you need to fill and file the IRS' 2290 tax form every year. To learn more about the form, visit the IRS website www.irs.gov.

Get an International Fuel Tax Agreement (IFTA) Decal

This agreement was created to streamline the process of reporting fuel consumed by trucks traveling through the lower 48 U.S. states and several Canadian provinces. The regulation enables your business to have one fuel license, and you are required to file fuel use tax returns every three months with the state where you are located. To get more information about IFTA, go to the website of the Department of Transportation in your state.

Complete a BOC-3 Form

Register a current BOC-3 form to get the authority to operate interstate. You need to register this form through the FMCSA. This form allows a person in every state where you conduct business to be your legal process agent. For example, if you are sued in a state other than where you are based, an attorney in the other state will receive the legal documents and convey the information to you and the attorney in your local state.

Obtain a Standard Carrier Alpha Code (SCAC)

This code is controlled privately and used to categorize different transportation firms. If you intend to carry intermodal, international, government, or military loads, you will require a SCAC code. Go to the National Motor Freight Traffic Association site to learn more about this code.

Temporary Permit

Temporary permits are basically expensive but critical when you are undertaking short-distance trips. This kind of permit will be required for oversize trucks, whether by weight or measurement. If you are going to a state where the vehicle is not listed under IRP, you will need this permit. Similarly, a Fuel Permit is required when going to a state where the truck doesn't have an IFTA license and decal. New York, Kentucky, and Arizona are the states where you will need to have Temporary Mileage Permits.

Proof of Insurance

The FMCSA requires that you provide proof of insurance before they can give you your authority. You are granted no more than 90 days to provide proof of insurance. It would be best if you did not relax during this period. Instead, make good use of the time by aligning your work, locating the first loads, and getting in touch with any brokers you may have the desire to collaborate with. There are many important things to do when waiting for proof of insurance.

Drug and Alcohol Tests

Anybody operating a car that needs a commercial driver's license should comply with the drug testing rules drafted by FMCSA. This comprises all vehicles that have a total weight of over 26,000 pounds. Additionally, any vehicle that carries hazardous material is also subject to this regulation.

Drug and alcohol testing comprises various requirements, which include:

- Written policy

- Pre-employment drug testing

- Employee education and supervisor training

- Arbitrary alcohol and drug testing, random consortium, or pool

- Post-accident, follow-up, and return to work testing

- Substance abuse professional

Fortunately, you can find a service that specializes in providing all the drug testing requirements in one place, such as the National Drug Screening. They have pocket-friendly prices.

Note that every state has its different transportation and cargo permit needs. Confirm with your home state DMV to determine which permits are needed for transport. You may require permits for crossing state borders, oddly sized or oversize loads, and for a hazardous haul. Make sure that you travel with any permits in your vehicle if you are stopped and requested to show them.

How to Keep Track of all Your Taxes

Keeping track of your taxes, permits, and requirements can be a daunting task. This is why most companies in this industry outsource this work to companies like Trucker's Bookkeeping Service (TBS), which can monitor everything for you. Instead of hiring one clerk in your company who specializes in ensuring that you are always complying with the law, a bookkeeping company like TBS can help you out at an affordable rate.

Remember that activities like being unable to fill your biennial motor carrier identification report might cause your DOT number to be deactivated, which means that you will have to pay heavy fines and have your trucks grounded. The penalties can be as much as $1,000 every day or more, as well as substantial tax levies for being unable to pay road taxes in good time. Monitoring taxes and permits is not a job that anyone should underestimate.

In the next chapter, you will learn how to get insurance for your trucking business.

Obtain Insurance

W hen you have a trucking company, you must ensure that you are adequately covered to protect yourself and your customers. In this industry, it is not sufficient to only have primary liability coverage. Commercial trucking insurance can be tricky, but you don't have to worry about it. This chapter will dissect the issue and teach you everything you need to know about trucking insurance. As a business owner, the insurance policy you will obtain for your trucking business will differ from your personal vehicle insurance.

Insurance is important for you as a truck driver for various reasons. For one, the Federal Motor Carrier Safety Administration (FMCSA) won't allow you to operate your business without it. The FMCSA and DOT—Department of Transportation—need evidence of liability insurance for your MC Number or Operating Authority application. A majority of shippers need proof of insurance before they will entrust your firm with their cargo. Your trucking business will also operate for the duration your insurance is in order. Proof of insurance usually requires to be on standby in case of an accident or inspection.

Insurance is one of the most costly purchases for this type of company. The premiums initially need a large amount of money, and the monthly installments can also be costly ($1,000s). But the benefit makes it worth investing in because an insurance firm protects your company and your clients.

When clients give you goods to carry, they trust you with their company. Your client wants that freight to arrive at its destination in perfect condition, since the freight is the source of their profits. Spoiled freight might make your customer close down their business. When you have insurance, your clients see that you can protect their livelihood in the event of an accident. You will also be protected by covering a percentage of the damages if there is an accident.

What to look for when buying business insurance:

1. Find an insurance policy that covers liability for normal damages that happen when carrying cargo and your vehicle.

2. Get an insurance company that can meet the needs of your business as you expand. Your insurance needs will grow as your assets increase.

Commercial Truck Insurance

There are numerous coverage options for commercial truck insurance firms. If you are transporting things such as hazardous materials, you will need to meet many requirements. You want to ensure that you have chosen a reliable insurance company to handle your insurance needs. This company can give you the right advice about your needs and help you get the appropriate coverage.

Certain insurance companies offer some coverage options that can protect your truck but cannot protect the cargo you are transporting. This could affect you adversely if something bad happens. As a professional driver, it is important to ensure that your driving records are clean, because that can be a big determinant when seeking coverage and the final insurance costs.

There are other kinds of business insurance that a trucking company may have, though they are not compulsory from a legal standpoint. These include trucking general liability insurance, motor cargo coverage, and business interruption insurance. These policies can prevent your company from dealing with losses and lawsuits.

Here are some of the different types of trucking insurance that you may require based on your circumstances:

- **Bobtail Insurance** – This type of insurance protects a tractor when used without attaching a trailer to it, whether delivering a load or not. Sometimes, people confuse this type of coverage with Non-Trucking Liability Insurance, which protects your vehicle when operating it for personal needs.

- **Limited Depreciation Coverage** – This insurance cover will assist you in covering the difference between what you owe on the truck and the amount that the insurance could pay out, or the price of replacing the truck.

- **Mechanical Breakdown Insurance** – This policy helps with cash costs for repairs.

- **Motor Truck Cargo Insurance** – This policy covers commodity or freight that is not hazardous and liability for a haul. It covers the cost of removing cargo that has dropped on a waterway or road by accident and replacing lost or destroyed loads because of collision, theft, or fire. It also protects against lost freight costs and legal expenses. For-hire truckers are usually advised to buy it.

- **Motor Truck General Liability Insurance** – Covers for hire truckers or motor carriers during claims for product and completed operations, medical payments, advertising injury liability, property damage liability, personal injury, and bodily injury. Additionally, it also gives you coverage for seven days or less for destruction to properties that have been rented.

  Drivers who use this coverage are restricted to a radius of 500 miles. It can only be bought in combination with the primary liability policy. Remarkably, truckers who run a business besides for-hire trucking do not qualify for motor truck general liability coverage. The following vehicles are also not qualified to seek this policy: ice cream trucks, passenger vans, buses, hearses, limos, cement trucks, and garbage trucks.

- **Non-Trucking Liability Insurance** – Offers coverage for the utilization of a truck for purposes that are not business-related when you are using the vehicle on holidays or days off.

- **On Hook Coverage** – Offers coverage of cars your business does not own during hauling or towing.

- **Optional Downtime Coverage** – This cover starts applying when your truck experiences downtime.

- **Passenger Accident Insurance** – Covers the driver if a truck gets involved in an accident when an uninsured person is inside the vehicle.

- **Physical Damage Coverage** – Covers your commercial truck when there is physical damage.

- **Trailer Interchange Agreement Insurance** – Covers damage to trailers that you don't own when damaged physically.

- **Commercial Umbrella Liability Insurance** – Working in vehicles and on roads puts your company at higher risk than other kinds of business, and costs coming from a covered liability loss can also be higher. This type of insurance stretches coverage beyond your general liability coverage policy limits.

- **Worker Compensation Insurance** – This is necessary for many states if you have staff. It insures medical expenses and prevents you from litigation if a member of staff gets an injury or falls sick due to their work.

- **Business Interruption Insurance** – This policy covers lost income plus operating costs and the cost of reinstating operations if a big calamity makes it impossible to conduct business.

- **Underinsured/Uninsured Motorists** – Commercial trucks are usually the biggest automobiles. If one of your trucks is involved in an accident that another driver has caused, there is a likelihood that the driver at fault does not have enough coverage to cater for your property damage and injuries. This coverage will help you cover the expenses instead.

- **Rental Reimbursement with Downtime** – Business owners who buy this policy can use a rental truck or get financial reimbursement if their commercial vehicle is unusable for business responsibilities after being damaged in an accident. This is particularly crucial to ensure that the trucking company continues to get regular income if a truck is momentarily unusable. When choosing this coverage, the limit you select affects the amount of money the insurance company will pay daily if the truck is ruined. The policyholder will get compensation for as many as 30 days to insure the cost of a rental truck. Several insurance companies, including Progressive, will also help locate a good rental truck as a short-term replacement.

Whereas most insurance companies provide rental reimbursement with downtime insurance as one policy option, some other companies provide these two as two different options. When provided independently, rental reimbursement caters for the values of a rental vehicle, whereas downtime policy caters for lost earnings if a rental truck is inaccessible.

Notably, not every commercial truck can qualify for this kind of policy. Only these vehicles are covered:

- Tractors

- Straight trucks with a weight of over 16,000 pounds

- Roll on vehicles with a weight of over 45,000 pounds

- Front loaders with a weight of over 45,000 pounds

- Dump trucks with a weight of over 16,000 pounds

- Tank trucks with a weight exceeding 1,400 gallons

- Stake trucks with a weight exceeding 16,000 pounds

- Refrigerated trucks with a weight exceeding 16,000 pounds

- Flatbed trucks with a weight exceeding 16,000 pounds

- Dually pickups

Trailer Interchange

Sometimes, trucks haul trailers belonging to other companies through a trailer interchange agreement. This is a contract that organizes the moving of a trailer between two different truckers to finalize a shipment. Basically, the trucker with the trailer bears the responsibility of covering the cost of any damages experienced when the trailer is in their possession. Because the vehicle's physical damage insurance does not insure borrowed trailers, they subsequently need extra trailer interchange coverage to insure any physical damage caused by an incident such as vandalism, explosion, theft, and collision.

Only pickups and semi-trucks or tractors qualify for this policy, and all vehicles should also buy primary liability policy. Be informed that trailer interchange is not obtainable in Virginia.

These requirements and needs can vary as a driver carries goods for different companies with different coverage types. An insurance agent can judge a driver's needs and look for the most suitable coverage varieties.

Commercial Truck Insurance Prerequisites

The prerequisites for acquiring commercial truck insurance are not as complicated as most people think. Nevertheless, you have to ensure that you provide adequate information about your company's status, so that your agent can get the most appropriate policy for you that is tailored to your needs. These are some of the things you will require, to start:

-

Avail the specifications for all vehicles you would like to include in the policy, such as Vin Numbers, Year, Model, and Make.

- DOT Authority and MC

- A commercial driving license if you are transporting over 26,000 pounds.

You can follow these steps to assess your coverage needs and buy policies.

Assess Your Risk Level

Your insurance needs are determined by how your business is exposed to lawsuits, accidents, and injuries. Think about how you are exposed to regular risks such as loss of income injury and the risks that are unique to the industry, such as

- An accident makes the load spill on the highway, ruining the product and incurring expensive cleanup expenses.

- An ice storm might delay your fleet for several days.

- A product belonging to a customer is destroyed because of wrong delivery.

The kind of truck you operate, the load you carry, and the routes you use (whether short haul or long haul) determine the insurance coverage you should buy.

Know Your Policy Needs

This coverage is popular among trucking companies such as freight forwarders and hire-truckers. The specific coverage requirements will be influenced by routes used, the kind of cargo you carry, and your company's size.

Shop Around for Coverage

You can use three methods to buy an insurance policy in this industry. These are through directly reaching out to individual insurers, going to an online marketplace, or an insurance broker.

Insurance broker

A broker is a well-connected person who is paid on a commission basis. You will tell them your business needs, and then they will explain the coverage options to you and give you quotes from different insurance companies. If you are new to the trucking business, you will find a broker to be quite important.

Advantages:

- They will assist you to know all about policy options and coverage needs

- Dealing with one person saves a lot of time instead of calling every insurance company yourself

Disadvantages:

- They have no obligation to look for the best rate for you

- Their services are not for free; they charge a fee or work on commission

Online insurance marketplace

You can consider these to be your online brokers. Fill out an online-based questionnaire, and the site provides coverage options and quotes from various insurers.

Advantages:

- You can look for an insurance company at your convenience, even when it is not business hours.

- Most websites allow you to communicate with an agent if you require assistance.

Disadvantages:

- You only get quotes from insurance providers who collaborate with the marketplace

- Policy maintenance, customer service, and claims are made through the insurance company and not the site.

Reach out to individual insurance companies

This option lets you bypass the broker and buy your policy straight from an insurance firm. The provider can give you a quote either by phone or online. Some providers are more willing to give someone a quote than others. Find as many different quotes as you can and compare the prices. You should know that some insurance companies use a third-party insurer for coverage.

Advantages:

- Obtain quotes from insurers you select

- Get a quote and get a policy fast

Disadvantages:

- You might not get customized support to assist you to personalize your coverage needs

- Shopping around for the best rates can take a lot of time.

Compare Insurers

It is crucial to obtain quotes from various insurance providers since the cost of business insurance for a trucking business can differ a lot, even for similar coverage.

Consider the following factors when comparing providers:

Price

Consider two primary costs, namely your deductible and your premium. The latter is basically per year, even though you may have the choice to pay every month. Insurance providers normally give you a discount if you pay the premium early.

Financial Strength

Commercial truck insurance is meant to insure events that would normally result in expensive costs that will be inconvenient for you, the business owner, to fund from your personal finances. With bigger and heavier cars, the financial loss caused by trucking incidents is greater than with a smaller commercial automobile or personal vehicle. Consequently, business owners must always assess the financial strength of an insurance company, because that will influence the insurance provider's capacity to pay costly claims.

You can always research independently, since public insurers are obligated to make their documents available to the public. Nevertheless, to compare various insurance companies effectively, it is beneficial to refer to the ratings provided by the main credit rating agencies, such as S &P, Moody's, and AM Best. Their ratings offer a clear picture of the financial health of a company.

Policy Coverage

What does the policy cover and what does it not cover? Notice the coverage variances between insurers. Most insurance companies offer basic policies such as property damage and general liability. However, your business needs could also require additional coverage like a non-trucking liability. In such situations, it is imperative to select an insurer who provides all kinds of the policies you require.

Additionally, it is important to comprehend the policy restrictions and coverage terms for every company to pick a plan that suits you best. Also, remember that some insurance companies do not operate in all states. Therefore, business owners who have across-state trucking services should make sure that they would be insured in every state they do business in.

Reviews

Go through reviews to find out what present and old customers are saying. Complaint databases such as the National Association of Insurance Commissioners and the Better Business Bureau can be useful.

Limits Of Liability

This is the highest amount an insurance company will pay out during your policy's lifetime and per incident. You can tweak coverage limits to be equal to your risk level. Greater limits mean greater premiums.

Some of the most reputable business insurance companies include Liberty Mutual, Huckleberry, USAA, State Farm, Progressive, Nationwide, Next, Travelers, Allstate, biBERK, Hiscox, Hartford, Geico, and Chubb.

Purchase Coverage, Review Yearly

Ensure that you understand the procedure for making a claim with your insurer. Is it through the phone, using an app, or online? Also, write down any important contacts—the claims department, your agent, etc. Coverage requirements can vary with time, therefore, check your policy limits and obtain new quotes every year.

Average Cost of Insurance

Trucking insurance rates differ according to the type of policy and the insurance company. For example, with general liability, it will cost you between $750 and $7,000 a year.

Trucking liability insurance costs between $2,500 and $4,000 for each trucker, while non-trucking liability costs range from approximately $450 to more than $5,000.

Factors That Influence the Cost of a Policy

Various factors will influence the cost of your policy. These include your:

- General aggregate limit
- Per-occurrence limit
- Number of staffs
- Deductible
- Location
- CDL's general safety rating
- Truck's mileage and weight
- Year of manufacture
- Engine type/miles/size per person
- Vehicle type
- Load type

Various factors influence how much insurance for commercial trucks will cost. The business owner can attune a number of them to decrease the amount of coverage needed, whereas others are an important part of doing business and cannot be altered. These are the most significant factors that affect coverage:

Amount of deductible and coverage

Basically, the more coverage needed, the bigger the monthly payment. Selecting a bigger deductible can reduce the cost of monthly payments. Nevertheless, this choice comes with financial risks. When you have a big deductible, if an incident happens, the company will have to fork out a lot of money before the insurance policy steps in.

Driving history

Like personal car insurance, driving history plays a huge role in the premium that a trucking business owner pays for their insurance policy. Nevertheless, since the risks are more with bigger automobiles, a driver with a history of accidents or violations will have a much higher increase in insurance expenses. Keeping driving records clean and devoid of violations and accidents is a great way to spend less on insurance and save money. A trucking company owner handling a fleet with many drivers should scrutinize driving records when hiring and may consider investing in driver safety training.

Cargo

Various kinds of cargo come with varying degrees of risk. More dangerous or heavier goods could cause more destruction than cargo with little weight during an accident. Therefore, the cost of insurance will account for this risk. Be aware that some kinds of cargo like livestock, pharmaceuticals, and explosives are not insured by most policies and would need extra coverage.

Vehicle Storage

The place you park your automobiles when you are not using them can impact your insurance premiums. The safer the location, the less the insurance expenses. For instance, commercial trucks parked in a closed yard or garage will be charged lower insurance rates than those parked in open lots or public areas.

Operating radius and location

The insurance cost is higher when drivers cover long distances between states or all over a region and not locally. Truck drivers with a bigger operating radius usually have greater risks of becoming involved in an accident, since there might be few stops in a route, or the driver may not know the route well. Additionally, different states have varying commercial truck insurance costs. Hence drivers in various states have a possibility of spending more on insurance.

Kinds of vehicles insured

Vehicles weighing more usually attract more insurance costs, since they risk creating substantial damage when there is an accident. Additionally, newer cars normally require more money to insure them since their replacement or repair costs will be higher if there is an accident. The bigger the fleet, the higher the cost of the policy will be.

What a Commercial Truck Insurance Policy Doesn't Cover

Apart from outlining what is covered, insurance policies for commercial trucks also list exclusions. These might include various kinds of occurrences or specific kinds of loads. Most omissions for commercial truck insurance are the same as what is omitted in commercial auto coverages. These are:

Damages that are more than policy limits

Each policy will have the highest amount that the insurance company will pay when you make a claim. Any extra damages that exceed the policy limit will not be paid for. Business owners can add additional liability or umbrella coverage to stretch coverage limits.

Property of others

Most commercial truck insurance policies will not insure damages to vehicles, personal items, or property belonging to others, regardless of whether the policy insures the person taking care of the vehicle or property. Suppose your firm frequently hauls property or vehicles owned by others. There are other coverage options that you can look into.

Intentional damages

Insurance companies will not insure injuries or damages caused by deliberate harm to another property or person. Inflicting intentional harm to trick the insurer into compensating for the damages is considered insurance fraud, which can result in criminal and financial penalties.

Various kinds of load

Additionally, specific kinds of cargo are omitted from commercial truck insurance policies. These cargos consist of valuables like jewelry and money, explosive materials, property in a different carrier's possession, live animals, contraband, pharmaceuticals, and drugs like tobacco and alcohol. In some situations, coverage options like Livestock Cargo Insurance are accessible to cover these loads.

How to Get Affordable Commercial Truck Insurance

As we have seen, commercial truck insurance is very important for a business. While insurance may be expensive sometimes, there are effective ways of saving on insurance and finding policies that work. These methods can help you save several hundred or thousands of dollars every month that you can direct towards other sections of the business. The major strategies that you can apply to save on truck insurance are finding discounts or selecting a lower coverage policy.

Discounts

- **CDL Discount** – For hire truckers who have had a CDL for not less than two years can get a discount on their liability policy.

- **Prior Insurance Savings** – Some insurance companies give discounts on the following year's insurance if a policyholder has maintained consistent insurance coverage for the past 12 months.

- **Business Experience Discount** – This discount is given to owner-operators who have been operating a business for over three years.

- **Paid In Full Discount** – Certain insurance companies will discount policyholders who pay off their premium all at once at the start of the coverage. For instance, truckers who have a policy with Progressive can save as much as 15% using this discount.

- **Less Coverage** – More coverage leads to greater monthly costs and vice versa. For instance, business owners may not require special insurance for cargo. Paying the most important insurance required by the state or federal government can help you save money.

- **Lower Coverage Limits** – The policy limit affects the amount of commercial truck insurance. Policies that have decreased coverage limits will qualify for reduced monthly premiums. Business owners need to think about how much coverage they will need instead of mechanically selecting the available high policy limit.

- **Higher Deductible** – A policy with a high deductible will decrease monthly payments, but there is also a danger of paying a huge amount of money if an accident occurs. A business owner can choose this kind of policy if the drivers have a spotless driving record.

The States with the Cheapest Truck Insurance

The top ten states with the least commercial truck insurance rates for across-the-state motor truck goods coverage are as follows according to Progressive's data:

1. Montana

2. Alaska

3. Wisconsin

4. North Dakota

5. South Dakota

6. Idaho

7. Iowa

8. Nebraska

9. Wyoming

10. Mississippi

For trucks that are being used within the state, the top ten states with the smallest commercial truck insurance premiums include:

1. South Dakota

2. Kansas

3. Montana

4. North Dakota

5.

Nebraska

6. Arizona

7. Iowa

8. Massachusetts

9. Wyoming

10. Mississippi

Important Points to Note

Most trucking business owners wonder whether they need insurance before starting a business. The answer to this question is that you need to buy insurance coverage for your company before you come into contact with any customer. Even though insurance prices may appear to be big for a new business, it is important to be proactive when securing your assets.

Truckers also wonder whether insurance will protect their businesses from all risks. This is not usually the case; your policy might have some exceptions, and some dangers may be uninsurable. Ensure that you talk about the scope of your cover in detail with your agent to avoid getting surprises when you discover that there are gaps in the policy.

Summary

Like any other business that involves vehicles, insurance is an important part of the equation, and you must include it in your company budget. Identify the most important policies for your trucking business and keep up with the payments. These include motor truck general liability and bobtail insurance.

In the next chapter, you will learn about the different ways you can raise money for your business as a trucking company owner.

Raise Capital For Your Business

S tarting a trucking company and becoming your own boss is an exciting prospect for anyone. But what do you do when you do not have enough money to start the business? Building a trucking business from scratch is not a cheap venture.

Despite being a profitable business, trucking also comes with a fair share of expenses. You will need to have a certain amount of capital when starting. For instance, buying a truck will cost you about $80,000. You will also need to have money that you will use to keep your trucks operating optimally. Besides buying a truck, you should also factor into your budget expenses such as accounting or invoicing software, truck maintenance fees, tolls, insurance, additional taxes, business licenses and permits, and registration and documentation. These expenses can add up. Therefore, it is unrealistic to think that you can start a trucking business without any money or with only a small amount.

Fortunately for you, there are many ways of raising money for your startup. In this chapter, we will explore the methods of raising capital that are available to you and how to go about applying these methods to your advantage.

You may not be able to raise all the money you require from just one method. Therefore, you will probably need to use a number of them, as most people do.

Savings

Of course, you may have figured out by now that you will need to save up for your business venture. To begin with, if you want to be a profitable business owner you should learn how to save. If you have not saved any money, start saving now and in a few months you will have a significant amount of money to invest in your business and you will also acquire an important skill that will help you in your new life as a business owner.

Try to think about ways in which you can reduce some expenses. Perhaps reduce the number of times you eat out and carry packed lunch from home. Take the bus instead of driving, and forego that Netflix subscription.

Another thing: do not spend all your savings on starting the business, rather, have some cash left for sorting unexpected payments that might emerge, or you might not be able to get on the road and start making money immediately. It is usually wise to keep some money aside for emergencies. Therefore, do not spend all of it.

Sell Some of Your Stuff

If you look closely, you will realize that you have something that you don't need that much or you do not use nowadays. Sell them and invest the money in something that will improve your lifestyle. This can be something like a car, a video game. Have a garage sale, and you will be surprised to know how much money you have been sitting on. Sell the things that are gathering dust in your house that someone else could make better use of.

Non-Profit Microlender

Many states have companies, basically founded by people who have succeeded in business and want to help the disadvantaged in society, which will extend loans to budding entrepreneurs who intend to open new micro-businesses. You will only qualify for a loan if they have no doubt that you can repay it. Having a solid business plan is the best way to demonstrate your capability.

SBA Microloan Program

The US government acknowledges that the economy relies on small businesses and that it is at its best when small businesses are doing well. They came up with the Small Business Administration to assist small businesses in getting established and expanding. The SBA Microloan Program helps offer loans to micro-businesses, such as startups. One of the good aspects of these loans is that they normally come with some business knowledge too.

Actually, the SBA doesn't offer loans. Rather, it simply guarantees them. Intermediaries are the ones that issue the loans. Finding the intermediaries is an easy process because all you have to do is visit the SBA website (sba.gov), go to the partners/lenders/microloan page, and search by state. For example, in New York, SBA intermediaries include Grameen America, Inc.; Community Capital New York, Inc.; and Renaissance Economic Development Corporation.

On the website's Funding Programs page, you will find crucial information, such as the special requirements for eligibility. These requirements include stating a solid business purpose, showing the capability to pay, meeting SBA standard size, exhausting funding options, having invested equity, conducting business in the USA, and being a business that is started with the intention of generating profits, among other requirements.

SBA loans are popular because of their favorable repayment terms, high loan amounts, and low-interest rates. Additionally, the SBA backs up as much as 85% of the loan's total amount if the person borrowing fails to repay it. These loans are excellent for helping you start your trucking company, however, they are relatively difficult to secure. You should be ready to deal with a lot of paperwork and have a good credit score as well as a lengthy and solid credit history.

Some of the Popular SBA Loans

The SBA 7 (a) Loan Program has seven varying financing options for companies relying on their needs. Businesses, where veterans own more than 5%, can get as much as $5 million via a Veteran's Advantage Loan. The 7 (a) Standard Loan is the easiest way for small businesses to get financing and can help them get as much as $5 million. The SBA can back up 85% of a loan of as much as $150,000 while more financing can be guaranteed 75%. Other choices are programs targeting international trade, 36-hour approval, (7a) Express Loans, and 7(a) Small Loans of as much as $350,000.

SBA disaster loans: these can be used for operating capital to meet operating costs and to cater for losses that insurance doesn't cover. From the beginning of COVID-19, these loans can boost businesses that have been badly affected by pandemic or natural occurrences. If you do not need a lot of capital, you can also consider an SBA Microloan. A trucking company must apply with a community-based organization or a nonprofit to get this loan of between $500 and $50,000.

SBA Express Loan

Considering the long durations linked to SBA loans, this program is meant to expedite things a bit. Therefore, instead of a bunch of paperwork and a 3-month-long waiting time, you only get a bundle of paperwork and can receive money in only one month. Sure, this period is longer than many loans that are not SBA. However, if you prefer an SBA loan and you do not have a lot of time to wait, then this loan would be perfect for you. Its requirements are the same as those in the 7(a) program even though they have lower dollar amounts. They also come with more limitations on how the money can be spent. There are three main ways that this loan can be used: debt consolidation, increasing working capital, and financing equipment.

SBA 504 loan

If some of your growth strategies consist of real estate, then this loan would be ideal for you. These loans are particularly designed for costs associated with a property. Approved uses are:

- Refinancing your loans to grow your business with equipment or facilities

- Buying machinery

- Renovating/modernizing as well as transforming current facilities

- Making land improvements, including landscaping, parking, utilities, streets, and grading

- Buying land

- Buying a current building

- Building new facilities

Your business plan should consist of any real estate projects your company needs to handle. If you have projects that are approved by this loan, you could gain from the targeted characteristics of this loan.

SBA Contractor Assistance

The federal government uses programs to ensure that small companies are given a small fraction of federal contracting money every year. The SBA offers contracting help to small enterprises via a number of programs such as:

- Women-Owned Small Business Federal Contracting Program: Not less than 5% of contracts are given to companies owned by women.

-

HUBZone Program: Concentrates on small businesses in areas that have been underused in history.

- 8(a) Business Development Program: Focuses on economically and socially disadvantaged small business owners for contracting based on SBA criteria.

- All Small Mentor Protégé Program: It connects small businesses with skilled contractors to offer mentorship.

- Service-Disabled Veteran-Owned Small Business program: It spares at least 3% of contracts for qualified small business owners.

Qualified trucking companies can hunt these chances for safe federal contracts, which can act as a dependable source of revenue.

Bank and Credit Union Loans

There is a wide array of bank loans. These are some of the most popular ones that most people use to start a business:

- Business Loans: It's normally difficult to obtain a business loan for a startup, however, there is no harm in trying. Under certain conditions, credit unions and banks will extend you a loan.

- Title Loans: If you buy a vehicle through a clean process, you can use it as security and obtain a loan, at times for more money than its real value. Certain banks will go to the extent of allowing you to refinance the loan on an automobile that has a higher value than your loan and give you the difference.

- Signature Loans: This kind of loan needs no collateral, therefore, banks will not normally lend you a lot of money.

- Home Equity Line of Credit: This is certainly one of the most preferred loans if you have a home in your name. Remember that you risk losing your home, so think carefully before applying for this kind of a loan.

Loans from Friends and Family

Be cautious about this one. Do not take funds if there is a possibility that it will jeopardize your relationship in the event that things go awry. Be straightforward about how you are going to use the money and the reason for doing it. Write the conditions of the loan down, so that there will be no queries later on.

Find a Partner

Doing this means that you are sacrificing your ownership. This should be your last option if your partner is only going to provide you with a loan once and they will not do anything else to help you run the business. If this is the case, reduce the size of ownership that you give to the partner.

Credit Cards

This is another choice that you should be cautious about. If you utilize credit card debt to finance your business, it is advisable to have a Plan B for paying for the credit card if the business cannot pay the expenses for some time. For example, you can use the income of your significant other if they have a stable job. Alternatively, you can reduce expenses somewhere else and use the money you save to pay for the payments.

You can use a credit card to pay for things such as buying equipment and tools, insurance or truck down payment. Keep in mind that you cannot use a credit card to pay for truck monthly payments, but many lenders will let you use it to pay for the down payment.

Business Line of Credit

A line of credit is basically a financial product that gives you the opportunity to borrow funds many times. You can borrow until you reach a specific limit and then you pay your debt. You can keep using the line of credit provided that the debt you owe does not exceed the limit.

The key difference between a credit card and a line of credit is that whereas a credit card is linked to and enables you to get access to a line of credit, you can open a line of credit that does not have a card linked to it. Essentially, all credit cards are also lines of credit, however, not every line of credit is a credit card.

When you own a trucking business, having a line of credit will come in handy because it will help you cover variable expenses that keep changing all the time. This form of funding will give you the flexibility to access funds whenever you need them as long as you do not go over the set limit.

Most of the time, businesses use a business line of credit like a financial safety net that helps them get money for emergencies. The credit limit is set according to the risk your company takes on, profitability, and market value. The lender is the one who decides what the limit will be. With this financing method, you can access up to $500,000.

Equipment Finance

A trucking company's success hinges on the equipment that it uses. Besides a truck, the business also needs other equipment such as vehicle jacks, computer systems, forklifts, trollies, and different trailers, including specialized trailers for transporting hazardous materials or liquids, auto transport trailers, refrigerated trailers, flatbeds, and dry vans.

Regardless of whether you are just starting a company or you simply want to offer better services to your customers and compete fairly with the competition, it is important that you use modern equipment to ensure that your business operates optimally and keeps customers happy.

Business equipment loans can help you buy the equipment you want or require without getting into too much debt. This kind of loan can give you access to up to $5 million.

Funding Operating Expenses

As soon as your truck goes for its maiden trip, you have to begin catering for expenses such as lumper fees, maintenance, and fuel. Unfortunately, you basically will not begin to receive payment for the tasks you do for about a month, or a month and a half, after you successfully deliver the cargo. Fortunately, as we mentioned earlier, there are services that you can take advantage of to eliminate this problem, including quickpays and factoring. Here are their pros and cons to help you decide which one suits your needs best:

Quickpays

Most brokers will give you this option. Usually, if you request this option, you will receive your payment in 2 to 7 days, which is better than the regular 30 to 45 days. However, you will have to pay a fee of 3-5%.

Pros

- You receive your payment within a short time.

Cons

- The price is normally 3 to 5%.

- You basically need to fill out a unique application for every broker, and there is usually a distinct process of submitting the paperwork.

Factoring

Just like Quickpays, factoring firms can also help you get your cash faster. They accomplish this by buying your firm's accounts receivable. Essentially, the factoring company gives you the money you have earned and deducts your fee within a day after you have delivered your cargo. The shipper or broker you transported the goods for will then give the factoring company the whole amount they owe you after 30 to 45 days.

Pros

- You will be paid within 24 business hours or the same day.

- They deal with all of the collecting and billing activities.

- You only deal with one individual who takes care of all the paperwork on your behalf. Therefore, you don't have to understand how the system of different shippers and brokers operates.

Cons

- The fees are 3 to 5%, according to how big or small your business is.

When you are choosing a factoring company, pick one that has a good reputation. Ask around for a referral from your fellow trucking business owners, because there are unscrupulous factoring businesses out there that make the good ones look bad. Another thing that you should be careful about is the contract. Scrutinize it carefully before signing it, and make sure you read the fine print well. If it is too long or if they refuse to let you view it until just before they want you to put your signature on it, these are red flags. If you have doubts about a contract, find a good lawyer and have them check if there is something wrong or not.

Financing an Already Established Business

A trucking business can generate good profits if it is well managed. However, a business like that usually needs high initial capital and operating costs. If you are joining this industry as a business owner, you need to have access to sufficient financing for use in buying or leasing trailers and trucks. There are numerous options for financing your business, such as capital ventures and loans, which will depend on the stage of your business.

Equipment Lenders

You can get funding from an equipment lender. Equipment lenders manufacture and sell trucks and similar equipment. They offer bespoke solutions for the people working in the trucking industry, providing them with attractive funding packages. Financed equipment, such as the vehicles, act as security for the loan.

Venture Capital

Even if the trucking business is perceived as being too segmented, you can get venture capital if you meet the criteria that equity investors set. Normally, if your company has a great management team that is doing a good job and is worth about twenty million dollars, it is possible for you to lure investors.

Franchise Agreements

You may think of getting into franchise arrangements with parties who are interested to assist your business in growing fast. Under an agreement like that, other trucking business owners operate their vehicles using your name and give you a franchising fee on top of giving a specific fraction of their proceeds. When you award the franchisee a license, you become responsible for offering the administrative services in the company's management.

Bank Loans

Bank loans can be used to improve cash flow or to grow the business by purchasing new equipment. However, banks set strict conditions. Usually, you need to have a good history of operating your business, because the bank will look at your balance sheet. Additionally, you will need fixed assets to use them as collateral, because in most cases, banks will not agree to use your vehicles as collateral.

How to Spot the Best Loan

There are certain loan pricing metrics that you need to focus on when choosing a loan. These include:

1. Annual Percentage Rate (APR): This metric shows the cost of a loan as an annual rate.

2. Total Cost of Capital (TCC): This metric basically adds all the fees and interests to provide you with a conclusive number.

3. Cents on the Dollar: This one shows the interest and fees that you will repay for every dollar owed.

4. Average Monthly Payment: This metric can assist you to gauge how a loan would affect your monthly cash flow.

Even though metrics are important assets, you should be aware that there can be discrepancies in the manner in which some financiers outline their fees. The ambiguity that results from these inconsistencies makes comparisons difficult. Luckily, you can solve this problem by using SMARTBox. This is a comparison software that assists you by placing loan options at the same level by emphasizing similar language and understandable disclosure principles.

Five Grant Resources for Your Startup

When starting a trucking business, it is nearly impossible to think of grants as a potential source of funding. The main advantage of seeking grants is that, unlike investors, business lines of credit, and loans, you will not have to repay them. This is a huge plus for businesses with little collateral or cash ready and cannot qualify for financing by most lenders.

However, free money can sometimes be costly. There are few grants for small trucking businesses. Finding time to fill reports and applications while managing a trucking business around the clock can be a daunting task. Moreover, grant terms can be relatively stringent, especially about how beneficiaries utilize their financing.

Even though most grants are given to government entities and nonprofit organizations, businesses in different sectors can also benefit from grants. When it comes to trucking companies, availability and suitability are determined by various factors such as the demographics of a business owner, number of staff, and geography. For instance, certain federal grants are specially meant for minority business owners, women, and veterans. In addition, different states offer different grants, so a grant provided by a particular state may not be available in an adjacent state.

Besides eligibility, grant proposals may require you to provide information and documentation that is similar to the ones required when applying for conventional financing or loans. Basically, funders have the desire to know that their money is being used wisely. Therefore, showing readiness through a business plan is normally one important element of an application.

Here are the five places to search for trucking grant opportunities:

USDA Rural Business Development Grants

This program offers training and technical assistance for businesses located in rural areas that have fewer than 50 fresh employees and under $2 million in gross profits. Rural areas are described as communities that are not within the urbanized boundaries of a city with at most 50,000 residents. Financing can be used for a few different reasons that are related to trucking companies, such as a revolving loan fund for new businesses, leadership training, and equipment.

Even though grant financing is used to help small businesses, privately owned businesses cannot apply straight to the USDA for financing. Rather, tribes recognized by the federal government, higher learning institutions, state agencies, nonprofit organizations, and municipalities have to apply, then later allocate the money to companies in their community.

Local Initiatives Support Corporation (LISC)

LISC was founded by the Ford Foundation in 1979, with the aim of bringing together private and public investment for assisting individuals and communities. In collaboration with Lowes, it presently provides funds of between $5,000 and $20,000 for qualified businesses via Rural Relief Small Business Grants. They approve applications after regular durations, as it is based on periodic rounds. Thus, it is important to constantly check the site for announcements to ensure that you can seize the opportunities when they become available.

Just like USDA Rural Business Development Grant program, suitable applicants need to be situated in a community with not more than 50,000 residents. For businesses such as trucking enterprises that do not operate in one location, the address where the automobile is kept will be used to gauge suitability. LISC gives the first priority to entrepreneurs who are women, those of color, companies situated in disadvantaged communities with little access to cheap capital, and businesses owned by veterans. Applications are also assessed based on the negative effects of the pandemic and the projected change in the community.

In addition, LISC offers regional small business grant opportunities. There is location-specific relief funding that is available to trucking businesses based in Chesterfield and Henrico Counties in Virginia, Boston, Los Angeles and New York.

NAV Small Business Grant Contest

This grant is awarded by a business loan company called NAV to two small businesses quarterly. The business that wins first place gets $10,000, and the second place winner receives $5,000. The moment an application is completed, enterprises get a voting link to share and accumulate votes to qualify as a finalist. NAV selects five finalists out of the 200 enterprises getting many votes online, Even though the grants offer little finding and allow few applicants, the process of applying is quite transparent and the grant terms are versatile.

National Association for the Self Employed

Most trucking business owners are their own bosses unless their business is a corporation. If you are part of the NASE, you can apply for a grant known as a growth grant for your business. Winners are picked on a monthly basis and given awards of $4,000 to grow their business. New members qualify to complete an application 90 days after joining.

Candid

Even though Candid's system of databases, community foundations, and libraries mainly deal with nonprofits, they also have information about business grant opportunities. Startups and businesses can utilize Candid to find financial assistance and relevant grant opportunities instead of surfing the internet randomly searching for grants.

Grants can be a beneficial source of capital for starting or expanding a business particularly if you want to start a trucking business without any money. Nevertheless, many trucking companies will probably require extra financing to purchase equipment, expand their business or hire new staff.

How to Use the Business Loan Funding

Besides using the loan money as capital when starting your trucking business, loans also come in handy when you want to expand your business. You need a substantial amount of working capital to run a trucking company.

Before submitting a loan application, ensure that you think carefully about the action you are about to take. Weigh all your options and see which one best suits you. When you evaluate business lenders, you need to find out the duration of their application procedure. This is particularly important if you require funding quickly. Mostly, alternative money lenders can approve your application within a day. On the other hand, banks can take weeks and sometimes months to respond to applicants.

Another element to think about when assessing trucking business funding options is the application requirements. These are the most common requirements for getting business loans:

- Bank Statements: Most of the time, business lenders will ask you to look at your bank statements. Besides helping you meet the requirements, these amounts can have an impact on your interest rate and repayment terms.

- Minimum Credit Score: A majority of financing providers will be interested in knowing your credit score. Therefore, if you have bad credit, it will be prudent for you to raise it before applying.

- Time in Business: Several financing companies have a time in business prerequisite, which means that new business owners may not qualify for loans with them.

So if you have been in business for some time and you have taken a loan, these are the ways in which you can use the loan money:

Increase your fleet

According to the research done by American Transportation Research Institute, trucking businesses that have big fleets normally have a high ROI. Besides saving on the expenses of shipping per mile, big companies can also save on expenses like tolls, fuel, insurance, permits, load boards, truck trailers and semi-trucks, and commercial vehicles.

If you have a small number of trucks at the moment, you might be forced to decline to take on some jobs. If you have to turn clients away, this will adversely affect your company's general profits.

When you increase your fleet, you will be able to accept more gigs, which will boost your business returns. Growing your fleet, in the beginning, is important in incurving out a niche for yourself in this competitive industry.

Hire more drivers

Having adequate drivers is important for your trucking company to survive. Nevertheless, there are many expenses associated with hiring that will require to be bought initially. To begin with, you may require to invest in hiring expenses including hiring a recruiter or posting on paid job sites. Additionally, you need to be in a position to personal equipment and staff uniforms, possible union costs, insurance, permits, commercial drivers licenses, and training. (We will dedicate a whole chapter to explaining all these expenses in detail later on). Even though these costs might appear to be many, your business will benefit in the long run. A business loan can help you attain this type of growth.

Upgrade trucking technology

Presently, there are more technology-based solutions for trucks than there have ever been before. Because of this, employing new technology is a great way of making your business have a competitive edge in the market. If you take too long to adopt and bring your technology up to date, you might end up being left behind by your competitors. There are many technologies that have recently been invented to streamline trucking business operations, such as electronic logging devices, improved routing systems, and enhanced camera systems. No doubt, these technological improvements will be expensive. A trucking business will help you achieve this objective.

Enhance your business logistics

The trucking business depends on efficient logistics. If your business does not have well-planned logistical procedures, there is a possibility that it will have a hard time meeting amplified demands. Besides operational success, when you ensure that your logistics are in order, it can help increase your business returns.

Enhancing your business's logistics entails doing various things, such as utilizing automated data systems, operation experts, and process engineers. When you apply for a business loan, you will get the funds to put into a system that can efficiently fulfill your needs.

Spend less on inventory

Usually, a majority of industries save on each unit when they buy larger amounts. After a while, reducing marginal costs is one of the most effective ways of boosting your profits. By utilizing extra working capital, you can buy more inventory for your trucking business. For example, you can purchase inventory like lights, mechanical equipment, and tires.

Other ways that you can use a transportation business loan include repairing vehicles, marketing your business, having some more cash on hand, diversifying services, and buying branding materials, as well as weather-related costs such as winter tires.

Summary

Becoming a trucking business owner can be a profitable endeavor, since the trucking industry is integral to the economy. Commercial trucks help keep the cost of transporting goods low. Even though the trucking industry will always be around, it is only a few trucking companies that will remain standing. Therefore, it is crucial to make useful investments that will separate your business from the crowd. Identify at least one area above that you can improve on and look for financing to enable you to actualize your strategy.

In the next chapter, you will learn the factors to consider when choosing a truck and how to buy a good truck.

Buy A Good Truck

One of the most important investments when starting a trucking company is a commercial truck. It is crucial that you select a good truck that will be reliable and help you achieve your business objectives. Some of the factors that you have to consider when choosing a truck are:

1. New versus used

2. Weight limit

3. Whether the manufacturers have many dealerships throughout the U.S.

4. Weather resistance

5. Your cab style of choice

6. Comfort level

7. Price

8. Whether you are working long-distance or locally

Like any car that you buy, you need to do a test drive. Some of the best brands to consider that can meet most of your trucking requirements are Peterbilt, Freightliner, and Kenworth trucks.

Another important thing that you need to do when buying a truck is to go with a mechanic to the truck dealership. Have the mechanic examine the vehicle and approve it before you pay for it. This advice comes directly from a trucking business owner who has been working in the industry for a while.

Think about it: you will be spending a significant amount of money purchasing the truck, so why should you take chances and go without an experienced mechanic?

Buy or lease

This decision depends on your purchasing power as a new small business owner, and each option has several pros and cons. When you purchase a truck with cash, your payment is finalized, hence, you will not need to pay monthly installments. You can also trade in the truck at a later date by taking advantage of the built-in equity. Definitely, you will also need to pay a bigger deposit, normally 10% to 25% based on whether you purchase used or new.

On the other hand, when you lease, the truck does not belong to you. You have to make consistent payments, and you cannot utilize equity to purchase a new vehicle. Additionally, you have to observe certain rules, such as mileage limitations and upholding its condition. One of the main advantages of leasing is that the person who leases the vehicle to you will usually pay for the maintenance costs.

Regardless of whether you purchase a new or used vehicle, acquiring trucks is usually a costly endeavor. The most important thing to keep in mind when you are shopping for a truck is the value of quality. It is okay to purchase a used vehicle, just make sure that it has a clean record and its last owners maintained it well. Some trucking companies like to buy the cheapest vehicles, regardless of the condition.

Doing this causes big problems later on, because maintenance expenses can become massive. You would rather spend more initially and save resources, money, and time in the long run. A good commandment when buying a used vehicle is to focus on trucks that are less than 5 years old. So long as the truck has been well maintained, it can be useful for at least ten years before it starts to become too problematic.

Whether you choose to purchase or lease, you will still have to find a way to fund your purchase. This is where the strategies that we discussed in the last chapter will come into play.

Types of Trucks

Since you will be dealing with trucks in your business, it is important that you learn the different types of trucks out there and what each truck is designed for.

Trucking companies can be categorized into two broad groups, namely long haul trucking and short-haul trucking. Long haul trucking is basically freight services that help clients transport goods to different parts of the country. Short-haul trucking, on the other hand, entails collecting and delivering cargo to nearby locations like a neighboring city or to a place that is two or three hours' drive away. Within these categories, there are various trucking companies that provide a mixture of freight services that enable people to transport nearly anything to any place.

As you are aware by now, there are as many types of trucks as there are goods to be transported. These are the specific types of tracks available in the market:

- Pickup trucks

- Box trucks

- Trailer trucks

- Tipper trucks

- Tankers

- Snowplows

- Logging trucks

- Livestock trucks

- Highway maintenance trucks

- Furniture trucks

- Flat-bed trailers

- Tow trucks

- Fire trucks

- Crane trucks or mobile cranes

- Chiller trucks/reefers

- Cement trucks

- Car transporter/car carrier trailer

- Boat haulage

- Australian road trains

There are many varying kinds of trucks on the road, as seen above. Some vehicles could appear the same, however, they often vary in the kinds of cargos they haul. Identifying precisely what is being carried can be difficult to tell, but one thing is apparent. In the trucking industry, there are numerous kinds of loads and trucks that keep the industry moving. There are also diverse types of trailers for certain kinds of loads. Here is a breakdown of the trailers, trucks, and freights in the industry:

Kinds of Truck Freight

Here are the different truck loads or truck freights:

- Hot Shot Load or expedited

- Partial Truck loads

- LTL (less than Truck load)

- TL Truck Load

A truck load is a full truck, thus more than 8,000 pounds, and needs a big space like the full trailer of an 18 wheeled truck. The other trucks in this category will be explained later.

Kinds of Trucks to Carry Loads

Trucks are classified into eight groups that differ depending on the weight and size. Here is how they are divided:

- Light trucks: These are the trucks in classes 1 to 3 that are usually non-commercial automobiles like pickup trucks, SUVs, and minivans.

- Medium trucks: These are the trucks in classes 4 to 6 that are commercial vehicles that weigh between 14,000 and 26,000 pounds. These include vehicles like big wall-in trucks, F-450 super duty pickup, school buses, delivery trucks, and box trucks.

- Heavy-duty trucks: These are the trucks in classes 7 to 8 which are the big vehicles that weigh more than 33,000 pounds. These include vehicles like 18 wheelers (Freightliners, kenworths, and Peterbilts), cement trucks, and garbage trucks.

Types of trailers

When you haul goods, you require a trailer. The trailer is a section of the truck and literally determines what you can and cannot carry. There are many different types of trailers. These are the most common ones:

- Reefer trailer: this is basically a refrigerator on wheels. It will be explained further later on in this chapter.

- Lowboy trailers; these ones are intended to be trailers for carrying heavyweights like industrial equipment and bulldozers. They have a deck that is quite low and very close to the ground. They can be heavy and weigh up to 80,000 pounds based on the number of axles used.

- Flatbed trailers: As the name suggests, they resemble a flat bed for normally weighty equipment that can be moved open air. These include construction materials, machinery, tractors, and cars.

- Dry Van Trailers: This is an enclosed trailer. It will be explained further in this chapter.

The trucks are further subdivided as follows:

Semi-Trailer truck

This kind of truck is commonly referred to as a semi, semitrailer, semi-tractor trailer, eighteen-wheeler, semi-truck, big rig, and tractor-trailer. It is made up of a tractor unit and a single or more semi-trailers to transport freight.

Styles of semi-trucks:

- Flat roof sleeper

- Mid-roof sleeper

- Raised roof sleeper

- Day cab

Box Truck

A box truck is also referred to as a box van, rolling toaster, cube van, and a cube truck. These kinds of trucks are basically 10 to 26 feet long and can be between class 3 to 7, which is 12,500 pounds to 33,000 pounds in weight. They usually have a rear door that resembles that of a garage and opens by rolling up. These kinds of trucks are normally used as moving trucks, carrying furniture and home appliances.

Dump Truck

This kind of truck is also referred to as a tipper truck or dumper truck. It is used for transporting dumps like demolition waste from construction locations or gravel and sand.

Garbage trucks

This kind of truck is a truck used to haul municipal solid waste to a solid waste treatment facility like a landfill. It is also referred to as bin van, bin lorry, dustbin lorry, bin wagon, dumpster, junk truck, and rubbish truck. Its technical names are refuse collection vehicles and waste collection vehicles.

Types of garbage trucks include:

- Rear loaders

- Front loaders

- Side loaders

- Manual/automatic side

- Automated side loaders

- Manual side loaders

- Semi-automatic side loaders

Tow Truck

This type of truck is also known as a recovery vehicle, a breakdown truck, or a wrecker, and it is used to transport indisposed, impounded, poorly parked, or disabled motor cars.

Styles of tow trucks include:

- Boom

- Integrated

- Wheel lift

- Lift flatbed

- Flatbed

Types of truckers (common niches in the trucking industry)

Dry Van Trucker

This type of trucker ships easy to move, nonperishable, and dry goods. It is usually packaged and moved in one rectangular trailer connected to a semi-truck. This kind of job is a great entry job for truck drivers, because they are not expected to unload the cargo that they carry by themselves. The trailer can be loaded without any hassle via the rear door, and the driver does not have to possess vast knowledge regarding how to secure commodities safely.

A dry van driver is required to have a Class A CDL license that enables them to drive across different states. A driver might require a Hazmat (H) endorsement depending on the goods they are transporting.

Flatbed Trucker

These kinds of trucks differ from tractor-trailers in their goods and shape. They come with open trailers which transport large or oddly shaped machines, dry goods, or vehicles. Drivers should possess specialized expertise and experience to drive flatbed trucks.

The drivers should be skilled at securing challenging goods with chains, tarps, straps, and come-alongs, among other equipment. They also need background information about the cargos they are carrying. The special skills that flatbed drivers need to have will mean that clients pay more for their services, hence these drivers earn more than dry van truckers.

Flatbed truckers require a Class A CDL which covers the total weight of the trailer and the truck. Endorsements for this kind of trucking differ by goods. When transporting dangerous goods, drivers require an (X) or (H) endorsement.

If a tank containing liquid is put on a flatbed, the trailer is viewed as a tanker and needs a Tank (N) endorsement. If possible, flatbed truckers are expected to have CDL endorsements for Hazmat/tanker transportation (X), dangerous materials (H), or Tank (N).

Tanker Trucker

Tanker truckers are some of the most popular kinds of trucks. As a driver of such a truck, you mainly transport gasses or liquids using a cylindrical tank connected to a trailer. The flatbeds or trailer beds carry the trucks in a horizontal position and are normally categorized as a semi-truck.

Just like flatbed drivers, tanker drivers are also expected to possess special skills. Drivers are tasked with the responsibility of hauling chemicals that can be dangerous to the environment or even fatal if exposed to the surrounding area. Thus, tanker truckers should be skilled in reading gauges, versed in transportation regulations, and experienced with record keeping and offloading liquids.

Nevertheless, not all tankers transport such hazardous things. Some of them carry products such as sugar, or milk. The most common types of cargo and tankers are:

- Dry Bulk Tankers: Plastic pellets, chemical powders, sugar, cement, and sand.

- Chemical Tankers: Hydrogen fluoride, chlorine, and Ammonia.

- Fuel Tankers: Jet fuel, gasoline, and other petroleum-based products.

- Food Tankers: Fruit juices, vegetable oil, alcohol, and liquid dairy products.

Drivers driving this type of tanker require Class C or A CDLs. A Class C license allows drivers to transport hazardous materials, and a Class A license covers the weight of both the trailer and the tank being towed. If the driver is shipping hazardous products, they will require a Tank (X) endorsement or (N) endorsement.

Heavy haulers

Heavy haulers are usually considered flatbed truckers who have an extremely big load. Nevertheless, the cargo and trailer design are different. Heavy haul trailers are made to transport items such as big construction tools, solar panels, or blades. Trailers that are meant for carrying heavy hauls include:

- Extendable or telescopic trailers

- Low boys

- Flatbed trailers that have removable goosenecks

- Step decks or two level trailers

A heavy hauler driver should be experienced in operating these automotives. They are quite challenging to drive because of hills, wide turns, steering, and extra weight. This is the reason why drivers who operate these trucks rely on a team of pilot vehicle drivers, loading specialists and route planners to guarantee safe delivery.

Heavy haul drivers should be Class A CDL holders. This license permits drivers to transport a greater weight than Class C or B licenses.

In addition, most drivers need to acquire a heavy haul permit. Each state has its unique requirements, but you should always have a permit for a width of 8 feet and 6 inches or a load weight of 80,000 pounds.

Refrigerated Freight Hauler/Reefers

These kinds of haulers transport food products that need to be stored at low temperature. These trucks can be operated across different nations or locally. Drivers who operate these trucks should possess special skills to keep an eye on temperatures and notice technical problems. Small repairs may be needed to ensure that the cargo does not go bad.

Time management and distance requirements are important, particularly in hauls that have freezer containers on them. Since these deliveries are sensitive, these types of truckers earn a sizable amount of money.

Basically, reefer drivers need a CDL classification that is unique to the kind of truck they are using. A refrigerated trailer or truck combination needs a Class A license, even though drivers can still operate straight trucks or refrigerated boxes with a Class B.

OTR/ Long-Haul Truckers

Over-the-road (OTR) or Long-haul drivers transport commodities from one coast to another. Truckers are classified as long-haul drivers when they take more than a day to complete their trip. Trips can take more than a week to reach to a destination. Nevertheless, most truckers who do this type of job enjoy the travel aspect of their work. Sometimes, two drivers are needed to operate one truck and drive in turns to ensure that they can reach their destination smoothly.

Expedited trucking service

Sometimes referred to as Straight Truck Delivery Service, this service is a type of truck used for getting goods from one point to another quickly, whenever and wherever. This method is preferred when goods are too big or too delicate to transport by air freight, yet they need to reach their destination quickly.

White Glove Service

This specialty service is perfect for transporting fragile goods or for when you need someone to handle the packaging and unpacking of the cargo for you. White glove services will come to a specific location, pack items and load them for you. They will ship the goods using a truck to where they are needed, then unpack and get rid of all the packaging materials. Drivers should have a Class A CDL to drive this type of truck.

Blanket Wrapping

Trucking firms can also specialize in blanket wrapping, which is another kind of transportation where goods do not have to be packed into containers or secured to a pallet. Firms that transport heavy equipment or furniture from one place to another are sometimes known as blanket wrappers or van movers due to the use of fabric to conceal the goods being transported. This kind of service is usually more costly than other kinds of services because there is a higher likelihood of damage when transporting them.

Other Types of Trucks Explained

Box Truck

A box truck is also called a cube truck, bob truck, cube van, or box van. This is a chassis cab truck that has a covered cargo area with a cuboid shape. On many box trucks, the cargo area and cabin are usually separated, but some box trucks have a door between the cargo area and cabin.

The difference between a van and a box truck is that the box truck is made by attaching a cargo box to a chassis cab while a cargo van only has one framework or it is unibody.

Box trucks are usually 20 to 36 feet long and can be categorized as class 3 to 7, which means that they have a gross weight of about 12,500 pounds to 33,000 pounds. They usually have a rear door that resembles that of a garage that rolls up when opening. They are usually used by companies hauling home furniture or home appliances. Sometimes they are used as moving trucks that individuals can rent.

Trailer Trucks

A full trailer is a phrase that Americans use to describe a freight trailer that is fastened by the rear and front axles which are dragged by a drawbar. In Europe, this vehicle is referred to as an A-frame drawbar trailer. It is almost two and a half meters wide and nearly 35 to 40 ft long.

Freight trailers are the kinds of trucks that truckers use to carry heavy products over long distances. Trucking companies can use them to move supplies and furniture or big cargos of raw materials. Consumers have to pay at least $2,000 to move house using a freight trailer.

Tankers

A tanker is usually used to carry liquids or liquefied material. This can include things like pesticides, fertilizers, liquid chemicals, water, gasoline, and oil. The containers are usually pressurized, insulated, and they are made purposely for either multiple or single loads. The tankers are quite challenging to drive, since they have a high COG (center of gravity). They can also be tremendously hazardous, due to the spillage of the products they carry.

Snow Plows

Just as the name suggests, this type of truck was designed to be used in removing snow from the roads to create a free passage for vehicles. It's used to get rid of ice and snow from surfaces outdoors that are being used for transportation needs. This phrase is used to describe vehicles that attach devices to work through the snow but they are not normally built for it. They are also classified as winter support cars.

Smaller snowplows are utilized for footpaths or sidewalks and underbody scrapers are attached to cars in cities for almost the same work as snowplows.

The history of the snowplow can be traced back to 1840 when it was used for the first time and dragged by horses. The first motorized plow was made in 1913 and was created to fulfill the requirements of the city streets of New York.

Logging trucks

A logging truck, or a timer lorry, is utilized in transporting big quantities of timber between widespread terminuses. They have combined, discrete tractor or flatbed units, in order to spread cargo between a dollied trailer and tractor units.

The first of its kind was made in 1913 to transport logs that were felled along river beds to the nearby towns or the city. Because of the start of World War I, the wood industry encountered a lot of demand, and many logging trucks were created to meet the demand sufficiently.

Livestock Trucks

These kinds of trucks are used to carry farm animals. It is a truck that is made specifically to carry livestock and keep them in a particular place. Certain trucks actually come with unique equipment to ensure that the animals stay in a fixed position and are fed well.

The vehicles are normally open a bit at the top, or the back, to see to it that the livestock can get air and daylight and not be restricted to a tiny area. This usually irritates them, making them uneasy. When it is not such a strong truck, they are quite sturdy, because they have to carry heavy animals.

Highway Maintenance Trucks

Highway maintenance trucks are fitted with very unique features, which let one person stand at the back and put cones on the road. This enables certain sections of the highway to be set apart for repairs to be made.

Additionally, the trucks have high-intensity lighting and a retractable crash barrier, in order for work to be performed in darkness. In addition, the truck is fitted with all kinds of tools and load space, so that the suitable materials can be transported for repair.

Furniture truck

These types of trucks are made for use in loading and unloading furniture. They are not only used to transport household goods when a person is moving, but also to transport big loads of furniture from manufacturers to dealerships. These trucks are not especially strong and tough, but they play an important role. They are fitted with a liftgate or a ramp if necessary. The drivers assist as much with manual lifting as well as with driving.

Fire truck

This kind of truck is made to transport the equipment required to put out a fire, where the fire has originated. It is typically equipped with sirens, hoses, and ample load room to accommodate a team of firemen. It is also equipped with breathing items, including oxygen containers and masks as well as automated lifting ladders. This is stored near protective garments, uniforms, and first aid kits, which the firefighters require to do their work efficiently.

It also has two-way radios, or walkie-talkies, to help the firemen keep in touch with the right authorities to address the problem promptly. In addition, the fire truck can house pumps and water to quell the fire when there are choices to link the hose to a fire hydrant at the location of a fire.

Mobile Cranes

This can be either a crane controlled by a cable and attached on carriers with rubber tires or crawlers or a hydraulic-controlled crane with self-propelled makes of carriers that resemble trucks. They are created to seamlessly transport to a site. It requires very little or no assembly or setup.

Car Carrier Trailer or Car Transporter

This is a single- or double-decker car carrier with many spaces created to keep cars in place over the course of a long journey. They can either be open or closed, and they are fitted with in-built ramps for heaping and removing the cargo to and from the vehicles. Most of the time, they are used to transport vehicles from the manufacturing site to dealerships. They differ from flatbed trucks, due to the fact that they are not fitted with winches or loaders.

Boat Haulers

A large car or an SUV can comfortably carry small boats. However, when it comes to transporting a big boat, you need a customized low loader called boat haulage, though sometimes a small truck can suffice. The boat haulage truck is particularly designed to carry the substantial weight of a boat, and it has superior stability. Speed is not its strong suit.

The average price of hiring a truck like this will depend on the boat being hauled. However, it normally ranges from $600 to $1,000. For small distances, the charges can be between $150 and $350.

Australian Road Train

A long combination vehicle (LCV), land train, or road train is a trucking vehicle that is used to transport road freight more efficiently than semi-trailer trucks. It comprises at least two semi-trailers or trailers pulled by a prime mover. Long combination vehicles are several trailers joined together and attached on tractor trucks. The most trailers ever hauled by one truck were 112. Road trains are common in Australia, where the road is straight from coast to coast, making it easy to pull trailers exceeding three.

Summary

There are many types of trucks on the market designed to transport different loads. Some of these types include livestock trucks, refrigerated trucks, Truck Loads, and Less Than Truck Load (or LTL), as well as Flatbed trailers and boat haulers, among others. There are also various niches that are common among truckers such as dry vans and heavy haulers. Some are more profitable than others.

In the next chapter, you will learn about how to price your load, explain what a freight load is, where to find clients, and factors to consider when determining your freight rate.

Price Your Load

B efore delving into the specifics of what truck freights are and how trucking business owners can get the best one, it is crucial to know what constitutes an ideal truck freight rate and how the rates are decided.

The Definition of a Truck Freight Rate

A truck freight rate is just the cost or price that a shipper or broker wants to pay a carrier to transport a load. Basically, it is what you will be paid to ship a load. We will only focus on truck freight rates for carriers with authority and owner-operators.

Where Do I Find Truck Freight Rates?

These rates are readily available on load boards such as Truckloads. The load board has more than three million truckloads every month, so you have to narrow down your search by filtering according to categories such as drop-off or pick-up dates, weight, trailer type, and location. Utilize free load boards like Truckloads to know the credit rating of a freight broker and duration before pay. You can even call brokers straight from the mobile app to reserve the most affordable freight rate for you.

Calculating Truck Freight Rates

These rates are calculated depending on numerous factors, such as the present market conditions, the kind of cargo being transported, distance covered, general size or weight, tolls, trucking insurance, auto maintenance and repair expenses, fuel costs, and demand levels. Various areas and routes will provide greater freight rates since there is a high volume of loads, hence the demand for carriers will be greater.

Remember that truck freight rates are usually decided by a freight broker. The broker takes a part of the overall rate that a shipper wants to pay and gives the trucker the difference. This rate can vary and it is usually negotiable.

If a shipper wants to transport highly-priced equipment that is quite heavy, there is a possibility that the freight rate will be very enticing for carriers.

Because the cargo to be hauled is precious, there is more willingness to hire experienced carriers. Definitely, you will require having the appropriate equipment and trailer needed to transport the particular load.

Factors Affecting Trucking Freight Rate Calculations Explained

Since trucking freight rates are calculated based on miles covered, we can aptly say that the most significant number when calculating these rates is the number of miles between where you are beginning and where you will make the drop. These are the explanations for the other factors that affect the calculations of truck freight rates:

Distance of Travel

Now that we know that the distance you will be traveling is essential in knowing the trucking rates for each mile, you need to make sure that you have the exact mileage from the start to avoid any issues along the way.

Confirm that your driver will not have to make lengthy detours due to road construction, or else you are in danger of suffering losses and wrong timing.

The Weight of the Load

After considering the distance, the next important thing to think of is the weight of the load. It is crucial to oversee the whole weight cargo for your fleet to keep expenses in check. It is best to look out for yourself and begin the negotiations with a higher rate, giving your customer a chance to haggle and at the same time making sure that your business makes a profit.

Shipment Density

This is another issue that will affect how much space a load will occupy in your truck. The moment you become aware of the weight of the load, calculating the density of the shipment is easy. You simply have to divide the weight of the shipment by its cubic feet.

Shipment weight divided by feet cubed = shipment density

Freight Classification

Freight classification is one of the most vital standards in the industry that you need to keep abreast with. The National Motor Freight Traffic Association (NMFTA) has described eighteen shipment classes.

Freight classification is influenced by features like:

- Stowability

- Handling needs

- Liability

- Product value

- Product density

Knowing intimately how to utilize these aspects to do your trucking rate calculations will help your business stay lucrative and competitive.

Even though these are the main issues that affect trucking rates, you should make sure that you have the fundamental industry knowledge to figure out the other factors that could determine your truck rates. This means that, for you to keep offering reasonable trucking rates per mile, you must stay updated on the changing industry trends.

Financing

This is also another issue that may affect the cost per mile. The price of purchasing trailers and trucks is somewhere between 0% and 30% of the returns.

What are the Best-Paying Loads?

For you to make a lot of money, you will benefit immensely from transporting cargo with the highest freight rate possible as many times as you can. Freight rates are usually paid for on a mile basis, and the rates can be as low as $1.50

and as high as $4.00 for every mile. Normally, flatbeds get the best rates but there is no guarantee that things will always happen this way.

A survey of 150 truck driver participants revealed that 59% of drivers think the best trucking freight rate is three dollars per mile while 32% believe it is two dollars per mile. However, these rates are usually hard to come by and the amount of freight-hauling at these rates is usually small.

Charge the Right Rate

As an owner of a small trucking business, you need to decide on what rate you want to charge your clients to transport goods. Your rates should be high enough to give you a good profit and cover all your operation costs. You must know what your rates are before you begin contacting shippers and finding clients. Keep in mind that when you contact shippers, you want to be more affordable than what brokers charge them. There is a straightforward method that you can follow to accomplish this:

1. Choose your freight lane

2. Visit a loan board

3. Get 10 loads that need to be ferried in one route

4. Contact the brokers and discover the amount they pay

5. Calculate the average

6. Add 10 to 15 percent to get the cost the brokers are charging shippers

7. Do the same thing for the opposite direction

Actually, experts advise that you should do the above calculations before you even start buying a truck so that you can know whether the money you will make is what you had in mind and whether this business is worth investing in. After doing the calculations, you will also be able to make other important decisions such as whether to change the home base or shipping line so that you can make the revenues you desire.

What are empty miles?

Empty miles are also referred to as deadhead or non-revenue miles. They are the miles that are covered by a truck when it is not earning any money.

This occurs when there is a cargo one way and no cargo on the way back. Empty miles account for about 30 to 40 percent of the total miles covered, which makes them very uneconomical for your trucking enterprise.

To minimize empty miles, try to reduce any unimportant transportation of goods and enhance your scheduling to ensure that your trucks are shipping cargo as many times as possible.

What is a Reasonable Rate Per Mile that Trucking Businesses Should Charge?

Even though it is hard to pinpoint an average figure when it comes to trucking rates per mile, if you stay updated about industry news, most of the time, you will have a clue about the average trucking rates.

These are the trucking rate per mile averages in 2022:

- Flatbed rates stand at $3.14 for each mile

- Reefer rates stand at $3.19 for each mile

- Van rates stand at $2.76 for each mile

Remember that these are just the average figures and your company can earn profits at another rate that differs from these ones. Offering the lowest rates might not be adequate to make you a profit, however, a rate that is too big might work against you and make it easy for your competitors to beat you.

Why are Trucking Rates Crucial?

Your biggest goal is to have a lucrative trucking business, and being up to speed with the average trucking rates is the ideal way to ensure that your business keeps expanding.

By being an expert in your industry and knowing its trends at any given moment, you will be able to provide attractive prices and woo more clients, which translates to more profits.

Summary

It is important to understand how much you should charge your clients to avoid making losses. The factors that influence freight rates include the weight of the cargo, shipment density, and the distance covered, among other things. To be able to set the correct rates, you need to know the industry trends and also ensure that you charge less than the brokers, so that you can easily attract clients.

In the next chapter, you will learn how to market your business, where to place the ads, and why you need a website, social media presence, and a blog.

Market The Business

Marketing is an important part of any business, and it should always feature on your monthly budget. Even famous companies like Nike and Coca-Cola still spend a lot of money promoting their products, which means that as a small business owner, you also need to put a lot of effort into creating brand awareness and making people aware that your business is their best choice. Failure to market a business is usually likened to a man winking at a woman in the dark. Definitely, the woman will not realize that there is someone trying to get their attention.

Whether you are a new trucking business owner or you have been operating your business for a number of years, marketing goals help you explain what you want to achieve with your marketing campaign. For trucking businesses, advertising your business usually means coming up with goals that target two distinct markets—these are the companies that require your delivery and freight services and the drivers themselves. Here are some of the marketing objectives that you might have as a trucking business owner:

Expanding Customer Base

Gaining customers who have never utilized your services before is a common goal for many trucking companies. For example, you may intend to have a goal of advertising to people who are moving and require a trucking service to assist them in transporting their belongings, such as furniture, to their new home. If you are a fairly new trucking company, your goal probably centers on acquiring local customers to build a good business image. To offer services to enterprises that require hauling products, your goal would state that you want to advertise to more businesses that need to transport goods from their manufacturing premises to centers of distribution.

Attracting Drivers

Getting dependable and experienced drivers is usually a big problem for many trucking companies, because the rate of turnover in the industry has been high in recent years. If you require drivers, you should have an objective that states the number of drivers you need and the kind of qualifications you expect them to have. You should also decide whether you will hire the drivers as your employees or you just want subcontracted drivers. Another goal to consider is an objective ensuring that your drivers are satisfied with their job, so that you can lower the rate of turnover.

Boost Marketing Efforts

Creating a brochure and modernizing your site are important objectives if you want to increase your marketing efforts. Another objective can be to use your website and marketing materials to get your current customers to give you more business. You can also make it an objective to use your sales efforts to attract new customers who require trucking services. Informing your current clients, such as manufacturers and brokers, that you have more trucks to handle more loads than you are presently transporting is yet another good objective to establish.

Increase Online Presence

The goal of making your online marketing strategy better and more effective could entail creating and upgrading your website, focusing on showing prospective clients that you transport freight and are open to hauling their cargo. A section of your online objective should also be to woo experienced drivers. Your goals should also include joining online directories to boost the chances that a freight broker or a manufacturer knows of your abilities.

Marketing Strategies for a Trucking Business

Design a Logo

Since you already have a catchy name, the next thing that you should do is design a logo. The logo should be remarkable. This should be the first thing to do when creating a marketing strategy. Take some time to gauge the impact of your logo and name by finding out what people think. This is important when establishing a brand and distinguishing your business from your competitors.

Create a Website

In this day and age, a young business that fails to take advantage of the internet as a marketing instrument misses out on a great opportunity to help their business. Your target market is always searching for your services on the internet, and if you don't have a site, you will definitely lose prospective clients to your competition.

Services like WordPress enable business owners to create and start operating a website even though they do not have any computer programming knowledge. Ensure that you observe the rules of Search Engine Optimization (SEO), so that you will get a lot of traffic to your site. Being active and having a community on YouTube as well as Google is crucial for online marketing.

More than 25% of people will visit the site that ranks the highest on a search engine, hence, it is crucial to improve the results of your company website. If you rank higher than your competitor's sites, you will enjoy greater visibility and get more sales.

Search engine optimization, or SEO, enables you to use keywords in your site and content design. This will cause your site to show up more conspicuously on internet searches, thereby increasing traffic to your website, ultimately expanding your customer base. You can reach more clientele by using SEO than you can with ordinary advertisements or word of mouth only.

You should select a domain name such as. You require a hosting provider to host your site, so set up a WordPress account and select a free theme that can be customized. After you have installed your website, explain who you are, what kinds of service you offer, and how prospective customers can reach you by providing your contact information.

Always include your web address on any kind of marketing that you will use, including social media profiles, digital marketing adverts, and print advertisements. Also, set up a Google My Business account to help it rank in the local region in search engines. Because people can visit websites with ease, you should make your site the epicenter of all your marketing initiatives.

Besides ensuring that your business information is available on your site, you should also make sure that the site is user-friendly. Speed is another important factor to consider. Ensure that you avoid putting many heavy images or other data-heavy components that can make your site take too long to load. Your site visitors need to be able to navigate with ease. Additionally, make sure that your site is designed nicely and is also mobile-friendly, because most people prefer to access the internet using their mobile gadgets, such as smartphones or tablets.

Start a Blog

An effective way to increase the usefulness of your company's site is to link it to a blog. This will ensure that your site stays fresh and assists with SEO by constantly putting out new content. Just a few posts weekly can assist you in directing traffic to your site while also being an efficient way to popularize your brand.

Use Social Media

There are different social media platforms that trucking companies can take advantage of to widen the reach of their enterprise. Even though using all the platforms is unnecessary, ensure that you use at least some of them. Platforms such as Tumblr, LinkedIn, Twitter, and Facebook can really help you advertise your company and get new clients.

Social media platforms will also let you state your shipping rates and share a link to your company's site, so that interested consumers can get more information. To capitalize on social media, consider publishing paid adverts.

Attend Trade Shows

Creating connections and selling resources is important to the survival of any enterprise and trade shows are the perfect place to do that and more. A trucking business owner should go to trucking trade shows and seize the opportunities they offer. Meeting owners and employees of other companies in the industry will help you get new business partners and grow your brand.

Trucking Load Boards

When promoting your trucking business, go to the customers where they are. Trucking load boards are created for both customers and trucking companies who require trucking services. These websites make it possible to market your business and link up with customers who are specifically searching for your services.

These sites below will let users do two kinds of searches. Transportation business owners can search for cargo that needs to be hauled and customers can go to the website and look for trucks in the region that can carry a load. These websites provide this service:

- TruckersEdge

- Landstar Carriers

- FreightFinder

- Trulos

- 123Loadboard

- Trucker Path

- Direct Freight Services

Adverts in Trade Publications

In most industries, print ads are just as effective as digital marketing; the trucking industry is one such industry. Trade publications target specific industries and are aimed at teaching the readers about trends in the industry. The advantage of placing adverts in these publications is that you are assured of an interested readership that is looking for information about trucking services.

When crafting your marketing strategy, think about which publications will be the best match for your adverts. For instance, you could place an advert in these publications if you are searching for new drivers. If you are marketing your services, you should choose to place your adverts in publications targeting the industries you work for. Use a database of trade publications that are grouped according to industries, such as webwire.com, to search for publications that have readers that you want to reach.

Remember that a majority of trade publications also have an online section. Even though many subscribers like the print form of industry magazines, most people will consume the contents of the publication online. The best thing to do if you want your marketing messages to be received by both audiences is to use digital marketing which can narrow your focus to businesses in your local area.

Trade Association Events

Just like trade publications, trade associations give you the chance to reach an interested audience. For example, if you desire to bring new drivers on board, you could erect a booth at a trucking industry trade show.

If you are advertising your services to other enterprises, you need to go to events that are B2B oriented. Go to sites like absoluteexhibits.com to check out upcoming trade shows and learn which ones focus on the trucking services that your company provides. Make an attractive and educational display to woo clients and bring marketing materials to send home with event-goers.

Having a stand at a trade show can be quite costly and be time-intensive. If you do not have the time to make an appealing display, think of becoming a sponsor. Usually, this will involve placing your marketing resources in swag bags, on-site advertising, and using adverts on promotional supplies. Your adverts will enable attendees to recall your company when they require transportation services.

Additionally, you need to review the online elements of these occasions. Discover if the business sells adverts on the registration website. By putting adverts on these websites, your company will be seen by every vendor when they register.

Email Marketing

Nowadays, most people have an email address. Emailing marketing links to clients will help market your services and ensure that potential customers are thinking about your business all the time. It is a good thing to remember when you are trying to come up with ideas about the marketing techniques for your company.

It is easy to schedule your emails ahead of time or personalize them individually to build relationships and provide customers with a great experience with your firm, which will motivate them to become loyal customers.

Marketing through email gives you a direct channel to attract more leads and get your company seen by as many people as possible at a considerably low price.

Email is effective in getting new customers and motivating existing customers more than other online marketing efforts.

You can create a personalized direct mail campaign and send e-newsletters to your customers. You may even buy an email list of businesses that are suitable for your market, like distribution businesses or auto-part makers. Also, prompt your website visitors to provide their email addresses when subscribing.

You can do this by making attractive promotions that visitors can access when they sign up with their contact information. After it starts operating, carry out appealing direct mail campaigns and use catchy headlines.

Creating an App

Tablet computers and mobile phones have permeated all aspects of our lives. Nowadays, owner-operators utilize their mobile apps and cellphones on the road to do various things, such as keep tabs on the weather, gas prices, traffic conditions, and book loads. A survey by uShip established that there has recently been a 16% increase in the number of truckers who utilize apps. It is important to remember to market through cell phones when coming up with the marketing ideas for your trucking business.

Making an app for truck drivers boosts your communication with customers and also fulfills your needs. It can also ensure that consumers do not forget about you. A trucking app can be anything such as load management tools, an affordable fuel finder, or GPS navigation, among other things to efficiently fulfill the needs of your customers on the road.

Online Reviews and Referrals

Word of mouth can be an effective marketing technique for your firm. When you make your existing customers happy, they become eager to market your business to their associates, family, and friends. Ultimately, your number of prospective customers increases significantly. You can also benefit from this influential strategy by simply requesting your customers give you referrals through your website or email.

When you conduct your business online, you can make reviews of your business readily accessible, allowing them to act as referrals from people you do not know well. Prospective customers will read the reviews prior to deciding whether they will hire you for your transportation services. Positive reviews put your services and products in a positive light, helping you retain existing customers and even helping your company rank well online.

In trucking sectors, reviews are uncommon. Hence, clients are not likely to think about giving you a review. Therefore, make it a habit to request clients leave one, because it is essential to making sure that your trucking business stays afloat. You should incorporate reviews with good quotes or even a "Reviews" section on your homepage, where new prospective customers will see them when they first access your site.

Building a body of favorable online reviews will positively influence people's business and purchasing decisions. Therefore, making sure that your business has readily visible reviews endorsing your services will improve your bottom line and help you compete fairly and effectively.

Retargeting and Google Adverts

Most people search on Google when they are looking for any type of information. Therefore, that is where they go when they want to find a company that satisfies their needs.

Spending money on Google ads will assist you in winning new customers, expanding your business, and gaining more leads. You can engage with prospective customers as they look for services and products that your trucking business provides.

Marketing on Google will also give your company site special treatment in Google's search engine, increasing your prospective leads and improving your web traffic.

Utilizing Google Ads also helps you advertise straight to prospective customers who visited your website recently due to retargeting. This method helps increase your client base and market your trucking business through promotions targeted at people who have shown interest in your business before. Retargeting also assists to make it highly probable that they will click on your advert, go back to your site, and eventually buy your services.

Social Media

Social media is an uncomplicated yet effective marketing tool. Currently, social media has 3.78 billion users all over the world, and it is projected to increase to more than 4.4 billion users by the year 2025. Based on these massive figures, there is no doubt that having a strong social media presence is a profitable move.

Building a social media presence allows you to link up with prospective customers and employees, increase your visibility, gain positive reviews, and build your company's image. By maintaining an active social media page for your trucking company, you can get access to a wide group of social media users. Utilize social media to assist you in creating awareness and promoting your branding, showing your experience in your field, and making your followers aware of your company values.

Managing your social media company pages does not have to be difficult. You can use a social media management tool by Constant Contact to enable you to manage your social media marketing t a c - tics.

Incorporating social media into your social media marketing strategies will increase your exposure, boost web traffic, increase quantity of leads—and consequently new customers—and lead to more profits and ultimately, more success.

Directories

These are an uncomplicated resource to keep in mind when creating marketing ideas for your trucking business. Online business directories help your online presence and assist prospective customers in locating you. Directories offer important information regarding your trucking business, making it effortless for prospective customers to get what they are searching for.

If you list with a directory, you will also improve your targeted coverage, so that you can concentrate your energy and time on networking with people who are aggressively looking for your services.

A good example of an online directory is Google Business Profile, which reaches numerous users and enhances the SEO for your company site. This in turn can multiply the amount of leads you attract and customers you reach.

Observe Your Competitors' Services

Beating your competitors is one of the best ways to promote your business. Observe what your competition is doing, then do it better, if you are able. If they are a bigger company that is providing an attractive deal, try to offer a better deal. Utilize your newsletters, website, and social media networks. If you are unable to compete with a competitor's prices, concentrate on customer service. Bigger companies usually have a hard time being friendly. Know the names of your customers and contact them to make them feel valued. Demonstrate to them why they need to work with you, even though you are offering higher prices than your competition. Generally, people like supporting smaller businesses, so give them a reason to do so.

Put a Plan in Place to Monitor Your Marketing Objectives, Results, and Campaigns

Monitoring the results of your marketing efforts is an important part of the marketing process, and more so if you are marketing when traveling on the road. Define distinct expectations for how you intend to market your business to your customers, what you anticipate achieving, and the timeline you intend to work from. No matter what you do, make sure that your plan is flexible. If you meet or exceed your marketing goal, shift the goal posts. Do the same if you fail to achieve your goal. Try a marketing strategy, evaluate the results, and proceed from there.

Go Viral

Going viral is not an easy thing, but it is still a great way to get publicity for your company. Before you create the content, ensure that it is something people would be interested in consuming and sharing with family and friends. Usually, photos and videos that are relatable and inspiring get a lot of attention, so you create a video such as a behind the scenes look at who your staff are and the ways they work. You may even consider going with one of your drivers from the pick-up point to the delivery spot. Think of anything, be creative, and put some effort into making sure that the end product is not only interesting but also of high quality. Maybe consider investing in a good camera up front.

Make Helpful and Interesting Industry-Specific Content

Create content on your social media pages and website which is important to your audience. Just like any other industry, companies in the transport industry can offer helpful and current information to assist their friends on the road. The content can be about anything associated with the trucking industry, such as weigh stations, coffee shops, rest stops, traffic reports, accidents, and weather. Rookie drivers would be especially happy to watch and consume such content.

Distribute Flyers

With the technological advancements of the modern world, most people do not like to use print media, and particularly flyers. Nevertheless, giving out flyers is not only an affordable method of marketing, but it is also beneficial in getting your company's name out there. If they have an attractive design, these marketing papers will attract people immediately. You can distribute flyers from any location, whether near a supermarket, inside a mall, or outside your office. If you hand out flyers to the market segment that you are targeting, they will undoubtedly identify your company. Alternatively, if they do not require your services, they can give it to their friends and family who do require it.

Do not ignore the idea of flyers; it is crucial to attract people's attention using colorful and high quality flyers. Make sure you write a compelling headline, proofread, let your audience know what your business can do for them, and organize the elements well.

Have Business Cards for Your Company

Giving out business cards to your prospective customers is an effective way to market your trucking business. Ensure that your business cards are visually appealing, and their concept and design should reflect your brand. Even in this age of the internet, a business card is still important, because it will help customers have a way to contact you if they ever require your services. It is also a way to make them aware of the existence of your business.

Create a Specific Advert

Remember that the message you convey on your marketing campaigns, be it online or print, is an important part of your marketing process. Before creating the advert, you should know the reason for advertising. Is it to acquire new customers? Do you intend to advertise your new branch or recruit more drivers?

You will make it easier for your audience to understand your advert if you make it more specific and avoid using any jargon. Also, ensure that your message centers on your marketing goals.

Additional Marketing Tips

- Brand your trucks using the company's brand name and logo.

- Ask your drivers to wear branded shirts when they are working.

Summary

Marketing your trucking company is an important aspect of your business. Combine both the modern and traditional methods of marketing to reach your target market. You will need to market when finding employees and when looking for customers. Some of the marketing methods that you need to use include advertising in trade publications, going to trade fairs, having a company website and blog, as well as using social media platforms.

In the next chapter you will learn how to grow your business, including the strategies that you need to apply to expand your client base and subsequently your business.

Grow Your Business

G rowing your trucking business is important because it will help your business survive for years to come, which is every business owner's dream. The strategies that you can use to achieve this are many and varied and can only be limited by your imagination. Most of the strategies have been discussed in the other chapters of this book, but we will briefly mention them here again and explain how important they are in helping your business expand.

Growth Strategies

Implement the Strategies in Your Plan

For starters, the business plan you write for your trucking business should be a roadmap for a lucrative business. It should contain marketing and sales plans, strategic plans, and provide a foundation for seamless operations, not to mention hopefully persuading an investor or lender to invest in your business. Writing a business plan might be an intimidating task for most people. However, you just need to view it as a list of answers to the questions that you ask yourself when you are starting a business. The answers will help you flesh out the plan.

To answer these questions, you have to research the market thoroughly, know who your competitors are, and give all these steps time. Once you have a comprehensive business plan ready, you will be able to do the important tasks that will stimulate growth. Some of the initiatives include hiring employees and building out crucial infrastructure. Additionally, you will have to ensure that the growth is maintainable by doing constant marketing to bring in new customers.

Offer Superior Customer Service

One important aspect that most people forget is customer service. If you want to attract new customers and keep the ones you already have, you have to offer exceptional experiences with your enterprise. Always engage your customers on social platforms. When customers say a good thing about your business, thank them and share their comments wherever you can. Undoubtedly, there are those who will complain about your services or your ability to deliver. Quickly address any complaints, because bad news spreads faster than good ones. Endeavor to compensate when essential, and make sure that bad customer involvements do not get out of hand or irritate a lot of people.

Increase Operational Efficiency

Increasing your operational efficiency can help you increase your profit margins. Basically, operational efficiency is how you capitalize on your revenue in relation to the money and time you put into your business. One of the best ways to do this in your trucking company is to utilize technology-oriented devices to automate the operations of your business. These are the tips for increasing operational performance and automating repetitive tasks in your trucking company:

1. Maximize fuel stops and route efficiency with smart route planning

2. Make use of load tracking apps, which minimize check calls

3. On the spot, digitally upload of proof of delivery documents

4. Do load bookings and load searches automatically

5. Select all-in-one technology that offers many benefits, such as the Trucker Tools free app for drivers

These technologies and more will be discussed in detail in the next chapter.

Reduce Your Cost Per Mile (CPM)

The most effective way to reduce your CPM is to be aware of your expenditure, including both variable and fixed expenses. For instance, you can decrease fuel consumption by being mindful of your driving habits and speed. Constant maintenance can help you avoid expensive breakdowns in the middle of nowhere and planning carefully can reduce out-of-route distances.

Raise Your Rate Per Mile

Charge shippers a bigger percentage over your expenses in order to get higher payments. Additionally, getting headhaul market cargos and taking them to backhaul markets could increase the rate per mile. Lowering deadhead miles by transporting LTL would also be beneficial. Using a reputable load board famous for highly valuable loads is also another method of increasing per mile choices. The best way to know how much you will charge shippers is by calculating the CPM. The formula for calculating CPM is adding fixed and variable costs and then dividing them by the total miles covered. Here's the formula:

CPM = (Fixed Costs + Variable Costs) ÷ Total Miles driven*

*With or without load

Therefore, if your CPM is $1.30, the amount you charge the shipper per mile should be higher than that.

Look for Well-Paying Truck Cargos

You can create a great name and increase your returns by hauling shipments that are harder to haul or ones that need more time or skill. You can also focus on shippers who require freight transported urgently; such loads attract high rates. The easiest way to maximize on high paying loads is to use load boards such as Truckstop.com and be flexible.

Have More Loaded Mileage

Loaded miles are the moments when you are driving while carrying paid goods. However, sometimes, you can have empty trailers. Ensure that you match your routes with clients' demand and be ready to accept backhauls to make sure your trailer is always full.

Lower Detention Time

There is nothing worse than spending hours waiting at a delivery or pickup site for more time than you had anticipated. Whereas shippers give allowance for a detention delay or to hours, occasionally, it can extend to three hours or more. Remember you will not be paid for that time. To make matters worse, it can make you late for other jobs. The easiest way to lower detention time is to increase loading and unloading periods. Also, stay away from loads from shippers or institutions that are famous for long wait times.

Factoring to Get Faster Payments

This is a service we discussed earlier. It entails selling your invoices to a financial business or a factor. You get your money immediately, but the company will deduct their fees. This service will help you have cash flow, especially in the first few months of doing business, when it is important to have money at hand to cover various expenses and keep the business going.

Let Professionals Handle Back Office Work

You can operate your trucking business more efficiently if you have experienced professionals to deal with all your fuel lines, cash applications, collections, and billings. An accountant will monitor your expenses and balance your accounting books more expertly than you. Hiring competent personnel eventually helps you save money. Basically, you need to delegate and stop attempting to do everything yourself.

Pay Yourself a Salary

Most owner-operators will factor in costs like load-specific costs, operational costs, and fixed costs into their budgets. But they will often forget one important cost: the owner's salary! If you are using your profits to meet your personal needs then you are denying the business growth and sustainability. Profits should be injected back into the business. Pay yourself the amount you would pay a driver. If you fail to do this, it means that you won't be able to pay another person in the future, whether it is a dispatcher or driver.

Proper Timing

Buying a second truck should not only be determined by the availability of customers. Rather, the operating and fixed costs of the business should be catered to by the business itself, without the need to add extra revenue for the first four months. Therefore, only bring in new trucks when you have considered the cost factor.

Treat Your Business Like a Business

Consider learning CPA to help you understand your profit and loss much better. Also, ensure that you have a good relationship with an attorney and a banker. Also, work smarter rather than harder. Stop thinking like a company driver and start reasoning like a shrewd businessman. Avoid cargo that needs you to drive more deadhead miles. Instead, look for loads that let you drive less but pay an equal amount of money. The advantages to shorter jobs are fewer miles are driven so you save on fuel, your truck wears out less, less time is worked overall, and therefore more money is earned.

Average Revenue Per Day

Find a way of ensuring that your average revenue per day is always high. If the revenue for each mile is small and the miles are many, then the revenue per day will be smaller than it is supposed to be—and some costs will also be higher. Equally, your revenue per day will be negatively affected if revenue per mile is up and miles are down.

Diversify Your Services

Another way to grow your business is to provide a wide range of services. Diversifying will help you spread risks and shield you from changes in the market. As a trucking company business, diversifying means owning different types of trucks and trailers that can serve different niches and industries, such as refrigerated trucks for meat and other perishable goods, a flatbed for hauling oversize loads, and a movers van, among others.

What Can You Do to Have a Profitable Trucking Business?

Besides learning how to grow your business, it is also important that you know what you can do to have a profitable business. Note that the more profits you can make, the faster you can expand your business, because it means that you can invest your profits back into the business. Here are the ways you can make your business more profitable:

1. Save on fuel; get that fuel card.

2. Better routing—an efficient GPS could save time and fuel.

3. Tires: make sure their condition and quality is top notch, because it affects the truck's fuel consumption and safety. Ensure that they are inflated to the amount recommended by the manufacturer at all times. Switch to Low-Rolling-Resistance tires to save more fuel.

4. Ensure that your truck is in a good condition all the time. Doing frequent preventive maintenance on your vehicles will help them to function better and serve you for a long time. Do not wait for issues

to emerge. Service the fleet, replacing parts and important fluids when necessary as well as examining all systems.

5. Proper driving habits: gentle accelerating and braking enhance fuel economy. Behaviors like idling and over-speeding waste fuel.

6. Know your actual expenses; knowing your cost per mile is important if you want to increase profits. You should first know what your costs are if you want to multiply your profits. Calculate both variable and fixed costs.

7. Use brokers and loan boards. These two are particularly useful for new companies which want to grow their customer base.

8. Negotiate competitive rates with shippers; when you are dealing directly with shippers, you could get reasonable rates. Even though load boards and brokers are helpful for seeking customers, they are usually expensive. Create your own network of shippers who you can haggle with for better rates.

9. Utilize non-recourse invoice factoring. Also referred to as transportation factoring or freight bill factoring, this is a great way to increase your cash flow for your trucking company. With this service, you will not only get immediate cash flow, but also you will enjoy credit protection on clients and can safeguard your business against loss from invoices that have not been paid because of customer bankruptcy. Other benefits that will save you money are the factoring firm dealing with your customer collection and handling billing.

10. Use cruise control; holding a constant speed becomes hard when you are on and off the gas pedal. Regularly reducing and increasing speed even in small measurements causes fuel wastage. Utilizing cruise control on the roadway allows you to maintain a more steady speed. Fuel consumption is decreased, helping you save money.

11. Decrease driver turnover. Statistics show that turnover costs a company $11,500 for each driver, on average. Findings of a survey that was conducted by Driver iQ discovered that the number one cause of drivers quitting is total compensation. The irregularity of paychecks every week is another reason. Many trucking companies use invoice factoring to solve this problem.

12. Intense marketing. Marketing is usually the biggest expense for most

businesses. Your business will not achieve any of its financial goals without effective marketing strategies. Spare no expense or opportunity in marketing your business, and when your customers start streaming in, you will be grateful you worked so hard to get the word out there. Remember that word of mouth and traditional ways of marketing are also effective in these times of the internet. Always strive to have a good reputation and satisfy your customers, so that they can refer friends and family to you, which will be free advertising for you.

13. Use credit cards and take out small business loans; these will help you increase your cash flow, and you need cash flow to expand your business. Have a reliable monthly repayment plan and only take the loan if you know that you have a good business plan.

14. Create an entity the right way; different states have distinct rules about how a business entity should be run, but it is advisable that trucking business owners create entities where their permanent tax and home address is based. Choices available are LLC, C or S corporations and partnership.

15. Know your taxes: determine the taxes you are likely to pay according to the present revenue. Planning for taxes can help you make big savings later on.

Common Scams in the Trucking Industry and How to Protect Your Business

While we have discussed a lot about what you need to do to save money and grow your business, you also need to be aware of the ways in which trucking companies get scammed. This is so that you can avoid becoming a victim of such incidents and lose your hard-earned money.

Cyberattacks

The trucking industry has a lot of technologies to make their work easier and more efficient. However, this has exposed the industry players to hacking or cybercrimes. One example of cyberattacks in the industry is the data breach against Total Quality Logistics. Apparently, hackers targeted TQL's systems and they stole confidential data about many customers. The data included bank information and social security numbers. The theft was so bad that it triggered a class action lawsuit in which TQL was charged and expected to pay damages of $5 million.

Identity Theft

This kind of fraud occurs when a person impersonates a company and then steals goods from a trucker. Sometimes, impersonators paid people $3,000 per month to repackage and transport goods, which is quite a common kind of scam. The individuals who pose as real logistics companies usually steal the credit card numbers of their victims in the process of stealing from them. Similarly, the actual company develops a bad reputation in the eyes of their customers—and the public in general. This could kill the business regardless of whether it is small or big.

Embezzlement

Embezzlement is another problem that you need to be wary about as a trucking business owner. There are many trucking companies in the U.S that have lost millions through embezzlement by their employees. Perpetrators of this crime are usually the accountants or other role that involves handling money directly.

For example, in 2020, a woman called Danielle Apadaca-Roberts was charged with embezzling half a million dollars from a Utah-based truck company, where she worked as a payroll manager. In another case, a woman was found guilty of embezzling $1 million from the trucking company she worked for in Las Cruces, NM. Sandra Roberto deposited checks into her accounts between 2011 and 2018. She worked in the accounting department. She could go to jail for 20 years.

Others

Other scams include DOT impersonation, phishing, fake tow service or repair shops, fuel advance scams, fake police, and double brokerage.

How to Prevent Becoming a Victim of Such Frauds

As a trucking business owner, it is important that you learn how to spot possible dangers early. This way, you can be safe from cyberattacks, as well as fraud. The first thing that you need to do is to find out which are the common scams at a given point in time. You can do this by listening to the trucking industry grapevine to learn of any new, emerging types of scams in the industry.

Another thing that you need to do is verify everything, even when a deal appears to be genuine. Every time an unknown person calls or makes an offer to you, ensure that you verify the validity of the source before getting into a deal with the person.

To safeguard against cyber-attacks, companies that deal with logistics need to practice safe internet habits, like using anti-malware software, using multi factor authentication, and avoiding clicking on suspicious links. They can also use passwords that are unique and hard to memorize and avoid using public wi-fi when accessing company databases. Bigger companies may even think of hiring an external cybersecurity services provider.

Summary

Every business owner has a great desire to expand their business and earn as much profit as possible in their industry of choice. As a trucking business owner, you probably also feel the same way. The above tips will help you grow your business and get it from a small trucking company with one or three trucks to a medium or a big company with hundreds or even thousands of trucks. Some of the strategies include having a budget, following the plans you laid out in your business plan, using factoring services to solve your cash flow problems, and looking for well-paying goods.

In the next chapter, we will examine the most important technologies that your business should adopt to stay ahead of the pack.

Technologies You Can Use In Your Trucking Business To Optimize Profits

B y now you must know that it will be nearly impossible for you to compete fairly and outdo your competition in the trucking industry if you do not embrace technology.

There are many add-ons that trucking companies can install in their trucks if they wish to. There are many companies innovating and putting out mind-boggling technology and gadgets, most of which are combining both software and hardware to connect with trucks with the promise that they have benefits that will improve the daily routines of trucks and make trucking operations seamless.

This is because it is a highly diversified industry to be working in which is made up of many sub-industries with many different kinds of trucks and vehicles dealing with their unique problems in conducting business. Technology is discovering methods to make it safer or more secure, less tedious, more precise, faster, and easier. Sometimes, technology has completely transformed certain aspects of the trucking industry.

The basic attraction is that it is going to improve lives for drivers and fleets. However, that is not what mainly makes fleets invest in these technologies. Transporting goods and freight or working with vehicles creates an environment where there is cut-throat competition, and most of the time, there are very small profit margins, hence most technology is advertised as a way to make your business more competitive.

In this chapter, we will concentrate on highlighting and describing technologies that could make your trucking business more competitive. You should be aware that utilizing different technologies is not an easy decision. Trucks are costly, and at times, fleets have many trucks. Fitting trucks with these technologies and ensuring that every truck in a fleet is catered to can be time consuming, and could take years. Most of the time, it needs maintenance and installation, which requires time and subsequently money. This is the main reason why technology firms are working hard to ensure that their innovations are installed or can be installed at the truck factory when they are new.

Additionally, truck add-ons need investment at the beginning and owners, operators, and fleet managers want to make sure that the investment is worthwhile. You should be able to get a high return on your investment, or at least notice tangible improvement, before and after installing the technology. Since the world is changing so quickly, a trucking company should ensure that it only invests in technology that will not become obsolete quickly. It would be very frustrating to train drivers how to use a certain technology, only to replace it with something else within a short period.

Due to this, it is wise for a company to adopt technology that has been in the market for some time. These are some of the best technologies in the trucking industry that keep evolving and are thus worth every dime spent on them:

Dynamic Routing

When working in this industry, you are constantly transporting workers and loads from one point to another, doing deliveries in different places. The route to use to accomplish your goal is vital. Dynamic routing is technology that works by improving flexibility and data to record routes used, particularly with weather and traffic in real time.

You can reduce unwanted miles and discover a faster route, or navigate around a huge collision or traffic, with constantly refreshed GPS data. Or, according to the condition of the business, drivers may manage to squeeze in more stops to improve route density and reduce the distance covered to every pickup point or subsequent delivery. Dynamic routing software is becoming better and can do most of these functions for you, which will help you save money and achieve automatic maximization.

All the time and fuel saved are important, because these are both some of the most expensive expenses for a trucking business. This technology can really help ensure that equipment and drivers are fully used, customers are more satisfied due to more efficient services, and expenses are managed better. Happy customers help improve your business's reputation and increase its chances of getting more clients in the future. A good example of this technology is CoPilot.

Forward Looking Camera System

Camera systems that are placed inside the vehicles have existed for many years now and have become quite popular. They are fondly known as dash cams. Over the years, their quality has improved tremendously.

Vehicle video systems have followed closely with the transformation of digital cameras, which have brought about major improvements in high-definition image capture, usability at night or low light, and image processing, because memory has increased storage capability while decreasing in size significantly.

Possibly, to start with, the purpose of adding video on a truck is to protect the driver and fleet in the event that there is an accident and possible fraudulent insurance claims. The people seeking a payday can try to hit a truck or make a false claim with the knowledge that fleets can be a good target.

Public perception is the other risk to trucks on the roads of America, which is even worse. Research from government agencies including the FMCSA have revealed that when passenger cars and heavy trucks get involved in an accident, 70% of the time, the crash is usually caused by the passenger vehicle driver, but when witnesses are questioned, they usually point their fingers at the truck and jump to the conclusion that it is the truck that was at fault.

Therefore, trucking companies and fleets usually find themselves paying when they are taken through the justice system, even though their trucks were not the ones that caused the accident. They also have to incur legal expenses fighting those accusations. Forward facing cameras can assist in showing what really transpired in accidents and save the business the expenses and bad reputation of being charged. Some of the best cameras out there are Lytx and SmartDrive. SureCam is a great provider of such cameras.

Driver Scorecards

This is a place where technologies have started to overlap and supplement one another. Gamification, or scorecarding, can trace its history back to the late 2000s, when fleet management systems were collecting telematics data to help identify where trucks were experiencing issues in their operation.

These were the notorious and stereotypical reporting of poor driving habits like acceleration and hard braking. They would signify careless driving that can cause accidents and also lead to more truck wear, which would end up in more maintenance expenses. Most fleet managers conducted meetings with drivers to call out the names of those who broke traffic rules or drove badly.

The concept has normally been straightforward. Therefore, even though your truck might have fuel economy, a truck driver is the biggest variable cost, since they can make up to 30% variance in mpg. Poor driving habits can make the truck consume more fuel and cause more regular crashes and other expensive incidents. Fleets can utilize driver coaching or scorecarding to reduce those expenses.

In modern times, scorecards have become more complicated, and they have also adopted a more positive method and incorporated more improved and intelligent functionality. Geotab is a great provider of this kind of technology.

Collision Mitigation Technology

Studies reveal that heavy trucks are usually excessively represented in fatalities and accidents. In a study that was done recently, the FMCSA realized that buses and heavy trucks totaled approximately 4% of vehicles that have been registered and 9% of overall miles covered, but were associated with 13% or total traffic fatalities and 13% of accidents.

It is somehow because of their bigger size and mass, which can create intense damage to passenger cars which are smaller. This is according to the agency's predictions. Although crash statistics evaluation continuously shows that it is the passenger vehicle driver who is usually in the wrong when heavy trucks and passenger vehicles crash, any big truck accident can lead to costly lawsuits and insurance claims.

Therefore, fleets have no choice but to minimize avoidable accidents as much as possible to not only safeguard profits but also protect the public. This is more so for fleets transporting dangerous materials such as fuel, because accidents can result in a lot of destruction and very costly cleanup.

Advanced collision mitigation technologies are integrating more detecting technology to keep track of accidents of different types and help make emergency maneuvers to steer clear of them. Modern systems are also reducing the quantity of false benefits that the initial similar products used to offer in the past. Due to the clear advantages they can provide if they function well, collision mitigation systems are common in most new trucks. Usually, they have an option to switch them off and can be fitted to older vehicles too.

One of the most praised systems in the market is the Wingman Fusion, made by Bendix Commercial Vehicle Systems, that utilizes video and radar to keep track of the roadway in front for hindrances and comes with an electronic stability program to safeguard against loss-of-control and rollover accidents. OnGuard systems, which were developed by meritor WABCO, provide the same capabilities. It depends on radar that is within a short range to sense obstacles.

Nowadays, there are also technologies that may provide more methods of dealing with collision reduction using driver behaviors. For instance, Drivewyze is popular for offering a time saving service that sends truck load and weight data to relevant inspection sites and weigh stations to let drivers simply drive past. It is available for free in the form of an add-on, and the company has also made an additional feature known as Driver Safety Notifications to notify drivers when they are about to drive through trouble zones.

Drivewyze collaborated with law enforcement agencies to know areas that have a greater need for security which would entail something like a certain highway or narrow road where the speed of a car leads to a high collision junction.

Electronic Logging Gadget

It is now mandatory that all commercial trucks that operate interstate in America possess electronic logging devices (ELDs). In the past, truckers have been using units known as automatic onboard recording devices (AOBRDs) which have been phased out even though they work in the same way.

Their work is to electronically track and record hours of service (HOS) for commercial truck drivers to make sure they are handling these trucks by following the rules and requirements put in place by the Federal Motor Carrier Safety Administration which is the regulatory body of the federal government. A number of owner-operators and drivers of small fleets dismiss the thought of using electronic logs, usually saying that they need to work for more hours than the usual HOS for them to survive in the industry that has stiff competition.

While some industry players don't see the need to use electronic logs,they will in fact make trucking companies and fleets more competitive. This increases their chances of succeeding in the industry. Remember that this is an industry that is usually plagued by high driver turnover, which means that a fleet could hire different drivers every year to replace its old team. This is quite expensive.

Omnitracs products are some of the best electronic logs out there. Matrack suppliers also offer reliable ELDs.

Trailer Tracking

This technology can make it relatively easier to find and control the usage of this equipment.

In this regard, you can also add GPS tracking as a method to keep track of what is happening with your trailers. Your fleet can be notified if your trailers are in risky areas where theft is common.

Trailers are costly assets, therefore, investing in technology that can help you monitor them will be good for business. Tracking a trailer does not just entail using a GPS transponder that is placed physically on the body of the trailer. Rather, it also offers an additional wireless device in the IOT (Internet of things) which means that a trailer tracking device can produce data that should be entered into a fleet management system.

Usually, the moment Big Data is included, there is a lot that can be accomplished. For instance, MiX Telematics provides its Asset Manager, which can monitor a shipping container with ease, just like a trailer. The firm said the tech can ease the process of managing assets like billing for a trailer that your company has rented out.

Services and technologies are joining forces to enhance trailer tracking. BlackBerry's product Rader tracking system offers analytics that, together with its tracking gadget, enables a fleet to manage maintenance and utilization, among others. For example, BlackBerry once partnered with Modagrafics, which is a fleet graphics service company, to do sales for trucking companies. When a fleet owner decides to do a marketing campaign using Modagrafics' graphics on their trailers, they can use BackBerry's tracking device to track where the trailers visited. The fleet can later observe if there will be an increase in sales in those places.

Additionally, trailer tracking could make it easier to do maintenance. FleetLocale Asset Management Solutions promises to solve this issue. This system can link maintenance records and data to a trailer, enabling a company to picture what has been serviced, what needs to be serviced, and create improved and more consistent inspection and maintenance plans. It is also easier for trucking companies with fleets to make informed decisions when buying equipment, because they will have better utilization and distinguishability of their trailers. Fleet Rabbit is another useful fleet maintenance app that you can consider using.

Last but not least, even the drivers benefit immensely from this technology, because it helps them find a trailer among many other trailers in a yard.

Record Keeping or Temperature Tracking

This is another group of technology which has become a must-have for most carriers. The Food Safety Modernization Act requires that the people who take part in shipping animal and human food, such as receivers, carriers, and shippers, should observe good practices for sanitary transporting.

It applies to items such as refrigerated food, keeping it safe while in transit and cleaning cars after unloading and before loading the next shipment, to avoid contamination. Shippers would want to ensure that they hire a company that has this technology. Shippers should stipulate in their contracts that they can abide by these rules and offer documents that prove that a truck had the right temperature at the time of delivering that type of food.

Many refrigeration units nowadays have integrated technology that can show the amount of temperature in the truck, as well as transmit results to the fleet management system using GPS. The fleet management platform can sync that data up with the requirements of the load and offer temperature documentations at the collection and delivery points, not to mention track the challenges between the two destinations.

One of the shortcomings of this technology is that it will force you to keep opening and shutting the trailer's door, allowing for the possibility of accidentally allowing in hot air. This is because you have to see those temperatures, but in case there is a problem, you can pull over and address it.

Like most things, when you notice the temperature issues early, you will be more likely to salvage the load. Additionally, having the ability to display documentation and temperature could be helpful if a reefer driver is inspected or asked to stop by the police.

Digital Freight Matching

These applications symbolize an interesting invention in transportation industry technology that has the capacity to help trucking firms boost profits. Just like Uber connects drivers and passengers, this technology spontaneously matches carriers and shippers, making it simpler for you to find clients. Drivers and shippers can be paired up according to a criteria like routes, dates and truckload capacity. The best digital freight matching applications include uShip, Uber Freight, and Convoy.

GPS Apps

Utilizing Global Positioning System technology, or simply GPS, for truck drivers is more complex than it is for regular car drivers. You must be aware which roads are open for trucks, where you can stop to rest or eat, and where you can find a place to refuel. Apps like Trucker Path contain GPS specially aimed at fulfilling the distinct needs of truck operators.

Telematics

This one mixes informatics with telecommunications technology. Informatics is the study of computer systems that are used to keep and obtain information. It includes dynamic routing and GPS, but it also goes a step further by making it possible for fleet managers to take actions like monitoring containers and drivers. Telematics providers like Samsara provide apps to assist fleet managers in using shipment and vehicle tracking.

Platooning

One significant use of telematics is synchronizing the movement of many trucks mechanically. This practice is referred to as platooning. It allows you to connect with different trucks and synchronize them in formations that could decrease wind resistance, enhance road safety for vehicles other than trucks, improve your efficiency, and decrease traffic conflicts. Platooning app providers include Peloton Technology. They can assist you in coordinating fleets of automobiles seamlessly.

Fuel Price Apps

Fueling is one of the things that gives trucking company operators sleepless nights, owing to how expensive it is. Luckily, fuel price apps like GasBuddy can assist you in reducing costs by comparing prices electronically, in real-time. Certain apps like Trucker Path contain features that assist you by confirming that a fuel pump has adequate clearance to handle trucks. When utilizing price comparison apps, select an area that has a low gas tax rate so that regardless of where you refill your tank, you will spend less on taxes. This way, you will ensure that you save the highest amount possible on fuel.

Prompt Digital Upload of Proof of Delivery (POD) Documents

An additional way to improve efficiency and receive payments quickly in your trucking business is to upload photographs of proof of delivery documents as soon as you complete a load. When you use the load tracking tool available in the free Trucker Tools driver app, you will be immediately prompted to send POD after a delivery. This tech enables 3PLs and brokers to begin payment quickly and is more effective than faxing, emailing, and scanning the PODs to them.

<hr>

Summary

In a nutshell, trucking technology is designed to help you:

- Analyze fleet and driver performance
- Evade insurance liability
- Save expenses on fuel and enhance safety
- Perform your operations better and faster
- Get loads to ship

Small businesses are usually derailed by repetitive tasks. Automating such tasks can improve your bottom line.

In the next chapter, we will look at the kind of positions you should seek to fill in your trucking company and what to do to attract and retain employees.

Hiring Employees

R egardless of the size of your business when you are beginning, you may get to a time when you will require hiring assistance. You will likely begin with subcontractors who work when you are overwhelmed with work. Perhaps you recruit a part-time driver who lets you handle office work one day a week or spend time with your family. However, if you grow some more, you will have to hire employees, regardless of whether they are a bookkeeper or drivers or scheduler or whichever duties require to be carried out to ensure that your business is not interrupted.

Selecting employees can make or break your company no matter if they are permanent or temporary. You should be surrounded by a reliable team. You will need to perform the following roles or hire a permanent or temporary staff member to do them:

Office Manager

This person deals with office-supply, clerical, and administrative tasks, such as answering phones, filing, ensuring that the office is clean and neat, and sometimes even coordinating employees.

Sales Staff

This is a person who is tasked with marketing your business and finding customers.

Director of Marketing

In a small business, a salesperson can double up as the director of marketing. The duties of a person in this role include getting well-timed publicity to the media, as well as handling promotion and advertising.

Bookkeeper

A bookkeeper monitors all business expenditure and could also do tax returns. If you find an accountant to work on some of the complex finance-oriented duties, you could manage the bookkeeping by yourself.

Note that you do not have to hire different people to do every role mentioned above. There is a possibility that you will end up doing most of the duties or all the tasks yourself.

Finding Candidates

After deciding the kinds of positions that you require to fill, you will need to communicate to potential employees by advertising the vacant positions. Do not take this step lightly. Use all avenues available to get the best staff.

Advertising

Think of putting your ad in your local as well as regional publications. If the role you are filling is a more executive job in your company, then also think about placing adverts in bigger newspapers and trade journals. National adverts are way pricier, therefore choose them only when the position is worth the cost and effort. National ads will possibly get the attention of candidates who will require a move to a different location, thus they will have high salary expectations to make the relocation worthwhile.

These are the other communication channels that you can use to market your job vacancy:

Online Job Sites

Advertising jobs on websites such as and has become quite popular lately. Nevertheless, by going this route, you will be marketing to a national audience whether you want to or not. Therefore, the best thing to do when using this form of advertising is to specify in your advert where the company is based to avoid receiving job applications from people located in far places who won't be able to move across states to do the job you are offering.

Online Newspaper Advertising

Confirm with the advertising personnel at your local newspaper to find out if they provide packages such as online only, print only or both kinds of advertising. If the newspaper provides an online choice, arrange with the newspaper to have them advertise both online and the print media.

Word of Mouth

This method of advertising never goes out of fashion. It is still as effective as it was since before print and online forms of advertising were invented. Tell your vendors that you are searching for employees.

Universities and Colleges

Universities and colleges usually have their own media and websites where you can advertise your job vacancies. This is a great place for getting capable candidates, particularly for minor positions.

Interviewing

When you start getting contacted by potential applicants, you should read their resumes carefully and group the unqualified candidates on one side and the qualified ones on the other side. If you created a precise job description, you should only have a few unqualified applicants. Neither should you have many in the qualified group because amazing employees are rare to come by. When reading through the resumes, utilize your rating criteria to determine which applicants to interview.

Interviewing Techniques

Make plans of interviewing between five and ten candidates for more executive roles and a smaller number for smaller roles. Once the candidates arrive for an interview, give them application forms to fill. You should ensure that you ask every candidate the same set of questions, guaranteeing a just process. If you need assistance in coming up with these questions, you can always look online for help. Sites like have great resources and content that can help you draft the questions. Additionally, get in touch with the trade association of your industry and they can give you appropriate questions that would be useful to your exact transportation company.

Write notes while the interviews are ongoing, so that you can go through them afterward and pare your pool of candidates down to two. Request that the two best candidates come back for another interview. Write notes in order to review the last two candidates' answers when the interviews are over and make the final decision.

Once the second interview comes and goes, you will be required to formulate an offer letter to the best candidate, outlining your proposal, benefits, and pay structure. After you and the applicant have both signed the letter, do not forget to inform the other candidate that the position has been filled. Give the bad news to the losing candidate only after the winning one has officially agreed to fill the position and become your employee. Sometimes, the best candidate that you have hired for the job might fail to accept the offer. If this happens, you will wish to hire the second candidate.

Pay

There are many factors to ponder when paying your employee. For example, the salary is usually greater in cities than in rural areas. The salary also depends on the employee's level of responsibility and experience. The labor department states that the average yearly salary for a truck driver is about $40,000.

Training

If it is drivers that you are bringing on board, there is a possibility that you will hire a person who has undergone some form of training. They could have a commercial license for the exact type of driving that your business needs, or at the very least have trained in a truck driving school. Bigger trucking companies usually have their own schools.

Regardless, you should still be prepared to train your employees, no matter whether they are schedulers, bookkeepers, or rookie drivers. These employees should be aware of the current trends in the industry and understand how to utilize the latest tools to work quickly and productively.

You need to be a great boss and find time to thoroughly train your new employees. When they report on their first day of work, demonstrate to them how you prefer things to be done, the basics of your business, and where to find the things they need to perform their duties. There is nothing more annoying to a new employee than not being given enough instructions about a job. Arrange to give every employee an exhaustive job description, explaining clearly what their responsibilities entail. Also, introduce the new hires to every person in the company, in order for them to meet the new team of people that they will be working with.

Why it can be difficult to get the appropriate kind of people to hire:

- There are many jobs to select from; the fact that the trucking industry has had a shortage of drivers since 2018 means that this is one of the most rapidly growing careers in the U.S., together with computer experts and health care workers.

- Many trucking companies are infamous for promising great things to new employees like high rates per mile, no deliveries to congested cities like New York, and time home each weekend. Later, when drivers start working, they discover that they were lied to during the recruitment process. After this occurs, rumors spread like wildfire, both through the trucking industry spheres and online. It requires just one or two dissatisfied employees to label you as a bad person.

- Trucking is hard; it needs a lot more than just the capability to operate a big rig. Truckers should be very responsible people who can cope with a continuously evolving work environment. They must know how to do the math, write, and read, as well as do well on written evaluations.

- Truckers have to get used to the challenges of living in a small space, eating food that is usually not so delicious or nutritious, and the health dangers that are associated with being inactive for a big chunk of the day. Additionally, there are the problems of encountering demanding dispatchers, weigh stations, and rude car drivers. When you combine all these issues, it is not hard to see why finding a good driver could be a problem for most trucking companies. If you want to outsmart your competitors in finding competent drivers, these are the strategies that you need to apply:
  - Market effectively and target a wide area, using the methods that we mentioned above.
  - If it is possible for you to employ trucking school graduates, go ahead and do it. A majority of these people have the determination and the intelligence to become good drivers, if they are given an opportunity.
  - Connect with groups that link employers with veterans. This can be a great way to get exceptional people, most of whom have acquired experience in handling transport machines when they were enlisted.
  - Consider employing a professional recruiter or be prepared to spend many hours hiring, particularly when you're first establishing your business. Looking for people is only a small part of what you need to do, because besides that, you also have to retain them for a long period. Consider that the turnover rate in the first year of employment is high in the trucking industry, nearly as high as that of the fast food business.

This can be a difficult task. Fortunately, there are things that you can do to help keep the rate of turnover low in your company.

How to keep employees working for you for longer

1. Avoid making promises that you cannot fulfill. If you are not sure whether your drivers can make it home every weekend then avoid saying that they can do it. Be honest from the onset about the number of miles drivers can anticipate regularly and the amount of money you will be paying them. This will help prevent your firm from being blacklisted as one of the companies that drivers should avoid working for.

2. Encourage your employees to share their opinions for making the company better and give them rewards when one of their suggestions is implemented. Small things such as praise from time to time can be quite beneficial, as can physical gifts like gift certificates to famous restaurants, cash bonuses, and achievement plaques.

3. Adopt an open-door policy. Basically, this means that your drivers are free to access you and discuss problems or questions and be confident that they will be treated respectfully, even though what they intend to say is not very positive. Listen carefully and assure them that you value their frankness. If you can find a solution to the issue and satisfy everybody, then make a genuine effort to solve it.

By going the extra mile for your employees, your business will have a good reputation, as the type of a company that drivers would be happy to work for. You will be surprised at how easy it will be for you to hire new drivers going forward.

Strategies that Key Industry Players are Using to Attract Employees

The need to hire new employees while retaining the workforce that commercial trucking firms already have is forcing companies to analyze their operations and pay more attention to improvement and development from the inside. This entails becoming innovative and repeatedly working with truck drivers as well as back-office staff, dispatchers, and technicians.

These are some of the strategies that some of the best trucking companies in the industry have been utilizing to ensure that they always have a constant supply of drivers, despite the shortage that the industry is experiencing.

Nonstop Engagement and Communication

The president and CEO of the National Transportation Institute (NTI), Leah Shaver, advises trucking company owners that it is important to improve an employee's experience during the first year. She says that the company should focus on constant engagement and training. She added that as people are getting used to working in a new company, it is vital to ensure that there is unending engagement and clear communication concerning what the future has in store for them, not to mention the rest of the company. She also observed that taking note of milestones made in the first year of an employee's time in the company and offering rewards as well as feedback to recognize how employees are moving ahead is crucial. Talk to employees about career path choices in the organizations.

She also believes that companies that are successful in hiring and retaining employees usually incorporate social media and technology to improve engagement across the company. She noted that newsletters are a good instrument to ensure that employees are up to date with important company communications, job announcements, or referral incentives.

Not Paying on a PrM-Mile Basis

Boyle Transportation's co-president, Andrew Boyle, asserts that his company does not just hire to fill positions or for the sake of hiring, rather, they employ drivers for their brain and not just their driving skills. They hire drivers due to their attention to detail and their knowledge about technology and their dedication to security, safety, and quality. He asserts that the company sells to customers security, safety, and quality, and therefore, they only employ applicants who have shown a commitment to these three principles.

The company is also committed to driver inclusion and feedback. Boyle also discourages trucking companies from basing their compensation on just the mileage covered. He explains that for over a decade now, the company stopped paying its drivers according to the mileage they had driven and it now pays them not less than $1,870 on a weekly basis during the first year OTR drivers.

The company also makes sure that drivers go home a minimum of two days for each week on the road. The co-president says that by refusing to pay people according to miles, and allowing them to go home regularly, the company is able to eliminate the stress for its drivers and gives them a chance to improve their productivity and work as professionals. He says that doing things right is more important than keeping track of the miles each driver covers. According to Boyle, when every employee is concentrating on what the customer values, then the business will do well.

Boyle Transportation was named as one of the best fleets to work for by Truckload Carriers Association and CarriersEdge for several years, consistently. It is no wonder why it has been making this list for years.

Listen to Employees and Drivers

Another top fleet, Garner Trucking, which is located in Ohio, is a family-operated and asset-oriented carrier. It has been in business for the last six decades. The company has been included in the "Best Fleets to Drive For" list for the last five successive years. Sherri Brumbaugh is the CEO and president of this company.

This company has improved communications with employees, including drivers through YouTube videos which are created and posted every week, company town halls, and podcasts. The firm also incorporated an app and updated its transportation management system to assist drivers to obtain load information quickly. The secret of the company's success and survival has been listening to employees and drivers.

The CEO says that the best way to find out the weaknesses in a company is to ask the drivers, and as long as they tell you in a respectful way, there is nothing wrong with listening to what they have to say. She asks the employees what they need to increase their productivity, and if they say they need more time at home with their families, she tries to fulfill their wishes.

The company also employs drivers who are hearing impaired and employees from different cultural backgrounds. The CEO notes that the employees simply speak a different language, and so the management just has to learn how to communicate differently. The company also tries to understand the cultural requirements of its employees' families. The company also has diverse services, which give drivers an opportunity to select the segment that suits them best. The firm operates dedicated segments, over the road, local, etc.

Recruiting and Retention Strategies Used by the Best in the Industry

Boyle Transportation is aware that there is a younger demographic that is joining the industry nowadays, which does not have sufficient experience like the older generation of drivers. Therefore, the company has adjusted its recruitment process to accommodate these young drivers. In the past, they used to take about three days to complete the onboarding process, but nowadays they take 5 days plus continuous training, and they offer tools that they can use whenever they need help. On top of that, the company also began a mentoring program whereby new drivers can look for guidance from older truckers who have more experience on the road.

Another company, Atlas Logistics, has been experiencing a problem with hiring technicians, because competitors keep poaching them and offering them higher salaries. To retain its employees, Atlas has been concentrating on creating a more comfortable work environment, as well as flexible work schedules. The company has also ensured that its benefits and wages are competitive, based on the marketplace. Atlas has also been assisting owner operators in buying liability insurance at affordable rates, and it has also begun an equipment leasing program for its drivers. All this has helped them get new employees. However, the most effective way of getting new employees for the company is through employee referrals. The company compensates its employees if the driver they recommended ends up becoming a valuable addition to the company.

Shaver says that the best strategy that she uses in hiring and retaining employees is recognizing their achievements and rewarding them. Also, she ensures that the company publicizes the action of rewarding the employees. This way, drivers in other companies will see what is happening in the other company and have the desire to join your company.

Drivers' Problems

Research done by WorkHound in 2021 revealed that most companies focus on raising compensation for its drivers, however drivers complain more about logistics and equipment than they do about money. The findings were based on more than 24,000 comments from over 10,000 people working in the trucking industry.

The survey also established that drivers who work for small companies with less than 200 employees reported having more job satisfaction than those working for big companies. Drivers from small companies also said that they are not likely to jump from one company to another and they are more likely to help their bosses deal with negative experiences.

Most employees cited the lack of praise by the big companies as the reason why they dislike working for the companies and prefer small ones. The preference for small companies is also evident in the way small companies are said to earn more than the bigger companies. However, this does not spell doom for the big players. All it means is that these companies can do better if they learn to praise their employees and make it part of their culture.

<hr />

Summary

In summary, hiring employees for your trucking company is an important process that should be given the seriousness it deserves. First and foremost, ensure that you screen the candidates thoroughly and have the experienced truck drivers do a drive test with you in the truck so that you can assess their skills. For rookie drivers, you need to do thorough and longer onboarding training for them and explain to them the kind of mistakes they need to avoid making, considering that they are inexperienced in the job.

Mistakes Trucking Business Owners And Drivers Make

Whenever most people start a business, they do it hoping that the business will last long and probably outlive them. Trucking business owners also entertain such thoughts, and with good reason. To ensure that your business survives for a long time, you need to avoid making the mistakes that others before you made. Some mistakes have devastating consequences, and avoiding them can mean the difference between your trucking business succeeding and failing. In this chapter, we will examine mistakes that a business owner and drivers can avoid to ensure that the business prospers.

Mistakes Trucking Business Owners Make

1. Buy the car the wrong way; do not overpay for a truck. Shop around for the best deals possible.

2. Getting loans with high interest; you need to shop around for the best rates possible. Do not just choose the first lender you come across. Looking for the best rate will help you find great savings.

3. Poor funds management: this is one of the major causes of trucking businesses failing. If you mismanage your finances, your business will not make it past the 5-year mark. Therefore, you need to be very good with numbers, as we have mentioned before.

4. Ensure that the truck is dependable; do not compromise on the quality of the vehicle you buy or lease. Search for the most affordable yet sound truck that you can use for a long time. Besides that, the truck should also consume less fuel to help you save money on fuel.

5. No experience: give yourself about two years to learn about the industry such as the types of engines and trucks.

6. Inadequate savings: always ensure that you have enough savings, because your vehicles will need repairs from time to time.

7. Problems with the authorities: failing to comply with the law is one sure way to make your business fail. This is because you will end up paying a lot of penalties and fines, which will deplete your resources.

8. Too many debts: if you incur a lot of debts before or soon after starting your trucking business, your credit score will be badly affected, which means it will be hard to get loans, and consequently your cash flow will always be low. Thus, surviving in the industry will be almost impossible.

9. Overspending money: as a trucking business owner, you must learn to avoid being extravagant. Spending money meant for business on unnecessary things, such as gambling or buying a sports car during the first few years of starting a business could kill it.

10. Reputation: your reputation is important as a business. Therefore, protect it at all costs. It will be very damaging if clients or drivers associate you with careless driving. Therefore, ensure that you discipline erring drivers. Consider having a hotline that drivers can report exceptional and reckless driving to.

11. Having inadequate money: it is very expensive to ensure that your truck is always on the road. If you are a rookie working for a big corporation, this may not be a huge problem. However, if you are an owner-operator, seeking the services of a factor is necessary.

More Do's and Don'ts for the Owner-Operator or Small Trucking Business Owner

There are numerous do's and don'ts when you are starting a trucking company and it is very easy to get overcome with the procedure and forget to focus on how to be successful.

Find the Freight First

The first thing that you should do before you even begin your trucking business is to make sure that the goods are available for you to transport. Many times, potential owner-operators begin spending money on leasing trucks, hiring drivers, and buying equipment, geting themselves into debt before ensuring that they have cargo to transport. Without getting the contacts to transport freight, your company will never become successful.

Have a Clear Plan

Another crucial thing to do before you begin to transport is draft a concise plan for your trucking business. Come up with a list of variable and fixed costs and weigh them against the amount of revenue you anticipate earning from transporting goods. Be ready to save between 20 and 30 percent of your projected profits to meet unexpected costs, like the repair needs of a truck or a hike in diesel prices, and understand how these will impact your personal spending.

Hire Qualified Drivers

It goes without saying that failing to hire a qualified driver is the recipe for disaster. The driver that you hire should not have more than one violation or a DUI, and they should have not less than one year of highway experience. When you do this, you will be saving yourself a lot of stress later on. Think about it: a trailer and tractor will cost you an average of $200,000. When you add the value of the cargo that the truck will be hauling, then you will appreciate that you are placing a huge responsibility into the hands of your driver. The best thing to do in order to find out whether you are hiring an experienced driver or not is to take them on a 30 minute road test. Observe keenly how they drive and see if they will make any foolish mistakes that can cost you your business. If you are satisfied with how they have driven then you have yourself a good reliable driver.

Have a Budget

The greatest mistake that owner-operators make is failing to draft a budget or do cash flow projections for their businesses. Record keeping and analyzing numbers should be an important function for an owner operator. However, it is shocking how many people downplay its importance. Ultimately, those business owners close down their businesses.

Writing a budget is a prudent thing to do. Actually, it is essential for a successful trucking business owner. The budget should contain your personal expenses plus your business costs. It should also contain strategies for contingency funds for emergency expenses like personal needs, freight delays, lack of miles, and truck breakdowns. It can be tempting to pay your bills and use the rest for your personal needs until you get another check. This is a dangerous move. You can survive like this for the short-term, but this habit will cost you down the line.

Advantages of Creating a Budget and Calculating Cash Flow

Cash flow calculations and a projected budget are easy methods for trucking companies to make crucial decisions like:

- They will help you determine if your business is profitable, and if it isn't, you will think of ways to make it lucrative.

- They will help you know an affordable plan for making truck payments.

- Help you know if your expected net profit is too small to maintain your business of personal costs.

- The number of miles the wheels should cover every month

- Are the present fuel prices too much for your truck, which is an older model and has huge gallon/mile utility?

- Will you be able to make a good profit operating the maximum number of miles every month, or will you be able to just cover the expenses? You may be forced to review the contract or decide to invest in a different industry.

One important thing that you will discover when you start thinking keenly about the money side of the business is that a lot of mileage does not necessarily mean a high profit.

Cash Flow Issues

At times, trucking businesses face cash flow issues. These problems are usually a combination of various factors, including having a lot of accounts receivable, unpaid invoices, low-paying freight, high operational costs, and few customers.

Use all the tactics possible to improve your cash flow. You can hire experts to help you if you are unable to do them yourself.

- Create cash flow projections for the days to come. Having a precise projection will help you prepare for trouble.

- Increase receivables; your objective should be to ensure that your customers pay you promptly. You can give discounts to the customers who pay their bills without delay, or ask them to make a deposit. You also need to invoice on time and follow up on pending payments. If you have clients who do not pay in a timely manner, then enforce a cash on delivery policy.

- Control your payables; monitor your expenses closely and ensure that your returns are not lagging behind. Ensure that you capitalize on payment conditions, and pay only when the deadline is about to elapse. You also need to maximize discounts and select suppliers who have versatile payment conditions.

- Anticipate declines in cash flow. These kinds of problems are normal for any type of business. The best thing to do is to expect them, so that you can get a line of credit to deal with it. If the banks refuse to give you any assistance, you can always request your suppliers to push your due date forward.

- Prioritize your expenditure: if you have trouble with cash flow, you need to select the bills that you wish to settle first. Suppliers and employees should be prioritized. You can also inquire of your supplier if you can make a partial payment or skip one payment.

- Factors. Using factors is one sure way to boost your cash flow.

Poor Management

Unfriendly and unprofessional managers intimidate good employees and make them quit. Research that was done by Acros Advisors shows that bad managers make the economy lose not less than $319 billion every year. In regards to truck drivers, they usually stop working for a company because they dislike the dispatcher or fleet manager. In the trucking sector, the issue is worsened by differing personalities. Drivers spend most of their time on the road by themselves. They have patience, but they do not like to be criticized. In addition, they require more structure. On the contrary, managers are more extroverted, and they prosper with limited rules and guidance in a fast-moving job environment.

Competent and straightforward drivers are not easy to find. Therefore, it is unfortunate if they quit simply due to your fleet manager's unaccommodating nature. Moreover, the trucking sector has been grappling with a driver shortage. According to the statistics by American Trucking Associations, the industry had an inadequate number of drivers by 60,800 in 2018. However, that figure is expected to increase by not less than 160,000 by 2028. If you lose a great driver when there is still a shortage, you might fail to get a good replacement. With inadequate drivers, a trucking business will be badly affected. You cannot complete orders, and it will strain your other drivers, who will be forced to work more hours just to match the demand.

Poor Managers Make Poor Business Decisions

Truth be told, anybody can make bad decisions, even good managers or leaders. However, bad managers repeatedly make dangerous decisions. Poor leaders have been found to make decisions according to what they perceive will help them advance careerwise. They are disconnected from employees, and are usually bothered by the big picture. Bad managers do not just push away good employees, rather they also do the following:

- Fail to seize opportunities

- Have a habit of mishandling resources

- Cause general performance to drop

- Fail to foster relationships with people they are supervising, making employees lose motivation and morale

- Make staff members to doubt senior management for backing up a bad leader

How to Avoid Hiring a Bad Manager

As we have explained above, a bad manager can harm your business by making it hard to retain good employees. To avoid all these problems, senior management should do certain things such as select the right manager, be clear about their expectations, communicate efficiently, and also train and teach managers about what high performance is all about. Selecting the correct manager can be a bit difficult, because not many people have leadership skills.

Vet potential managers thoroughly and treat the process as seriously as you would the employee recruitment process.

Failure to Care About Compliance

As a trucking company, you need to know and adhere to different compliance needs. That is because breaking these rules could be quite costly, and in some situations, the U.S. Department of Transportation can give orders that your business should be closed.

If you fail to observe the rules, you could really have a hard time surviving in the industry. For example, the FMCSA raised the fines when you violate federal trucking rules. Nowadays, the fines begin at over $300, and they can be as high as $191,000. The amount of your fine will be based on the nature of your trucking business and the law you've violated. If you ignore it, the DOT can make you stop operating momentarily or ask you to close the business. If you go on operating when you have been suspended, you will be given an additional fine of $24,017. Fortunately for you, you can use the checklists that are available online to help you obey different regulations. Apart from these checklists, there are three other things that you can do to make sure that you observe the regulations governing your industry.

1. Know the hours of service and other relevant regulations.

The FMCSA has a certain number of hours of service for this industry. Read through the criteria to understand which of your cars are regarded as CMVs. You also need to know the documentation that you require for your drivers. Additionally, there are periods when seasonal or part time drivers plus mechanics are affected by hours of service rules. There are also state alternatives of HOS rules. These regulations differ in different states.

2. Track your BASICs and CSA score status.

The FMCSA's safety measurement system establishes where you are in the Behavior Analysis and Safety Improvement categories. Your history of violations and inspection results determine your status. This process will enable you to get accountability, safety, and compliance scores. Here are the seven categories:

- Crash indicator that contains any history of being involved in accidents

- Dangerous driving that comprises seatbelt violations, wrong lane changes, careless driving, inattentiveness, and speeding

- Car maintenance, which consists of not doing repairs and any faults that the vehicle has

- Complying with hours of service, which consists of incomplete or incorrect logs

- Driver fitness, which consists of invalid licenses and medical problems

- Dangerous materials compliance, which comprises the utilization of leaking containers, erroneous placards, or wrong packaging

- Alcohol or controlled substances, which comprises the possession and use of controlled substances, like alcohol and drugs

To know your BASICs situation, visit the FMCSA website. If you have safety concerns, you will be able to address them there.

The Importance of Tracking Your CSA and BASICs Score

For starters, it will give you an idea of where you are compared to other companies and your competitors, in regards to safety on the road and off. It will also enable you to be aware of the areas that need improvement, and make adherence much easier in the future. Additionally, you can avoid safety issues. Drivers must always comprehend the HOS rules and keep complete and correct logs. They should also know every part of driver inspection reports.

Training them once is not enough, you need to have them undergo regular training or refresher courses. These courses will handle not just the basics, but the updates of new rules.

3. Use technology to enhance logging and inspection.

Drivers could already understand why it is important to log their time. However, they may be overwhelmed by the paperwork. If this is the reality, they may be violating regulations by constantly postponing the task. Mercifully, there are technologies that can help you mechanize logging.

Problem with the Industry or Economy

Sometimes a trucking business can fail due to reasons that are beyond your control. There are instances when your industry goes through difficult times. In 2019, several trucking companies closed down, both big and small. For example, Falcon Transport, which had 585 drivers, and Terrill Transportation, which had 36 drivers.

Driver Shortage

The reason cited for causing this problem is that the legalization of marijuana in some states is making it difficult for companies to get drivers who can pass a drug test. This is one of the requirements for getting hired. Moreover, it is only a few people who are applying to become truck drivers. People just prefer more comfortable jobs.

Fewer Class 8 Vehicles

Class 8 orders are for heavy-duty trucks. Back in 2018, the demand for these vehicles rose sharply, but the next year the demand went down. The decline was occasioned by the reduced operations in the manufacturing industry. Nevertheless, facing difficult times should not be a justification for failure. If you plan your business properly and understand your cash flow, knowing the intricacies of the trucking industry and other strategies will help you survive the challenges that come your way.

Mistakes Rookie Drivers Make

With the driver shortage that the industry has been experiencing lately, you might end up hiring a rookie. Advise them not to make these mistakes.

These are the common mistakes they make:

1. Misjudging a corner. A driver could be swinging too wide or failing to swing wide enough. It is good to check their clearances and spacing regularly.

2. Failing to get clear directions to a pickup or delivery. If you are a trucking business owner, make sure that you give good directions to drivers to prevent a situation where the vehicle gets stuck in a weird location where it cannot be turned around or the driver gets lost.

3. Not having focus when backing the vehicle up. The driver should make sure that they back up correctly. They can do this by stepping out of the vehicle and observing the surroundings first. They should look for clearance and obstructions. They should do it safely and gradually, and consistently concentrate on their driver aids, such as cameras and side mirrors. Backing up requires practice and a lot of experience, so find time to learn and practice.

4. Hurrying. A driver should avoid hurrying at all costs. Rushing results in blunders. Mistakes can be deadly when they are a professional driver. Always take as much time as they need to do things right.

5. Being overconfident. Qualified drivers and especially those who have been truck drivers for a long time have the tendency to be overconfident and become complacent. Pay attention to details, concentrate on driving a hundred percent of the time, and never assume anything. Complacency could lead them into big problems.

6. Getting distracted. Some truck drivers tend to text or listen to music while on the road. This is a very dangerous habit, because when they are operating such a huge machine as a truck or trailer, they need to concentrate 100% on what they are doing. Failure to do so can end up causing an accident, because by the time they realize something is wrong, it will be too late to control the truck and avoid disaster.

7. Relying only on the GPS. A GPS is a great device, that is designed to help them know their directions. However, they should avoid relying on it entirely. The best thing to do is to clarify the information they have by contacting the people involved to ask for clear instructions. They can call the shipper, receptionist, or anybody else who might have the information they need.

8. Using a car GPS instead of a truck GPS. A car GPS will give them the directions that a car can take. Keep in mind that when they are driving a truck, they cannot just use any road available. Some have bridges which can become obstacles when they are driving a huge vehicle, and they are bound to get stuck under the bridge or cause damage to the vehicle. Therefore, it is important to be sure which road and route they need to use.

9. Driving down a hill too fast. When they are driving one of these massive trucks, they need to drive slowly when they are ascending a hill, because if they are speeding up, they can get into an accident which can cost them their life.

10. Stopping at the wrong stop. Some rookies can make the mistake of parking in a lot that is not meant for trucks. This is a big mistake, because they will have a difficult time getting in and out of the lot, since there will be cars swarming around them.

11.

Failing to see that the air tanks are always drained, especially during the winter, and failing to ensure that their clutch is adjusted.

12. Forgetting to check the doors when pulling up from a pickup or drop off point. It is important to check that the doors are properly closed before moving, because the door could get damaged and they might end up spilling the goods down the road as they drive.

13. Failing to check the hub oil or wheel seal leak. Replace the oil if it has run out, and have the car repaired if it has a leak.

14. Hauling the incorrect load. Be alert when picking up cargo from the pickup point to avoid wasting fuel carrying the wrong load.

15. Taking a turn too sharply; when they do this, they could ruin good wheels, and they can wind up in a ditch, which would result in so much down time. Therefore, they must give themself room when taking a turn.

16. Bumping a car when they are changing lanes. Make sure that when they are turning, the lanes are clear to avoid colliding with another car. This could result in a lot of expenses and downtime.

17. Tailgating. This is the behavior of a driver driving just behind another car, without leaving enough space to stop without colliding if the car in the front stops abruptly. Some rookies tend to make this mistake on the road.

18. Forgetting to lift the landing gear. It can cost them time and consequently money.

19. Leaving a truck at the fuel island. Be mindful where they park the truck.

20. Setting the wrong temperature on a refrigerated truck. Check the relevant documents when picking up the load, see what temperature is needed, and set it. If the shipper asks them to use a different temperature than the correct one indicated in the papers, have them sign somewhere that they are the ones who asked you to use the wrong temperature, so that when they arrive at the delivery point and the cargo has spoiled, the signee will be held liable for the loss.

21. Refusing to grow as a driver. Most rookie drivers just want to stay as good drivers instead of working hard to better their skills and become great. Do more than just drive, get involved in the other aspects of

the job, such as negotiations and accounting. They should grow as a business person.

22. Heeding advice from anybody. If a rookie is told something that sounds too good to be true, then know that it is possibly not true. They can ask their fellow drivers for advice, but they should not believe everything they are told. They can listen to anybody's opinions but should use their own judgment about anything concerning the load or their career.

23. Having a lot of expectations. Being a trucker can be a rewarding career, but it is not as stress-free as most new drivers think it is. It is not easy to be away from home, and fighting homesickness when they are trying to be an expert truck driver can be a bit tricky. This blunder that rookie truck drivers make is not essentially risky in regards to safety, however, it is crucial to always remember it, since it is associated with their individual happiness and mental health. Understand that life on the road can be hard, but most of the time, it is worthwhile in the long run.

24. Failing to take safety measures seriously. They might be well versed about the operations of their truck, but that does not mean they should ignore the specifics that they think could be unimportant and silly. Protecting their load should also be something that they take seriously. Even if there are methods of preventing haul theft, there is still a possibility that it can be stolen. Some thieves are willing to go to great lengths to acquire what is in your truck. Regardless of whether they are rushing to meet a deadline or they are trying to avoid particular weather conditions, they should always ensure that they inspect load tie-downs or do a truck inspection. This blunder that many new truckers make can result in bad injuries to other road users, hence, it is not something that can be overlooked.

25. Failing to take good care of themselves; A very rampant rookie error is not taking care of themselves. This is not as straightforward as it sounds, since adjusting their lifestyle to cope with life on the road can make this difficult sometimes. At times, they will be required to transport a cargo when they are tired to the level where the big vehicle they are operating could harm themself or other drivers near them. That would be the perfect time to rest. There is no employment or quantity of money that has the same value as the risk of them killing or injuring someone on the road. Being a professional driver entails,

among other things, understanding their limits, hence looking out for themselves will mean they will be safer and more successful in the end.

26. Not being organized. All paperwork and documents needed for them to be on the road are definitely very crucial, hence, they should ensure that they are completing logs and monitoring paperwork and receipts after arriving at the drop off and delivering the goods as well as everything else that is associated with driving. Being an organized driver will enable them to save time and assist them in feeling more relaxed when they are beginning as a driver.

27. Listening to family or friends. A lot of damage has happened due to the mere fact of listening to the advice or disapproval of friends and family more than anything else they can think about. It appears so natural, and it even appears as if it is the wisest thing to do. If they don't know about something, they should just begin by questioning other people. Definitely, we always want to begin with the people we are most familiar with and trust, who are friends and family. Nevertheless, this is a risky move for many reasons. These include:

Emotional Attachments

You have history and grudges with friends and family that can become an obstacle to good communication. They could think they are helping you out, but in most cases, they will give you lousy advice for what they are convinced are good reasons. Family and friends' main concern would be to prevent you from making mistakes. This is amazing, however, this is not very important when you are considering making a huge life decision. For instance, if you are planning to purchase a truck, you are likely to make mistakes during the process of buying the equipment. However, you should focus on ensuring that you do not make too many mistakes, but you should not avoid mistakes by doing nothing.

If you do take action, family and friends may be too motivating, since they are afraid of telling you the truth or discouraging you. No matter what you do, you will not be receiving the best advice that you should be getting. You require valuable advice from persons who comprehend what you are attempting to achieve. Bad advice provided for positive reasons is still not good advice.

Inexperience

Even if your family or friends have been owner-operators in the past, or are one at the moment, there is no guarantee that they have adequate experience to give you beneficial advice. Do they know the important steps that you should follow when buying a truck such as spec'ing, finding, searching, inspecting, and haggling for a truck, or did they buy without doing any due diligence like most people do? How many vehicles do they have on the road? Have they ever made any mistakes when buying trucks and can they acknowledge that they did?

Someone can get lucky and buy a good truck without following the right process. However, it is not wise to operate your business based on luck. Some people might have been in the trucking industry for many years, but that does not necessarily mean that they are fit to give you sound advice. Most people get comfortable and stop learning about the business, and don't continue to expand or grow their knowledge. Therefore, you should only seek advice from people who keep on growing and studying.

Bad Communication Skills

Even if people have the correct knowledge or experience, they are not usually talented communicators, thus they will not be able to communicate what they know in a clear and effective way. Actually, most of the time, they can create more confusion through being unable to advise someone properly. Some people have the knowledge in their minds, however they have never been able to organize it in a manner that is understandable and is useful to another person who might not have the same experience or background.

There are many people who suffer from this problem. The best way to overcome it is to find time and write and arrange your knowledge, ideas, and thoughts about a topic in a manner that can assist you in comprehending the ideas. However, very few people manage to do this. Therefore, how do you counter this problem? You can circumvent it by seeking advice from as many people as possible and then sitting down and analyzing it all to see what is important and what isn't. But when you are asking them for advice, the best thing to do is to ask them to give you the reason behind every piece of advice that they offer to you.

Summary

To sum it up, there are several things that you need to be careful about if you want your business to avoid becoming a statistic by failing within the first five years of starting. This includes ensuring that you comply with the regulations that the government has put in place to regulate the trucking industry. You should also have a budget and a cash flow plan to ensure that you always have money to pay wages and salaries, as well as catering to important expenses such as fuel and repairs. Another important thing is to ensure that you hire competent drivers, give them clear instructions, and if you decide to hire rookies, train them well and let them know the common mistakes they need to avoid. Also, teach all your drivers how to protect their loads from theft while in transit.

Next we will look at why it is important for you to know and monitor your expenses as well as which tools to use to do it.

Know And Monitor Your Expenses

A s we have seen, one way to ensure that your business does not go under is to make sure that you keep track of your finances. It is wise to be constantly aware of what is going on with your business instead of waiting until the end of the year to check whether you are making any profits.

Essentially, the trucking industry is vital to the U.S economy. Many industries would be badly affected if no trucks transported goods across the state boundaries. When you are an owner-operator, two options are available to you to monitor your finances.

You can either do it yourself or outsource the work to an expert. Many companies offer such services to small businesses. Just make sure to look for the right company with reliable and reputable services. If you decide to go hard and learn all the maths and accounting involved, you will still run a successful business. Just be sure to master the calculations and analysis.

Besides having a solid business plan and budgeting for your business, you should also do the following:

Understand Your Expenses

You can avoid closing down your business due to bankruptcy by understanding your expenses. When you monitor expenses like repairs, truck maintenance, office expenses, trailers, truck finance payments, fuel, and salaries, you will appreciate how much money you need to operate your business. When you realize how much you are investing in the business, you will know whether you are making profits or losses. Most trucking business owners monitor their costs through a spreadsheet on Excel. Some like using paper and pen to write data. However, trucking management software, or TMS, is the most efficient way of monitoring costs.

There are typically two kinds of operating expenses for trucking business owners. These are fixed fees and variable expenses. Knowing your fixed payments will assist you in understanding how much it costs to run your business. Costs such as license plates are paid on an annual basis. On the other hand, variable expenses differ according to the number of miles your vehicle has covered that month. If you ship goods over a longer distance in a particular month, you will spend more on fuel and repair and maintenance costs. You will discover that the more distance you cover in a month, the more you will spend on your variable expenses.

Planning and Maximizing Routes

When you spend time optimizing and planning your trucking routes, you acquire the strength to optimize the general efficiency of your fleet and keep high profit margins.

You have to consider various factors when route planning for your employees. You will also need to think of scheduled stops along the road that comprise compulsory driving breaks as overnight stays.

Remember that planning a specific route and hoping that the driver will reach there by the estimated arrival time is not enough. Delivery trucks, particularly those hauling time-sensitive goods, have an essential delivery time window and schedule that the driver must observe. Whereas map apps like Google Maps or Waze may be perfect when planning a vacation or making personal trips, they are unsuitable for truck routing. You need to input information about your stops by hand, and the highest amount you can include on Google Maps is ten. Luckily, when you use TMS, you can plan each route for your trucks and add information about all the essential stops along the road, which will help you become knowledgeable and organized.

Indeed, a TMS will simplify your life as a trucking business owner. Besides keeping track of your records, it will also monitor truck maintenance records, driver pay records, management reports, mileage reports, invoices, IFTA payments, and dispatch reports and records.

Labor Costs

You also need to factor in your labor fees. If you have employed drivers, you will need to pay them. There are also people to get the loads on and off the trucks who also need to be paid. Labor fees form a significant percentage of your annual expenditure.

Strategies to Save Fuel

Besides reducing idling time, avoiding overspeeding, and using fuel cards, there are other ways to reduce fuel consumption. Aerodynamics is one such technique that will help you spend less on fuel. Heavy trucks use too much energy fighting air resistance, particularly when moving at highway speeds. The best thing to do in this case is to enhance your truck's aerodynamics. Doing frequent vehicle maintenance is another way of reducing your expenses as a trucking business. For instance, driving a truck with low pressure tires will utilize more fuel. You also need to constantly evaluate the axle placement because pulling the wheels sideways consumes more fuel. You can also arrange an engine refurbishment if your truck is an older model. Also, remember that the newest tires usually have more roll resistance than older ones. Thus, if your tires can still cover additional miles, do not be in a hurry to replace them.

Besides the tires, you should also closely monitor and maximize these parts of your trucks:

- Oil levels: failing to lubricate your trucks well means that the engine could overheat and result in expensive repairs and replacement.

- Exterior features: if you don't notice even the tiniest scratches or dents, you could be forced to spend a lot of money on replacing a big external part of your truck's body.

- Fluid levels in components such as the radiator.

- Wiring

- Brakes

- Lights

Other measures that can help you save on fuel are using the correct fuel for your truck, using the air conditioner only when absolutely essential, and buying roof fairing.

Protect Your Goods From Theft

Stolen trailers and goods are a big problem for trucking companies, and the outcomes can be expensive. Thieves are creative in finding methods to steal from your fleets. Therefore, it is crucial for both you, as the company owner, and your drivers to know the effective preventive measures that you can take to protect loads and prevent theft. These could include:

- Establish which goods are usually stolen.

- Evaluate the places where there is a high chance of items getting stolen and what duration during the day.

- Park intelligently; it is wise to use available objects and surroundings to create an obstacle for unwanted entry. Shunning dangerous areas and parking close to security cameras is also advisable.

- Be wary of any suspicious driving behavior; if you suspect that someone is following you, you should get in touch with your manager for assistance or try to get rid of them while driving, but do it safely.

- Use reliable safety gear; examples include security programs such as alarms and padlocks.

- Make sure that you associate yourself with honest people who can be trusted.

- Choose transportation companions carefully.

- Offer security education to employees.

- Employ security personnel at base locations.

Select Your Market Niche Cleverly

Depending on your trucking business's kind of niche, you will need to invest in various equipment and decide your general rates. With this in mind, it would be wise for you to work in a niche that practically provides more financial benefits than others. For example, most people do not think a dry van is profitable. However, as we had mentioned before, niches such as the mining industry, oversized loads, tankers, hazmats (hazardous materials), luxurious meat products, and fresh produce are pretty profitable. The latter generates good profit because it is recession-proof, as people will always require those products.

Understand When to Outsource and Which Business Functions to Handle In House

If you can outsource some functions to other firms, do so, because it could free up time for you to do other vital tasks in your company. These companies can handle things like development programs, training, health and safety management, workers' salaries and wages, payroll, and employee benefits. If you try to do everything yourself, you might become overwhelmed, and the quality of the work you will produce might be sub-par, because one person can't be good at everything. On the contrary, if you outsource all the areas of your company while you can manage some of them yourself effectively, it could be counterproductive. This is because you might end up losing money. If you can find time to do various tasks, your employees could be more qualified to handle some managerial functions in the company.

Running a Proficient Back Office

Beginning a trucking business requires you to do more than just be available and prepared to transport goods. Having a back office that functions efficiently is vital for establishing properly organized trucking company processes and keeping them operating like a Swiss watch. It becomes even busier when you begin employing drivers you will be dispatching in real-time. This is why overseeing the day to day operations of a trucking company can become challenging.

You can have brokers or dispatchers do your back-office tasks. However, this option can be expensive. In the beginning, you can do it yourself. Thanks to technology, you only require a comprehensive employee management app, such as Connecteam. It combines the features of a trucking dispatch mobile app and fleet management and GPS tracking software. Therefore, you can efficiently handle your back office tasks during your breaks while on the road with just a smartphone and this app.

Connecteam is a reputable management app for small businesses that assists many small businesses to save funds and time on day-to-day operations and improve communication with partners, suppliers, and teammates. This will help you keep tabs on the operations of your business and know how well it is doing. Some of the things you will be able to do with this app are:

- Fast and easy scheduling and dispatching; allocating routes, organizing deliveries, and offering pertinent information like special instructions, address, and time. Send reminders and notifications, notify the company owner when they reject or acknowledge a shift, complete their assignment, or report to work late.

- GPS-enabled mobile time trucking with precise time-monitoring enables our employees to use their smartphones to clock in and out of work. A real-time GPS location and timestamp are notified every time an employee reports to work and leaves at a chosen location.

- Export timesheets easily by simply clicking a button and relaying to Quickbooks Online and Connecteam's synchronization for error-free payroll.

- Receiving updates reports from the field as they happen, to improve reporting from field to office with the latest digital reports to be delivered instantaneously, including vehicle inspection and truck repair requests, among other things.

- Effective team communication equipment for operational and logistical communication, real-time private and group chats, announcements, and crucial updates.

- Easy task management for assigning one time jobs to your teams who do not have an office space. It also contains built-in reminders for your employees to complete a specific task and electronically receive updates instantaneously about completed tasks. One time projects include things like annual vehicle inspection and license renewal.

- Safety and compliance protocols via forms that need to be signed and quick access to crucial safety reading materials and resources, like safety protocols, real-time safety reporting, and continuous safety training.

- Easy remote training for new employees: quickly and effectively onboard your drivers and update them about your company's operations and design a well-planned onboarding process with PDFs, videos, quizzes, read and sign forms, among other things.

Summary

Operating your own trucking company can be challenging enough without the extra stress of security and financial management. You might be tempted to fill your trucks with cheap fuel or outsource all of your business functions, thinking that this will solve all your predicaments. However, as we have explained above, there are other ways of reducing costs that you can consider implementing to keep your expenses as low as possible. Making sure that you are aware of where you are spending your money, whether on maintenance or loan payments, plus knowing any small thing that you and your employees could be doing to save money, will be necessary.

Truck Maintenance

T ruck driving is a back-breaking profession even for the fittest person. According to a New York Post article, the extreme toll that truck driving has on drivers is the cause of the spiraling shortage of drivers in the USA and Canada. Despite the steep rise in remuneration and improved working conditions that hauliers adopt to woo drivers, truck maintenance is still essential to minimize inconveniencing and worsening their plight.

Besides, a stalled truck exposes you or your hauling business to liability claims, such as carrier's liability or performance bonds if your contract does not have a force majeure clause. Not to mention, the average cost for towing a heavy, medium, or light-duty truck loaded to capacity in the middle of nowhere is very high. Fortunately, there is an array of truck maintenance tips that you can adopt, enabling you to operate seamlessly and maximize your margins.

By reading some of the possible mistakes that a truck driver can make, you may have noticed that they can be prevented if the driver knows how to do maintenance. If you are a small trucking business owner, you may have to learn some of the essential maintenance techniques by heart so that you can ensure your trucks are always in their best possible shape. If you have drivers, ensure that you train them on maintenance and detecting problems early. These are some of the standard truck maintenance tips that you should know.

Check the Oils

The essential fluids that your truck contains include the engine, coolant, and antifreeze oils. The coolant oil is vital to ensuring that your engine does not overheat in summer or freeze in winter. When selecting your coolant oil, ensure that the vehicle manufacturer or vehicle dealer recommends whatever product you use. Failure to adhere to user manuals can invalidate your warranty in case you have one.

The engine oil prevents the wear and tear in your engine following all the tension and friction as the pistons grind. It not only extends the life of your truck's engine, but also improves the horsepower and fuel economy of your vehicle. You can also consider other types of oil, such as gear oil, which protects your truck gearbox from corrosion or contamination. Although there are numerous DIY oil change guidelines, you should identify a reliable service provider to be checking the oils for you. The professional will drain the oil and refill the oil compartments in most cases.

Check the Brake System

According to the U.S. Department of Transportation, 29% of truck crashes are caused by brake failure. The effects are often catastrophic, and they make headlines all over the news, which can damage your reputation and subject you to professional negligence lawsuits. Sadly, most drivers only discover that their brakes have failed while on the road. Salvaging the situation can be nothing less than a harrowing attempt to minimize potential damage and injury to the public.

A hydraulic braking system contains fluid. The liquid is graded according to two main components: viscosity and operating temperature. As you use your braking, the liquid can leak and corrode the components, due to heat changes. Over time, sludge can form, and the liquid line can break, not to mention damage to your braking system components. The earlier warning signs do not occur as flicker lights on your dashboard, but you can notice that the stopping distance has deteriorated. One of the mitigation efforts that oil manufacturers have adopted is adding detergents to the hydraulic liquid to clear impurities and minimize corrosion. Nevertheless, always prioritize hydraulic systems check in your maintenance routine.

Checking Tires and Wheel Suspension

A standard truck suspension system entails linkages, springs, and shock absorbers. Shock absorbers cushion the truck from loads by using pistons and cylinders. Road surface obstructions reduce the spring oscillations and smoothen the travel, which is essential, primarily if you transport items of a brittle nature, such as glass or flammable substances.

On the other hand, springs maintain the truck's stability on uneven surfaces by absorbing the bumps and shocks and maintaining the vehicle's orientation. Lastly, the linkages attach to the vehicle's axles and connect the wheels, springs, and shock absorbers. Other parts of the suspension system, such as ball joints, kingpins, knucks, tie rods, and more connect the parts and reduce friction between the components. Due to friction, the system should also be oiled and greased, and worn-out parts should be replaced to mitigate the risk of the whole system breakdown.

Regarding the wheel, the most basic thing to check is to ensure that the rims are tightly fastened into the axle. Another issue is to ensure that the tread is satisfactory to give the vehicle a better grip on the road, minimizing skidding. Tire pressure is also essential, and it is always important to consider the wheel manufacturer's air pressure recommendation.

While checking the tires and the suspension system, it is essential to inspect the wheel alignment. A misaligned wheel can drag your truck, which can affect performance and efficiency.

Verify the Electrical System

Most truckers rarely contemplate checking their electric system until the engine fails to start after a stop in a motel in the middle of nowhere. A truck's electric system is an intricate web of circuit wires that run from the battery. Other than checking the acid level and the buildup of residue on the anode and cathode, it is not easy to tell whether a battery is in good condition.

However, if the alternator, starter generator, or powertrain is in good condition depending on the make and model of your truck, you are unlikely to experience an electrical hitch. A dim headlight and dashboard can indicate that your electrical system has an issue, and you, therefore, need to check the battery or the alternator.

Summary

Preventive maintenance should be your routine if you expect the performance of your truck to be top-notch. Additionally, if you have a mileage or time warranty, you are always more likely to claim successfully from your dealer if you prove that you have taken all the due diligence to maintain your truck. Additionally, other habits, such as routine cleaning of the vehicle, removing clutter from the cabin, and ensuring that you have not overloaded the car, can keep your vehicle in pristine condition.

Next, we will focus on some of the most common jargon that individuals working in the trucking industry like to use and their meanings.

Common Terminologies In The Trucking Industry

T he trucking industry is unique and those involved have their own language. Here are a few of the terms you may run across.

Anti-Lock Braking System (ABS) – To keep from skidding and prevent uncontrolled stops, sensors held to monitor the wheel speed so that the ABS will be triggered if the wheels try to lock up.

Air freight – Freights which have been transported for some distance by air.

Air Ride Suspension – The suspension uses air bags so that the ride is smooth which helps if the cargo contains fragile freight.

Anchor it – During an emergency, this uses the brakes to quickly stop the vehicle.

Axle – The wheel rotates on this shaft and are connected on the other side of the trailer or truck. There are four types: front and rear axles, tag axles,, and pusher axles.

ATC (Automatic Traction Control) – Inspired by the ABS, this helps to stop the drive wheels from turning when driving on a wet, oily, or icyroad.

Backhaul – This refers to the return trip to home base with a load.

Bear – Law enforcement officers such as police or highway patrol.

Bed bugger – Someone who professionally moves household goods.

Belly Dump – A type of dump trailer that instead of the bed lifting and dumping the contents, the trailer uses a hopper underneath it.

Bill of Lading (BOL) – This is a receipt of sorts that lists the contents of the cargo to be transported.

The BOL is handled by all parties – the carrier, consignee, and consignor. The consignee and the consignor receive a copy of the BOL, and then there is usually a third copy given to the bank. Contents of the BOL contains:

- Conditions of payment

- Rate of freight and the total amount

- Specific handling instructions

- Features and quantities of the products

- The consignee and consignor's contact details

Blanket permit – This is a kind of terminology that is used in the trucking industry to mean a written authorization. The Department of Motor Vehicles issues it.

Bobtail – This is a tractor that operates without having a trailer attached to it. It is also called a straight truck.

Brake Lining – Another valuable and interesting terminology in this industry. Basically, it is a sturdy frictional substance like cotton, wire, or copper attached to the shoe brake. The shoe brake usually comes into contact with the brake drum when braking.

Carrier – The carrier is the person who is tasked with delivering the items to their last drop. A carrier usually bears the responsibility of getting the bill of lading and safely hauling products to the consignee.

Cartage company – This firm offers local pickup and delivery services within a municipality, city, or town.

Chassis – A commercial vehicle's framework, to which cargo compartments, axles, fuel tanks, cab, transmission, and engine are attached

Consignee – This is the person who will receive the items being transported. Another word that can describe them is a buyer, and they can either be a company or an individual. This person or entity must show up to receive the shipment when the consignor delivers unless they have specified in the bill of lading that they will not be available to accept the goods.

Consignor – This word refers to the entity or person shipping the cargo you are hauling. They are usually known as your client or the seller.

The consignor can be:

- Anybody who has signed a contract to ship cargo

- A distribution facility

- A manufacturing firm or factory

The consignor retains the shipment's ownership until the consignee settles the full payment. However, that does not automatically mean that they also retain the liability for the goods.

Converter Dolly – This is an auxiliary axle component fitted with a coupling device or fifth wheel, hauled by a semi trailer, holding the front of and hauling another trailer.

Coupling – Attaching a tractor to a trailer or connecting two trailers when towing doubles.

Drayage – This is a word that entails transporting cargo at a short distance through ground freight. Essentially, it is the practice of transporting a big container to your vehicle. This could be an additional expense that you need to think about when giving your client a rough estimation of the total price of your services.

Exempt carrier – This firm hauls goods that are not governed by the Interstate Commerce Commission economic rules.

Full Truckload shipping – A full truckload shipping or FTL manifests a shipment that occupies a whole trailer. Regardless of the truck's size, it is still a full truckload if it takes up all the space available. Basically, FTL freight will be more than 15,000 pounds. FTL will typically cost more per mile, because your vehicle is full.

Free onboard point (FOB) – Free on board is also referred to as freight on board, which is a terminology used to state if the seller or the buyer bears liability for cargos that are destroyed, damaged, or lost during transportation.

The FOB transportation section states that the title and accountability of goods move from the seller to the buyer when the cargo is put on your truck. On the contrary, an FOB designation signifies that the seller is accountable for the goods until the cargo is delivered to the person or entity buying it.

Hundredweight (CWT) – A hundredweight is a unit of measurement. The British take a hundredweight to be one hundred and twelve pounds, whereas, in North America, this word is equivalent to CWT.

Back in the day, packages that occupied less than a full truckload were weighed using CWT. However, it is rare to weigh packages using CWT. Nowadays, measuring by kilograms and pounds is normal for most people. The authorities also expect you to use these measurements.

JIT(Just in time) – This manufacturing system relies on regular, tiny deliveries of supplies and parts to ensure that the inventory in the company's premises is as little as possible.

Landing gear – These legs can be retracted, which hold the anterior part of the semi trailer when it is not attached to a trailer.

Less than truckload (LTL) – This is the opposite of an FTL. An LTL does not occupy the whole trailer, however. It may require transport between automobiles during the transportation process. Trucking payment rates will differ according to how far your business will be hauling the shipment.

Linehaul driver – This is a truck driver who uses a particular route from one city to another and usually goes home after every shift. They are also referred to as regional drivers.

Logbook – This is a book that truck drivers carry in which they indicate their hours of service (HOS) and their duty status every 24 hours. This is a requirement for cross-state commercial trucking by DOT, or the Department of Transportation, in the U.S.

Loss and damage – Being a carrier, you will occasionally have to deal with damage or loss claims. A damage claim entails damage that can be seen to the storage container holding the goods or to the goods themselves. The damage must be written on the bill of lading or a different delivery document.

A loss claim is made when it seems that a shipment was delivered, yet the recipient has not seen it, or when a shipment is not delivered. This can result from typography mistakes in the bill of lading, causing the shipment to be taken to the wrong destination.

Over-the-road driver – This term refers to the driver who drives across the nation to make freight deliveries and usually sleeps inside the truck cab. This kind of driver usually covers about 100,000 miles every year.

Owner-operator – This is a truck driver who operates a truck that belongs to them.

Pallets – These are easy to carry platforms used to cover goods for freight transportation. Pallets are available in varying sizes; however, the most common dimension that you will get is the average 40" by 48" size to transport products. Pallets make it easy to load and unload goods, and they also make it possible to use the maximum space in the truck. This could lower your total expenses and enable you to offer more profitable trucking rates per mile.

Payload – This refers to the weight of the goods being transported.

Peddle Run – This is the route with many delivery stops.

P&D – Pickup and delivery. Also known as a city driver.

Rig – Refers to huge tractor and truck trailer units.

Safety Audit – This is an evaluation of records of a motor carrier that the Department of Transportation carries out to confirm that the vehicle follows standard safety management controls according to FMCSR.

Sleeper – A compartment designed for sleeping in, which drivers mount behind a truck cab. It is at times fastened to the cab or sometimes made to be an essential section of the cab.

Sliding fifth wheel – This is a fifth that is attached to a device, enabling it to be transported forward and backward, to spread the weight distribution on the axles of a tractor.

Spread axle – This trailer has many axles that do not directly align next to each other as they do on regular trailers. They are usually found on flatbeds and flatbeds.

Straight Truck – This is a vehicle that carries goods in a body fastened to its chassis instead of on a trailer hauled by a vehicle.

Stop Keeping Unit (SKU) – This identification code for services. They are usually written in alphabetical order or a barcode. SKUs make it easy to track goods in the warehouse because they include all the aspects necessary to spot them like:

- Packaging

- Color

- Description

- Size

- Manufacturer

- Material

Tanker – A baffled and closed trailer used to tow wet or dry bulk cargos such as cooking oil, gasoline, dry concrete mix, and flour.

Tractor – This is a truck made purposely to haul a semi trailer using a fifth wheel placed over the last axle.

Tri-Axle – This trailer, tractor, or truck has three axles combined at the back.

Trip leasing – It means lending a vehicle belonging to a company to a different transportation services provider for one trip.

Unladen weight – The weight of an empty vehicle, which is also referred to as tare weight

Waybill – A document that a carrier issues, outlining crucial details and directions about a specific shipment.

Yard Jockey – A driver who moves trailers into loading docks and out within the distribution or factory facility. Such a person is also known as a spotter.

Introduction - Freight Broker Business Startup 2023

The transportation and shipping industries are two of the oldest in our world. With the former being 500 years old and the ladder close to 5000 years old, the transportation and shipping industries are two that have shaped our world for many years. Working together they make up the majority of how goods and resources are shipped not only nationally but internationally as well.

If you look at just the definition of each industry they are quite easy to understand. The shipping industry deals with crossing waterways to transport goods whereas the transportation industry uses other sorts of carriers, oftentimes trucks, to bring goods and commodities across the country.

However, even with a simple definition there are many complex and moving parts that make up the transportation and shipping industries. Because these two industries are not going anywhere, and are essentially the backbone of much of our economic success, the need for individuals working In these industries is consistently high; in turn, making these jobs incredibly lucrative. Unfortunately however, many individuals are hesitant to break into these industries because more of the well-known jobs require specific skills, or long training sessions and formal education.

So how are you able to break into these industries and begin making a large annual income without having to attend expensive training or specialized skill? It may be easier than you think.

There is one role that acts as a sort of center point, and organizational crux, for these industries; a freight broker. Becoming a freight broker does not require specialized training or formal education. What's more, is that you can create your own freight broker business and become the ever-important middleman between the shipping company and the carrier that brings the merchandise from point A to point B.

Although creating your own freight broker business is not a complicated task, it is labor-intensive. There are a few important steps and tasks you have to accomplish in order to create a legitimate and successful freight brokerage. To help guide you through the process this book has been divided into three parts. The first part, titled "About The Business," holds 6 chapters that are meant to explain some generalities about the freight broker business. Topics in this first part include top mistakes and challenges for the business, how freight brokerages fit into the shipping and trucking business and mention some of the already popular and well-known freight brokerage businesses.

It is in the second part of the book, however, where we get into the nitty-gritty of making your own brokerage. Titled "Making Your Own Business" this second part will go through the 10 steps it takes for you to create your own freight broker business startup from the ground up: training, registration, brokerage authorities, process agents, security bonds, insurance, tax regulations, business plan, financing, broker contracts, and miscellaneous. We have devoted one entire chapter to each of these steps. In doing so we have ensured to give you all of the information you need to be successful in your startup.

The third and final part of this book, titled "Myths, Misconceptions, and FAQs," is reserved for miscellaneous information about both the freight broker business in general and about starting your own brokerage. This part includes chapters that list and break myths and misconceptions about freight brokerages and frequently asked questions by those who are looking to start their own brokerage.

Essentially what we have collected for you is an all-encompassing, one-stop-shopping kind of experience for everything you need to know about starting your new journey as a freight broker.

The Shipping And Trucking Industry

I n order to fully understand the purpose and value of a freight broker-age—and in turn, start 1 yourself—there are two other industries and businesses that you have to first understand. They are the shipping and the trucking industry.

As was mentioned in the introduction, the shipping and trucking industry, as spin-offs of the trade industry, have been around for centuries. As such they have an incredible amount of history and details associated with them. Since the focus of this book is on free brokerages and not the shipping or trucking industry, we will quickly summarize for you these two industries so as to simply better understand the freight brokerage business.

The Shipping Industry

World trade is the process of sharing goods from other countries all over the world. While this concept may seem straightforward and simple, enough the gravity and importance of this business cannot be overstated. It is from international shipping and world trade that we receive about 90% of goods worldwide.

Being one of the oldest industries, the shipping industry has cultivated some impressive statistics. For instance;

- There are over 150 countries around the world that participate in the shipping trade.

- There are over 50,000 cargo ships currently in use for international shipping trade.

- There are almost 2million individuals working as sailors and crewmen on these cargo ships.

- At any one time, there are around 20 million shipping containers that are being used and shipped across international waters.

In short, since water covers over 70% of the Earth's surface, shipping over waterways is one of the most important, commonly used, and lucrative shipping businesses in the world.

Categories of the Shipping Industry

The shipping industry is made up of a number of different parts; it is not just one type of shipping. In fact, there are 5 distinct and separate parts that, together, make up the shipping industry.

Maritime Industry

The maritime industry is anything that is associated with trade and shipments over waterways. This includes, of course, the ocean and the seas. But it also includes any technology related to navigation equipment and the ships that are used for maritime trade. It also includes the ports at which the ships dock and leave from. With the world being over 70% water, the maritime industry remains the backbone of the shipping industry playing a role in the majority of trade done the world over.

The Shipping Business

The shipping business is related to the carrying and transporting of goods from point A to point B. This includes the ships in the maritime industry, but also the trucks used for road transportation.

Freight

Fright refers to the cargo or the goods that are carried and transported between different ports, countries, and places.

Logistics

The logistic part of the shipping industry is the services that are at play to get the cargo from point A to point B. Whether it is from a manufacturer's warehouse, a country, or a port, the logistics are the planning and processes that let the trade take place.

The Supply Chain

This is the process that underscores the entirety of the shipping industry. The supply chain dictates what country is in need of what and from where they can receive their items and goods. Also sometimes known as supply and demand, the supply chain traces the movements and process of the materials and goods involved in the trade.

The Trade

This is the basic concept of economics that explains the exchange of goods and services for others of the same value.

The Trucking Industry

The trucking industry is the second industry that employs and uses a freight brokerage. Generally, the trucking business includes some sort of road-based transport that brings goods and trade items from one place to another. Although it is equally important as the shipping industry, the trucking industry takes a backseat as most of the trade movement is done overseas. That being said, the trucking industry still is responsible for transporting about 70% of goods all over the world. This includes clothes, food, raw materials, and other items.

Necessities of the Trucking Industry

Permits

Not everyone can simply load up their truck and drive across the country to legitimately deliver goods. There are special taxes and permits that have to be paid in order for someone to have a trucking business. That being said, a trucking business does not have to have multiple trucks; it can still have a single driver with a single truck. As long as the taxes, permits, and licenses are acquired, then a trucking business can begin. These registrations include special licenses to drive certain vehicles, and registrations and permits to carry certain kinds of materials.

A Home Office

A trucking business also needs a sort of home base. This home base acts as an office for the truckers. This home base is usually where the trucks will load up and deliver their goods from. The office can range from an actual office to a warehouse. No matter the format or structure, the home office is the starting point of most if not all of the trucker's journeys.

This office also acts as a sort of logistics center. This is where the routes are planned and the schedule is made. It dictates which truck goes where with what items and when the route is scheduled to begin and end. Lastly, this office also acts as a command center to receive marching orders. Clients will call this office to schedule and higher the trucking services.

People

There are a variety of roles and people that are needed for a successful trucking business to run. First, you need office people. These are the ones that help with the logistics and the scheduling of the trucking route. These office-bound individuals also deal with payroll and any sort of filing. You also need the truckers themselves and those who drive the vehicles. In some cases, you might also need guards or security people depending on the cargo of the truck.

Even if the trucking company is only one truck with one driver, there are many rules that have to be filled in order for this company to thrive.

Both the trucking and the shipping Industries utilize freight brokers as part of their business, To help them organize and schedule their routes. But what is a freight brokerage?

What Is The Freight Broker Business

What is a Freight Broker?

Freight brokers act as a sort of middleman for other parts of the shipping industry. The freight broker is the business that deals with the communication between the shipper and the carrier in any one shipment and transaction. As such they are the company and part of the process that ensures that communication is clear and correct between the two parties. They are also the part of the shipping transaction that works to make sure that certain parts and details of the shipment are followed through, such as the receiving date and the condition of the goods.

Shipping companies opt to work with freight brokerages to help avoid miscommunications with their clients and to, perhaps, increase the number of clients they can take on, in turn boosting their own work.

As such some of the responsibilities of a freight brokerage are:

- marketing to advertise sales
- choosing and finding service carriers
- making quotes for shipment cost estimations
- scheduling and coordinating with carriers
- keeping track of all shipments and orders

- coordinating with shipping companies, dispatching companies, and carriers

- preparing orders and loads

- negotiating prices

Parts of a Freight Brokerage

There are many different people or positions that are involved in a freight brokerage, in order for it to do its job successfully. Let's break them down.

Freight Broker

The freight broker, your position, is to maintain a path of communication between the shippers, the motor carriers, and the shipment of goods itself.

Shipper

The shipper is the person or company that has a collection of goods and wishes to trade it or transport it somewhere else.

Motor Carrier

The motor carrier is the person or company that provides the transportation service of the goods. This transportation is done using trucks.

The shipper can have its own motor carrier business or they can hire another, or third party, carrier company to transport the goods. The former is known as "private" while the latter is known as "for hire."

Freight Forwarder

A freight forwarder is often time confused with the freight broker in a shipping transaction. While the names are similar, their jobs are different. Freight forwarders are actually in possession and have traded and shipped goods at one point in the transaction. They take smaller shipments of goods, combine and consolidate them with other smaller shipments that are going to the same place, and make one large shipment. Freight forwarders deal with a variety of different transportation kinds, not just motor transports and carriers.

Import-Export Broker

The import-export brokers are those individuals and companies that deal specifically with importers and exporters; that is shippers that want to transport their goods to other countries. They deal with the customs offices of the respective countries and international governments. They are not used for domestic trading and shipping.

Agricultural Truck Broker

The agricultural truck broker is only used for motor carriers when the goods and products are considered except agriculturally speaking.

Shippers Association

Shipper's associations are a collection of groups, created by shippers, that are considered to be exempt or nonprofit. These associations help to limit and decrease the cost of transportation.

It is important to note that although you will not be working with each of these individuals with every shipment and transaction you do as a freight broker, it is important that you understand these roles.

How Do People Select a Freight Brokerage?

One way to ensure that you will develop a successful freight broker business is to understand your customer and clientele. Knowing how your customers will be evaluating, judging, and ultimately selecting your business can help you to improve different areas of your business.

Communication

This selection criteria is perhaps the most important since your entire job entails professional and effective communication. Your clients will ask how well you present your company and your business plan? How well do you communicate your services? These are potential opportunities for you to show off your communication skills before entering into contracts. Be prepared for your clients to ask you for references or testimonials from previous clients to prove your communication skills are up to the task.

Reliability

Your prospective clients will also be looking for reliability of your company. Do you have a track record of always following through with your communication? Do shipments that go through your company get to where they need to be unscathed? Again, to find these answers your new clients will look at the comments and opinions of your previous contracts and partners. If you want to continue to get clients you are going to want to make sure that you are providing not only good service but reliable service.

Size

Size is an interesting category to be evaluated. This is because your clients will not always be seeking a large freight broker; rather they will be looking for the freight broker that is the right size for them. After all, the reason shippers seek out the help of freight brokers is to save them money in their shipment. They do not and will not want to pay for the use of a large brokerage when it is not needed.

What is important for you to know is that you should choose which kind of brokerage you wish to be and stick within those parameters and limitations. If you only have the capital to be a smaller brokerage and deal with shipments of a small distance, then stick with that. Your client has specific needs, you do not have to do everything, you just need to fit their needs perfectly.

Responsibility and Accountability

Another business detail that your clients will be looking for is how responsible and accountable you are. They will ask how well you deal with unexpected problems? Do you crumble under the pressure or do you thrive to fix them?

It will be rare that you will never have any problems with your shipments; after all, you will have to deal with weather conditions, roads, and a range of other variables that can affect your shipment. It isn't the fact that nothing is perfect, it is, rather, how you deal with the imperfection when it happens.

Is your brokerage known to solve problems or is it known to be plagued by them? You should strive for the former option. Take responsibility for your business and work to ameliorate it at every chance you get.

Available Resources

Your clients need to know that you and your company are up to the task. You need to be able to prove that you have all of the available resources, technology, and experience required to fulfill their freight broker needs. Be clear with the carriers you have used in the past and where you have experience shipping. It isn't about being able to do more tasks, it is about being able to do the necessary tasks properly.

The freight broker business is meant to help ease communication between the shipper and the carrier. It is also meant to help cut the cost associated with the shipment. While this may seem simple there are, as you can see, many parts and details that go into having a successful freight brokerage. Now that you are familiar with what your brokerage will do, the key positions of your business, and what your clients will be looking for in your business, we will now move on to some chapters detailing some of the keys to making your business successful.

The History Of The Freight Broker

A freight broker is an individual or business that helps to match a shipper with a carrier. This position falls under the employment category of "transportation intermediary." This means that they are between the shipper and the company that actually moves the cargo from one area to another. The freight broker, usually, does not own any assets or cargo, nor do they usually have any hands touching the cargo. Their role is merely an administrative and organizational, albeit an integral one.

As the president and CEO of the Transportation Intermediaries Association has said, freight brokers balance and combine their knowledge, organizational skills, investment and technology, and resources to help companies share their products with the world.

Any shipper and any size motor carrier are likely to use a freight broker. For smaller shipping companies, a freight broker can help them become organized and make sure that their products get to where they need to go; likewise, for smaller motor carriers, they can help put the carrier company on the map—so to speak—and get consistent work. On the other hand, larger shipping and motor carrier companies will usually use freight brokers simply because it alleviates a lot of the responsibility and pressure of shipping goods nationwide.

Although freight broker businesses seem to have seen an incredible surge in popularity and interest over the last few years, they are not a new industry. In fact, they have been part of the transportation and shipping industries for the majority of the 20th century. However, before the 1970s, restrictions placed on freight brokers were so high that many shippers were unwilling to take on the job. That being said, when the importance of the role became clear, restrictions began to subside and popularity of becoming a freight broker increased.

To some, the advancement and development of the transportation industry is the one thing that has led human civilization to continually develop year after year, decade after decade. After all, it is the ability to ship and move goods from one place to another that allows for economies to form, interrelation to develop, and for civilization to develop.

Let's trace some of these important moves that the transportation and shipping industry have made that have led us to our present day.

The "Early Days" of Shipping and Transporting Freight

- **4,000 BCE** – It was around this time in history when horses were captured and trained from the wild in order to be used as a means of transportation. Items and goods were stored in bags that were slung over the horse's hips or the horses pulled sled-type chariots to carry goods.

- **3,200 BCE** – With the invention of the wheel, vehicles were now a new means of transport. Of course, they're not the vehicles that we used today. Instead, they were carts and chariots that were still pulled by larger animals.

- **770 CE** – It was around this time that iron horseshoes were invented. These were strapped and attached to the horse's feet to allow horses to travel further distances. This improved the transportation industry as horses were able to travel further distances and for longer without tiring.

- **1787** – When the steamboat was invented in the late 1700s, it changed the transportation and shipping industry. Now goods were able to be shipped faster and in larger amounts over waterways. What's more, was that the steamboat was a much more reliable form of waterway travel than its competitors. This meant that goods were more likely to arrive at their destinations and more people participated in waterway and international trade.

- **1807** – The railroad and canal systems were built around the world in the early 1800s. As a result, goods were able to be more readily available in areas other than where they were produced. It also created more jobs within the transportation industry as more shipments were made and more men were needed to drive the trains, load the trains, and make sure the freight and cargo got to its destination safely.

- **1820** – At this time the railroad has monopolized the freight and transportation in America. Any shipment made overland was done through the railroad system.

- **1869** – It was in this year that the 3500-mile-long transcontinental railroad was finished. It connected the state of California to Chicago, cementing and ensuring trade across the United States.

The 20th Century

- **Early 1900s** – Cars and Automobiles become the most popular form of transportation; albeit still rather expensive and reserved for those who are wealthy.

- **1935** – United States legislation passes The Motor Carrier Act. It includes different regulations and specifics about the trucking industry. For instance, it limits the number of hours a driver can be on the road and regulations for shipping companies.

- **1950** – Around 173 billion ton-miles of freight are transported by truck between cities.

- **1956** – The Interstate Highway System is established. This results in 41,000 miles of new highway. This also brought about improvements in the trucks that carry the freight.

- **1970** – Trucking increased from transporting only 1% of goods to 25%.

- **The 1980s** – In this decade the freight trucking industry nearly doubled.

- **The 1990s** – Legislation became more lenient which brought about an increase in how many trucks were on the road. Motor carriers went from 18,000 to about 500,000 by the end of the decade.

What Does the Future Bring?

It may seem like now the freight broker business is as advanced as it can be. We have new technology that helps to make scheduling easier; we have weather-predicting technology to help make planning trips more effective; we also have more advanced motor carriers making transporting goods safer and more reliable in general.

However, experts in the field say that there are some developments in the transportation industry that we can expect to come in the future.

More Digitization

First, it is predicted that there will be even more digitization of the job. This does not mean that the freight broker job is at risk of being completely replaced by technology, but it does mean that even more aspects of the job will be over technology. For example, in the future shippers may not even talk to the broker; perhaps there will be an ordering system that is completely online.

More Automation

Another prediction is that there will be more automation. There will still need to be the freight broker to have the final say in the route; you will always need to have a truck driver to drive the truck, but there will be aspects to be automated. For example, unloaded cargo, maintaining shipping journals, and predicting weather may all become automated.

◄O►

But where do freight brokers, specifically, fit into this history and future image of the transportation industry?

The Old Days

Freight brokers were not always viewed in the positive light that they are today. Before the regulation of the transportation industry in the late 1940s, brokers were seen as pirates. They were considered to undermine and go around the local government in order to help shippers and carriers deliver their goods.

Then again, you have to consider that thousands of years ago, individuals had less understanding of the goods that were being transported. Therefore, if there were some illegal goods being transported a freight broker would be used to help sneak past authorities.

The Fear of The Freight Broker

However, once the government and shipping companies deemed freight brokers to be legitimate, there was then push back and resistance by the carriers themselves.

Motor carrier companies would warn their customers that freight brokers needed only to be used sparingly. I would say that freight brokers did not actually offer any sort of stability or benefit to the shipping process. It would only make the process more complicated and more expensive for both the shipping company and the motor carrier company.

A Clearer Picture In the Present

However, in the past three decades or so, as the transportation and shipping industries have had another boom in productivity and popularity, nearly everyone agrees that freight brokers are a necessary part of the transportation and shipping processes.

With the incredible influx in the number of goods being shipped all over the world, freight brokers have proven their value in how they help to organize the shipping routes. Of course, the increase in shipping has led to an increase in the number of freight brokers; but with the ease that freight brokers have brought to the industry more freight is able to be shipped, leading once more to a need for more brokers.

In this way, brokers will never be undervalued again. In fact, so many freight brokers are needed that motor carriers are trying to hire and keep a freight broker on staff to help fill the need.

Ultimately, the transportation and shipping industries are two of the oldest industries in our world. Even if it wasn't officially labeled as such, these industries have been present ever since people have been sharing goods with others.

Thankfully, freight brokers have come into popularity as well. Without them, the transportation and shipping industry would be much more convoluted and hectic. Considering the number of shipments in transportation that are made daily, nation and worldwide, there needs to be a position that helps to organize all of the moving parts.

So how does one become a successful freight broker?

How To Be A Successful Freight Brokerage

I n order to be successful in the freight broker business, you should look to those companies that have come before you for advice and suggestions for what to do.

The following are only some of the suggestions and tips given by those successful brokerages, that you can use to help bring your company and business to their level.

Go With the Flow

The shipping industry is one that changes and fluctuates with the tide of the ocean. The trends, costs, and regulations that are to be followed change throughout the year based on season, economic trends, and world events, among many others. For this reason, it can be incredibly difficult to control.

This is why the first key to running a successful freight broker business is that you should try your best to move with the ebb and flow of the industry itself and focus on controlling those aspects that you can control. You may not be able to truly control if a client chooses you, but you can control how your brokerage is presented to them. You may not be able to control the weather, but you can prepare for certain weather events. You may not be able to control the prices and costs of shipping, but you can control how much your charge and ensure that it is reasonable for the client.

Showing yourself as flexible, you will present your company as being professional and are likely to be trusted and chosen by clients. It will also lead to less stress in the job. Knowing that you cannot control certain aspects will help you to focus on and perfect those aspects you can control and bring about a more enjoyable experience as a business owner.

Be Proactive in Your Communication

Communication can be a key factor in the success of your business. As you will see repeated in the following chapters, open, honest, and consistent communication is one aspect that can make or break your company. Although it may be easy to only deal with the items you are shipping, you cannot forget that those items belong to a person. This person wants to know what is going on with their items, where their shipment is, and if their shipment was received safely. Your clients do not want to have to wait to be told, nor do they want to have to ask themselves.

This is your responsibility as the broker service. You should have consistent communication with your client, initiated by you, to let them know about the process and status of their shipment.

Be Ready to Negotiate—and Know When to Concede

While you will have your set prices and costs for your services, there will be plenty of opportunities for you to negotiate. You will be able to negotiate terms of contracts and prices most often but that does not mean that is all.

This is where knowing to negotiate can help build the success of your freight broker business. Knowing when to give up in order to get what you want is key. Alternatively, however, you must also know when to concede. Getting exactly what you want is not always the best idea. Clients need to know that you are working with them and understanding their needs and desires; not that you are pushing for what you want. Knowing when to negotiate and when to concede to their wishes is key to ensuring good customer service and building the success of your business.

After all, if a client is proposing a contract that is not profitable for you, you will want to be able to negotiate properly and respectively to ensure it is lucrative.

Develop the Relationship with Your Carriers

Your carriers are those individuals that complete the shipment process. Seeing them as individuals and not just people associated with your business will go a long way in creating a successful brokerage. Get to know them, get to know their likes and dislikes with the business, and begin to see them as individuals who are working a job. In doing so you will develop strong relationships with them.

Be strong relationships with your carriers will go a long distance—pun intended—you will likely have their loyalty for work for many years to come. Even in business transactions, individuals want to be seen as individual people, not cogs in a machine used for a purpose or a means to an end.

Have the Right Technology

It is hard to find an industry that is not reliant on technology. In fact, as different technologies develop, it would seem that the shipping industry is one that relies most heavily on these new technologies. Whether they are technologies to help increase environmentalism or technologies to make the shipping process easier, you will need to know and understand how to use all technologies associated with this industry.

Not only will you need to know the technology you will need access to the right technology. Flashy and new technologies are not always what is needed. Be selective with the technologies you choose to use in your freight broker business. Having the right ones working for you can make the difference between a successful and an unsuccessful brokerage.

Understand That Experience is Ongoing

It can be easy to think that you know everything. Especially if you have prepared yourself accordingly to begin your business journey, and if your freight brokerage is doing well. You may think that you know everything there is to know about the industry and business. This is, however, not entirely true.

While the base of the industry may stay the same, the specifics will change violently. The costs will increase and decrease, methods of transport will differ, ethics are likely to evolve over time, and—not to mention—the technologies will be advanced as well. This means that as the industry changes your knowledge of it becomes out of date. While it will still be useful it will always be lacking in some areas. As long as you know that you will always be learning and gaining new experiences in this position, those areas of missing knowledge will prove to be opportunities to grow rather than sources of stress.

Showing that you are willing to evolve and continue to learn and grow as a company and business will not only help to strengthen your company but will also help to attract clients to you.

Know That It Will Be Costly

Beginning and sustaining a business is not cheap. There are the costs of different registrations and licenses, there are the costs of hiring employees, and there are the costs of administrative items like computers, the internet, etc.

When it comes to the shipping and freight broker businesses, these costs increase due to the number of different regulations needed to function, and the high cost of trucks and supplies used to ship items around the world. Knowing that your business journey will be a costly one will help you move forward as a successful business. Coming to terms with the fact that it will be expensive in certain areas will help you avoid cutting corners to avoid spending too much and losing the quality of your service.

Follow the Law

Although it may be obvious, we cannot forget to mention that following the law is one way to help your freight broker business to succeed. Breaking the laws, such as not following proper tax requirements or not keeping up-to-date records of registrations and licenses can hurt your company in a number of ways. You can lose all of your profits to fees and fines; you can lose your business entirely, or you can present yourself as a business that is unreliable to clients. After all, if you have no respect for following the necessary laws and legislation surrounding the freight broker business then you will also likely not respect your clients.

Although it can be a lot of paperwork, ensuring that you are always following the law and maintaining proper registrations, you can help raise your brokerage above others.

Put in the Time

Do not be fooled, because you are the owner of the business does not mean that you can sit back and do nothing. In fact, in the freight broker business, it is the owners of the business that have to put in the time and effort to ensure that their company is going strong. You have to cultivate relationships to get contracts and nurture those established ones to ensure continuous work. One thing that makes clients come back and feel comfortable with your company is a connection with the boss and owner.

It can be hard work, but through dedication and commitment, the hard work will raise your business to the level of success and become enjoyable.

Gain Experience

When you embark on any new business journey you do not want to enter it with no experience at all. The same is for a freight brokerage. To give yourself a leg up in the competition, and to give yourself the best chance possible to be successful in your business, you should gain experience in the associated industries. Specifically the shipping and trucking industries. Working at ports, driving transport trucks, or even working at loading and unloading different shipping vessels can all help you gain the necessary experience for opening a freight brokerage.

The idea here is to learn about how the entire industry works; how to intersect with others in the business and network with those individuals already in the business.

Be Sure to Understand a Bond and a Trust

There are different licenses and insurance that are required to open a freight broker business. It is easy, and understandable, to get confused about what license is for what? Two types of registrations that you should fully understand, however, is the difference between a bond and trust. They both are registrations that are meant to help you in instances of damage or if you are sued. Freight brokers are required to have a bond or a trust of $75,000. You can choose to have either one but a bond is a more preferred choice; as the brokers, you will pay far less on any claims made against you.

To go into the difference between each would be to stray too far from the point of this chapter. What would be wise would be for you to seek out a financial advisor for your business to help you set up and decide which is best for you.

Network, Network, Network

Along the same reasoning as to why you should gain experience in the field, you should always do your best to network within the business *before* you launch your business. By networking before, you will have clients and relationships set up already and will be able to hit the ground running, as it were, when you officially launch.

If you launch without having done the networking, you will be losing time and money trying to establish clients and partners after the fact. The more you can set up before you officially launch your business the better it is for you.

Establish a Communication System and Method That Works for You

Freight brokers are based on communication and organization, therefore establishing a communication system is imperative to having a successful business. You should make sure that you have incorporated and have taken into consideration all kinds of communication technology; that is to be sure individuals can reach you—and you can reach them—in a number of different ways. We are not saying that you need to learn morse code or teach pigeons to deliver messages. Simply being available through all of the modern and present-day technologies should be enough.

This includes over the phone, email, texting, and even over fax—the medium is not completely out of date yet. This also means that creating social media accounts for your business can also play to your advantage when it comes to communication.

You must also be sure the communication system works for you and that you maintain communication with your clients. If you set the expectation and promise that you will return all communication within 24 hours—which is a strong policy—you have to make that you in fact follow through with.

As you can see, there is much more to communication in running a freight broker business than meets the eye.

Use the Right Technology

The freight industry has come a long way and has incorporated many different kinds of tech in its operations. What is important for you to know is what technology is necessary, what technology is superfluous, and which technology is nice to have but can be expensive. Seeking out the best and most tech for your business before you are established can actually yield counterproductive results as it can set you in the red financially.

Therefore make sure you are using the right technology and try not to get caught up in the newest and fanciest tech. You will have lots of time to upgrade once you have established your company.

Continue to Learn

Establishing and running any successful business is not a one-time thing. You will never know everything that you need to know for your business. That does not mean that you should give up. On the contrary, you should always be sending your employees and yourself to update and upgrade their training and licenses. Keep up to date with and learn the ever-changing trends of the market and industry, and continue your education in the field. This will not only set you apart from other companies in the field but assure your clients that you are the best company for their needs.

Marketing

Launching your freight brokerage will do nothing unless you advertise and market it. Reach out to online forums and platforms to help you advertise there. You can also send emails to your partners, and advertise on loading docks, ports, and warehouses.

Showing your clients what you are and the services you provide is imperative to your business thriving; without clients, you have no business. You cannot rely entirely on word of mouth to bring in your clients and partners. Marketing and advertising will do most of the work for you, so be diligent in how you present yourself and your business to the world.

———————◄O►———————

The freight brokers business is one that is fast-paced and hectic if not organized properly. Together, these two aspects of the industry cause many up-and-coming brokerages to fail. That being said, having the above tips and pieces of advice in hand, will set you apart from other brokerages competing for the same contract you are. If you follow the advice given above, you will raise your freight brokerage to success while others fall.

Top Mistakes To Be Made

I ndeed it is important to know the business tactics that set certain freight brokerages apart from others, While the mistakes to avoid can be deduced from those prices of advice, it is always more helpful—especially for those individuals who are trying to start their own business—to hear what specific mistakes and bring your business to fail.

Poor Communication

The freight brokerage business is not one where the service given to the clients all happens in one spot. The entire service is one that spans the globe. Individuals who hire a freight brokerage can be in a completely different country than the brokerage itself. Not to mention both the brokerage and the client can be in different countries than the items that are being shipped. For this reason, it is important that communication is maintained to ensure that everyone knows what is going on with the product and the shipment.

This is why having poor communication skills is one of the largest and most devastating mistakes a freight brokerage can make. Many times communication will be lacking if there is an issue with the shipment, as the brokerage does not want to admit to damage or shipping delays. However, even if these unfortunate events occur, you have to still communicate with a client. Being honest and connecting with the client in a timely manner is key to keeping your client in the loop.

Not having full disclosure and transparency when it comes to your client's shipment is one mistake that can lead to a freight brokerage's downfall. After all, if clients can't trust you to communicate with them, then they will likely not use your services.

Betting on Only One Contract

As mentioned above, freight brokerages rely on contracts to stay in business. You will be hired by a company or by a client to help ship their items from one place to another. Usually, the contract begins with your receipt of your client's item and ends with the completed shipment of all your client's items.

Keep in mind that you will need to bid on these contracts and compete with other freight brokers in order to receive work. Large clients that offer consistent and repetitive contracts may seem to be the best bet. That is, they may seem to be the most important contract of the land as they will yield consistent work for you and your worker. However, bidding on only one contract, and putting all of the eggs in their basket so to speak, is not the best idea. You are likely to lose out on other contracts if you are focussing on one in particular. By losing out on these other contracts that are perhaps smaller or not as attractive, you could be potentially losing out on a large sum of money and income. Not to mention the fact that you will be hurting the relationship with other potential clients by rejecting their work and contracts.

This is a mistake that small and budding freight brokers businesses make; especially when first starting out. It is wise to take and bid on any job that you are able to complete. Once you become more established, then you will be able to be slightly more selective with the contracts.

Not Paying Attention to the Market and Its Trends

Just as with any other business or industry, there is a market that has different trends associated with it. In shipping, the market trends can affect what gets shipped, how it gets shipped, and the countries to which things are shipped.

Most specifically, and recently, one of the trends in the shipping business is to become more environmentally friendly. For this reason, freight brokerages are moving to make their vessels more environmentally friendly in addition to making their business itself more environmentally friendly. This can include going paperless or cutting down on unnecessary travel in order to connect with clients; to do so, certain freight brokers have opted to use paperless billing, and choose to communicate with their clients on the telephone or over video calls.

If a freight brokerage does not keep up with this trend of trying to be more environmentally aware, then they are more likely to lose out on contracts. Indeed, this example of the environmental trend is an individual one but it represents the importance of knowing what is going on in the market and industry of shipping. If your brokerage does not keep up with the trends of the business, you will likely be deemed out of touch and not an expert in your industry. Although your brokerage may be suited and able to fulfill all of your client's needs, if you do not present yourself as such, then your client will not think so.

Being Complacent

Another grave mistake that a freight brokerage can make is being complacent. When you are first starting out in any endeavor it is commonplace for any individual to try very hard and to work long hours in order to yield results quickly. However, it is equally common for once results are seen for the individual to become complacent. Complacency is simply trying less. It is not trying as hard as you once did in order to yield the same results.

When it comes to businesses, especially freight broker businesses, it can be easy to maintain your effort at first because things happened quite quickly in the beginning. Setting up your business, getting contracts, and completing those first few contracts, are exciting times for any new business. However, once you see that your business is becoming successful, you have a steady influx of contracts, and you begin to make money, it can be easy to fall back on some bad habits, cut corners, and not put as much effort in.

To put it another way, in order to be fit and lose weight, one healthy meal and one workout does not do the trick. Indeed you can feel good about yourself and you may even see results that quickly. But in order to maintain those results, you have to maintain your diet and exercise routine. The same philosophy applies to your freight brokerage.

You should put the same amount of effort into every contract and for every client as you do the first few. In doing so, you will show your client that every one of them is important and valued. As a result, you are more likely to have repeat clients and consistent work for your brokerage.

When your brokerage starts picking up speed do not pump the brakes. Keep going forward.

Not Growing

Related to the idea of complacency, another mistake that freight brokerages make that can be fatal to the success of their business is not moving beyond. It is not enough to not fall back to complacency, you have to always look for opportunities to grow, expand, and do better. It will be incredibly rare if every shipment and every contract goes off without a hitch. Every shipment, but in this case is an opportunity to learn and improve as a business.

Not looking for these opportunities to grow can be just as damaging as falling back on what is easy and what is complacent for your business. It shows the clients that you are not looking for the newest trends; it lends itself to the idea that you are not an expert in your field and it shows your client that you do not care enough about the business to ensure that you are always improving and willing to move beyond past mistakes.

To avoid this mistake, do not be afraid to seek out the help of other brokerages. While you are all competing for the same work and contracts, there is camaraderie needed in the shipping industry. Not just one company and brokerage can be used for all of the shipments made worldwide. For this reason, you should feel comfortable seeking out help from those who offer it and from those who are willing. Not only will you help your own business to grow, but you can build important relationships and partnerships through seeking out these opportunities to grow.

Too Much Overhead

In an attempt to have the best technologies, the best services, and be the best freight brokerage there is, many beginner brokers tend to have too many expenses and too much overhead. Flashy new technologies, and ensuring you are set up for everything and every possible contract and situation can put you in a financial situation that is difficult to overcome and get out of. Indeed, spending money to make money in business is a necessity in some cases. However, you have to be strategic with what you spend your money on. Having too much overhead and showing too much money will result in less money in your own pocket, and less money given to your employees. After all, if you don't have enough to pay your employees your employees will likely leave. If you don't have employees, you don't have a business.

When you are first starting out try to keep your expenses at only the necessaries. Then when you begin to become a more lucrative business, then you can look into expanding. Whether that is a partnership with other brokerages, getting loans from other companies to expand, or investing in the newest technologies, you need to be strategic with what you spend your money on and when you spend it.

As you can see, the secrets of a successful freight broker business are not that different from the mistakes that any business should avoid making. It just goes to show that running a freight business can be a difficult one. However, if it is done properly, it can be rather lucrative.

Top Challenges

Before we move on to the stops you must take to create and establish your freight brokerage, we would like to take some time to give you a better understanding of the business that you are entering into. While the freight broker business—not to mention the shipping industry itself—is a rather lucrative business for anyone to enter, it does not mean that there are not any challenges.

In fact, because of its size and importance, there are some rather significant challenges that anyone breaking into the freight broker business needs to be aware of.

Challenge #1: Communication

As we have discussed through the last two chapters, communication in a freight brokerage business is paramount and closely linked to the success or the failure of your business. Too little communication, communication that is lacking information, and communication that is unclear or dishonest can lead to the early downfall and failure of a brokerage. That being said, maintaining communication is easier said than done.

As mentioned before, the structure of the freight brokerage business does not allow for the client and the broker to be in the same room at all times. What's more, is that it does not allow for the service the broker is providing to be close to home so to speak. For instance, the broker, the client, and the shipment can all take place and be located in different countries.

For this reason, certain technologies are a must. Telephones, video calls, and anything that allows you to communicate clearly over large distances is necessary. There needs to be humility and honesty coming from you as the freight broker. Customers need to know that they can trust their broker with their shipped goods. What makes this more complicated is that it can be difficult to communicate certain ideas in written form or not face-to-face. You may also have a difficult time getting a hold of the client or conversely the client getting a hold of you. Lastly, due to the nature of the shipping business, it can be nerve-wracking to admit to a mistake surrounding the shipment.

The best advice that we can give you to help alleviate this challenge is to have good communication with the client right from the start. In addition to being honest, transparent, and consistent with your communication. Make your company available 24/7 so as to allow the customer to reach you no matter their time zone or time difference. You can even set up consistent or schedule check-ins between yourself in the client to ensure that the communication is consistent and the expectation of your surface remains high.

Challenge #2: Quality of Service

Another challenge that freight brokers face is maintaining high-quality service. Again the service you are providing is one that spans the globe. It is also a service that you do not have your hands on—so to speak—at all times. Whereas a contractor or an architect is able to see the process of their building being constructed step-by-step, you as a freight broker do not have such luxury. Once the item is shipped, or even in the process of being, it is physically out of your hands. As a result, it can be difficult to maintain quality because it will take time for you to even know if the standards of quality and of service have fallen below what is expected and acceptable.

What makes maintaining quality service even more challenging is that the shipping industry is not one that is expensive. In order to keep costs low, brokers feel the pressure of cutting corners. As a result, they find themselves in a balancing act of how much quality can suffer in order to keep costs low.

The advice that we give in order to help with this challenge is to provide the best quality of service that you can. If you find that there are shortcomings, try to fix them as quickly as possible. Keep in mind that it is important to not hide any past issues. Be honest and forthcoming with any instance of poor quality or poor service and be determined to ensure that it never happens again.

Brokerages that are keen to maintain high-quality service and are ready to improve on any instance where service was lacking are those that are chosen more often by clients and have consistent work.

Challenge #3: Consistency with Pricing

As mentioned above, the shipping industry is not one that comes cheap. And it can be difficult for freight brokerage to not only have consistency in their pricing but just stay true and stick to a quoted rate.

Just like every other business and industry, prices increase more often than they decrease. Repairs for ships become more expensive, the cost of transportation, in general, becomes more expensive, and the cost of supplies, in order to run the business, becomes more expensive. As a result, it can be difficult to stay competitive and affordable with your prices. Setting your price too high to ensure that you are making a profit may lead you to miss out on contracts. Alternatively, setting the price too low may lead you to not make a profit at all or can negatively affect the quality of service. After all, doing things cheaply does not necessarily mean doing things right.

What's more is that you cannot continuously increase your prices as the market changes because past clients, who were charged one price in the past, may not appreciate being charged an increased price in the future.

Our advice to help streamline this challenge for you and your freight broker business is to try and be as consistent as possible with your pricing. However, when consistent pricing is impossible, due to increasing the market itself or due to unforeseen expenses, we suggest being as transparent and honest as you can with the customers. Letting your customers know why you have to charge them an increased rate and letting them know that you are trying to give them the best quality service for that price can go a long way in charging those increased rates.

Challenge #4: Staying Accountable

Another challenge that comes with a freight broker business is being accountable. Stemming from the challenges above poor communication and the difficulty with service comes the challenge of being accountable for your business. You want to ensure that your client feels comfortable and knows that their shipment will not only make it to the destination but will make it there safely and on time.

Being a brokerage that consistently shows up late or consistently damages the goods is not one that will likely be successful. Unfortunately, the shipping business is one that relies on many different parts and aspects that in themselves can be inconsistent and unexpected. For example weather, repairs, and shipping accidents can throw a shipment into delays or worse.

To alleviate this challenge we suggest just trying to cut down on instances where a shipment is compromised in one way or the other. Alternatively, continuously putting the blame for delays and damages on external factors can become problematic as well as you will be presented as a business that does not have the capacity to avoid or work around problems.

What we suggest is thinking ahead as much as possible. Look into those factors that are at fault for the most common delays or issues and put safeguards in place to help move around them with ease. You should, again, always be honest with the client. Good brokerages not only try their best to remove potential blockages and problems but also are honest with the clients about any issue. Let your client know what has happened and specifically what you are doing to fix and remedy the issue.

Challenge #5: Consistent Work and Availability

While world trade and shipment is a consistent business and lucrative industry, it does not mean that the work for one company will be consistent. A variety of factors can be at play to ensure you have consistent work or that you miss out on work.

For example, depending on where your brokerage is located and where you are able to ship and travel to, you may be fighting weather conditions. On the other hand, you will also be fighting and competing for work with other companies and brokers.

What we suggest to help you get through this challenge is to set yourself up for the best possible amount of work possible. Ensure that you are not making the fatal mistakes we have explored above so as to ensure that you are presenting your brokerage as one of the best. This way you will likely get more work from clients to choose you and to choose you over and over again. Furthermore, if weather conditions are factors that are unavoidable, then it is wise to prepare for those months, perhaps the winter, when you will be out of consistent work. Putting money away or providing different services during those winter months can help you stay afloat during times where little work is inevitable.

Challenge #6: The Pay Clock

The pay clock is a term used to refer to the time between the job being done and when the payment comes through for that work. The problem that many brokerages face is that their pay clock does not match up or work with their expenses. In other words, freight brokerages find they have to pay out their expenses and carriers well before they get paid by their clients. In fact, some brokerages have to wait between a month and a month and a half—or even longer—before they get their invoice paid.

Of course, some reasons why this length of time between invoice and work to actually getting paid, are set out of legal reasons. For example, most business laws state that you have to allow your client a minimum of thirty days between receiving your invoice and getting paid to give them the opportunity to rebut the invoice and charges.

Thankfully, there are ways to make this pay clock smaller and shorter, while still following the law. The easiest way to do this is to ask for payment in advance. This means that you can set a perceived budget and send that as an invoice to your client—asking it to be paid within 30 days—before you do the job. Then send a secondary invoice or refund some of the money if the job ends up costing more or less than what was guessed. Of course, this can cause some tensions and issues between you and your clients if unexpected costs arise, or if you do not get their refund back to them in a timely manner.

You can also receive money from a third party then pay back that loan when your invoice is paid; this is called factoring. However, this is dangerous because you may have to pay interest on this loan, which can eat into your profits.

A third option is of course to balance your expenses so you are not struggling to get by while you wait for your invoice to be paid.

In the end, the freight brokerage business is not any more challenging than any other industry in theory. If you have done the proper preparation and research, breaking into and developing a successful freight broker business can be relatively easy. That is as long as you are prepared. Knowing the keys to success, the role of a brokerage in the shipping industry, understanding the mistakes to avoid, and familiarizing the challenges that are associated with this industry are all factors that can help prepare you for your journey ahead.

Now that we have gone through some of what you should expect once your business has been created and established, it is now time to move to the specific steps you must take to actually form and create your brokerage.

Business Summary

As we have mentioned, there are multiple steps to running a freight broker business. While each step will be discussed in detail in the following chapters, we have summarized the steps here for you so you can get a good overview of each step before diving into them individually.

Start with Training

While you do not necessarily have to go to school to run a freight brokerage, schooling and training can be helpful and make a difference in how successful your freight brokerage is.

Training for freight brokerages is easy to find. Much of the training can be done online and over a short period of time.

Again it is not legally required of you to go through any training programs or special qualifications to begin your freight brokerage however, such programs can help you get to know the business and prepare you for what your job and business will entail rather than entering into the industry completely blind.

Courses like logistics management, dispatcher training, and even shipping management can all help you become a better freight broker. Essentially, when you are looking for which courses to take, you want to take those that are related to your field. For example, the qualifications and certifications that are required to be a trucker or carrier is a good place to start. Alternatively, you may want to look at some low-level business courses, or even human resources as they can help you with the administrative side of your business.

These courses usually cost money, even though they take only a few weeks to complete. Therefore if you are looking for a way to train without it costing you too much money, you can get a job as a dock worker, a loader, an office worker, or any other position in a shipping or carrier company. Again, in doing so, you will learn the ropes of the shipping business, however, you will be getting paid for your training.

Register Your Brokerage Company

There are a few different registrations that you have to go through when you begin your freight broker business.

Every freight broker has to complete a Unified Carrier Registration and then pay the annual fee that comes along with it. The fee is not too expensive and ranges from $60-$80 per year.

On top of this registration that is specifically associated with the shipping industry, you also have to think about the business itself. When starting your own business, you have to register it as a business. This is because it lets your government bodies know that it is how you are going to be making money. The different registration levels for a business. They are a sole proprietorship, a partnership, or a corporation. A sole proprietorship means that you run the business and you have no employees that you pay or higher. A partnership usually is when you go into business with someone else. Registering your business as a partnership also means that you are not the sole owner of the business but you share ownership with at least one other person. Then there is a corporation. A corporation does not necessarily mean that you have a large company with many many employees. Rather if you incorporate your business it is usually for taxes and insurance reasons.

During this step of registration, you will also have to choose a name for your business.

Apply for Brokerage Authority

If you are a freight brokerage that does not deal with other states, and you only stay within your state, then you don't have to apply for a brokerage authority. However, it is interstate commerce where the majority of the money is in this job.

Brokerage authority can be applied for through the Federal Motor Carrier Safety Administration or FMCSA. There is usually a small fee for processing the application and it usually takes between 4 to 6 weeks.

All a brokerage authority does is allow you to cross state borders with your goods and shipments. The Federal Motor Carrier Safety Administration is a subsect of the United States Department of Transportation; therefore it helps to regulate and enforce rules associated with commerce between states.

Select Process Agent for Your Company

A process agent is just a formal term meaning a person that represents your company and who will receive court papers if any legal proceedings or issues arise.

You will have to choose a process agent in every state with which you do business. However, you can choose a process agent business that offers you a sort of blanket coverage for the entire country or geographical area of the country.

There must be a physical location of your process agent and an address that can receive mail.

Acquire a Surety Bond

A surety bond is your next step. It is required that every freight broker have a $75,000 dollar surety bond. This is meant to make sure that the freight broker has the money to cover the asset and load in the chance that something goes wrong.

Surety bonds can be applied for and gotten from your insurance company, as long as the payments are not consolidated with your insurance payments.

There is a chance that you will have to get more than a $75,000 dollar surety bond. However, that will depend on your company size, employees, where your shipments run, and what you are shipping.

Get Insurance

Along with your surety bond—a specific kind of insurance—you are also going to need other kinds of insurance for your company. These kinds of insurance can range from insurance for the building you use for your office, to insurance for your machinery and technologies, to your employees and clients.

Because you are dealing with people from all over the country, and you do not actually have physical control over what happens to the shipment as it is on route, it is important to get insurance to cover and protect everyone associated with the shipment; you, your employees, your partners, and your clients.

Know the Tax Regulations

You will have to pay taxes for your business. You will also have to charge tax on your invoices to your clients, in addition to paying taxes when you cross certain borders.

While there are some tax regulations that are universal and nationwide, there are others that are state-specific. You will need to familiarize yourself with these different tax policies to ensure that you do not default on paying or forget to charge tax.

Failure to do so will not only make your business look less professional, but it can also result in serious legal ramifications.

Create Your Business Plan

This step is often overlooked as a step at all. As a result, many up-and-coming businesses forget to create a business plan, ultimately leading to their failure. Business plans do not have to be official or incredibly formal. It just needs to outline how you plan on setting up your business; the future vision you have for your company; and a number of other details about how your business conducts itself.

Find Broker Contracts

A necessary step to being a successful freight broker is having contracts. The job of a freight broker is unique in that you will not be given work to do. You have to go out to find it. These are called freight broker contracts. There are agreements between yourself, the shipping company, and the motor carrier company.

Finding a freight broker contract is not a difficult task to do but it can be complicated. In this section, we will outline some stuff and methods of how you can find surplus contracts. Remember more contracts equals more work.

Set Up Financing

You will likely not be able to build a startup with your own capital. Instead, you will have to seek out different types of financing to help you.

There are a variety of different kinds of financing methods out there, and understanding them is key to making sure that you actually use the financing methods to your benefit. In this chapter, we will talk about the different kinds of financing that are available to you, and some of the benefits and potential downfalls.

Conduct Business

Once everything is set up, the only thing you need to do now is conduct your business. While the specifics of your day will vary, we have compiled a template day for you, to help you understand and know what to expect in the day-to-day dealings of a freight broker.

Let's look at each of these steps in more detail.

Step 1: Start With The Training

W e should start this chapter off by saying that you do not legally or necessarily need any sort of training or formal schooling to become a freight broker. That being said, starting this journey with some sort of education or training can help you set yourself apart from others who are trying to do the same thing.

But if there are no formal or legally required schools; then what sort of training can you get?

What Kinds of Training Are There?

Freight brokers are an integral part of the transportation and trade goods industry. They helped to organize the entire shipment. They match the shipping company with the appropriate carrier and help to plan the most cost-effective, quickest, and safest route for the shipping company's products to be delivered to their desired location. Within this job description, there are a variety of smaller roles that a freight broker does.

Thanks in part to this variety of hats a freight broker wears, the training that you can get to help make you a successful freight broker is also varied.

Taking any sort of business administration course, or business management course can help you exponentially. In business administration and business management, you learn how to schedule and manage your time, delegate, and how to appropriately communicate with clients and employees. Since communication and scheduling are two of the most important jobs of the freight broker, these courses can be useful.

But what about on the other side? Is having the good business sense all you need to become a successful freight broker? In fact, it is not. It is also smart to be trained and have experience in different areas of the transportation industry itself. A freight broker should have a general working knowledge of how the transportation industry works, and all of the moving parts that are associated with this industry. For example, you should understand economic trends, in addition to being familiar with the shipping industry and the trucking industry.

For this reason, getting a job as, or getting the training to become, a truck driver, a docking attendant, a freight loader, or even a freight forwarder, can all help you understand the transportation industry, and in turn, help you become a more well-rounded freight broker.

You can even speak out about shipping companies and begin apprenticeships or part-time employment with them. In doing so, you will learn what the shipping companies are looking for in a freight broker, and what they want out of their shipping experience in general.

In the end, the more you know about the transportation industry the better freight broker you are going to be. Thankfully there are numerous opportunities for you to learn about these different aspects of the industry.

Another option is to seek out successful freight brokers and ask for them to teach you. Usually, a successful freight broker is qualified by having completed over two hundred million dollars worth of shipping contracts, and has close to or exceeds 100 clients. Although these are general numbers, it can help you gauge which sort of freight broker is experienced enough to help teach you the ropes and guide you into your own freight brokerage.

One course of training that seems to be favored among the potential freight brokers is a freight broker certification course or freight broker school.

What Is Freight Broker School?

Now again we want to make clear that such courses are not necessary or legally required. However, due to the increasing need of all freight brokers in the transportation business, some companies have taken it upon themselves to develop a curriculum that holds a generalized version of all the information you need to know to take off the position. This is what is known as a freight broker school.

Like any other sort of degree where completing it gives you a well-rounded knowledge of the subject, freight broker school gives you a sort of crash course in what to expect when you become a freight broker.

Freight broker schools require a little bit of research to find. However, depending on your area, you may be able to find in-class schools at your local community center. Sometimes they are listed with other sorts of secondary jobs or business starting horses.

But if you are not fortunate enough to have one of these in-person courses available to you, there are many freight broker schools available online; in fact, this is probably the primary format and message through which individuals receive a freight broker certification.

The online format allows for the certification to be self-paced. This means that once you begin you can continue through the course as your schedule and timetable allow. It also allows you to take a longer amount of time on more difficult areas and breathe through subjects that you perhaps are already familiar with.

Even though they are self-paced, freight broker schools usually have enough content to last you about a month to two and a half months. Of course with the self-paced structure, it can take you shorter or longer to complete. These courses will also include quizzes, pamphlets, downloadable documents, and other sorts of resources that can help you to become a successful freight broker. These training programs usually end with a sort of final exam which you need to pass in order to receive a certificate. Again, and we cannot state this enough, passing or failing this final exam does not have a direct or legal influence on whether you can become a freight broker or not. All it means is that you have either successfully or successfully completed the course.

These courses are not necessary; they are merely supplementary to help individuals interested in becoming freight brokers learn about the industry. This certificate also looks nice and professional in your office when you begin your freight brokerage business. It shows your prospective client that you care about the industry so much that you chose to learn as much about it as you possibly could.

Another important note about freight broker school and freight broker certification is that taking and passing these courses does not make you an upper-level freight broker. There is only one level of a freight broker. The more certifications you get, whether it be freight broker school, truck driver training, or even a business school diploma, it does not increase the level of freight broker that you are. It can perhaps increase the chance of you getting a client as you will be seen as more knowledgeable than others; but legally speaking and professionally speaking, it does not increase your level of freight broker status.

What Will You Learn at Freight Broker School?

Freight broker school provides you with a curriculum that covers most if not all aspects of the freight broker job.

Some of the better freight broker schools will include the following subjects in their curriculum:

- How to set up your business and create a business plan

- What it means to become a freight broker

- A thorough definition of what a freight broker is and its role in the transportation industry

- It will list and explain the different roles and other jobs that you will deal with as a freight broker

- How to contact shippers

- How to find carriers

- How to cultivate strong relationships between shippers and carrier

- How to find the perfect match between shippers and carriers

- Necessary paperwork required

- How to negotiate a shipping or carrier contract

- Understanding and calculating proper rates of service

- How to send and pay invoices

- Business etiquette

- Skills and knowledge of different office technology

- Explain the different registrations, bonds, insurances, and rules back freight brokers must follow

And the list can really go on.

When you are looking at the curriculum to decide which freight broker certification course is good for you, take a good look at the specific lessons. If it does not seem like they are covering enough of what you should know, perhaps go to a different level of certification, or change certification companies altogether. Legitimate certification courses will show you sample curriculum or curriculum schedule before your enrolment so you can have a good idea of what to expect. If you cannot find this information on the website, feel free to email the administrator of the course. They should be happy to provide you with any information you need.

How Much Does Freight Broker School Cost?

Freight broker school and certification, just like any other sort of course, is not free. Depending on the level of detail and comprehensiveness that you choose for your certification, the course can cost anywhere from $100 to $2000.

Remember the level of certification you get means nothing in the eyes of being a legal freight broker. The level of certification only relates to how much information is going to be given to you in your course. Usually, a more expensive course is the more comprehensive and detailed the information you get. An increase in cost can also mean a few other things. It can mean that the teachers and instructors of the course perhaps have more experience and certification and therefore expect to be paid more. Increased costs can also mean that you need more resources to complete the course; for example, you may have to pay to download the audiobook rather than to get free PDF files. One last reason why a freight broker school can be more expensive than others is that it can include other types of certifications. For example, some freight broker schools can offer business management courses alongside freight broker school.

What's important to remember when trying to choose which certification is right for you is to look into what you are getting for your money. A more expensive certification does not always mean that it is going to be better. On the other hand, a more expensive certification does not always mean that they are simply gouging you for money.

Take your time and really look through what the course is offering and when possible look at some samples of the curriculum. This will help you to decide which course is best for you. If you are still unsure, you should always feel free to contact the company or administrators of the course. You can ask them for some sample curriculums or maybe even some testimonials of past students. Legitimate courses will be happy to provide you with the necessary information that will bring you on board. You want a course that is transparent in what it is offering and has a reasonable cost associated with it.

In the last chapter of this book, we will provide you with some of the more prominent and popular companies that offer freight broker certification.

One last piece of information before we move on to the next step in becoming a freight broker is that your training does not have to be completed and its entirety before you go on to the next step. While we do suggest you have some sort of training before you begin this journey into the freight broker business, it is not necessary.

You can begin your freight broker training before or after you begin the process of registration and applying for authority, setting up your process agents, getting your surety bonds, etc. As you will learn in the later chapters, there is about a month waiting period between when you apply for your registration and when you find out if you are accepted. Those 21 days can be used and filled with freight broker certification school.

At this time let's move past this idea of training and towards the next step: registering your brokerage company.

Step 2: Registration Of Your Brokerage Company

There are two ways in which you have to register your business when you are beginning your journey to become a freight broker. You first have to register your business in the general sense and name what kind of business structure you are using for tax purposes. You also have to register your business as a freight broker business with the proper authorities.

Registering Your Business Structure

There are three general choices to choose from when it comes to registering your business, in terms of its business structure. These choices are sole proprietorship, partnership, and a corporation. Let's look at each one on its own to discuss the merits.

Sole Proprietorship

A sole proprietorship means that there is only one owner, and usually only one employee, of the business. This one employee is usually also just the owner. In a sole proprietorship, all of the profits, proceeds, and income, go to the owner. There is no lower-level employee that gets paid out. What's more, is that all of the responsibility and liability fall on the owners as well. They are responsible for filing all necessary paperwork, and they are the ones responsible for any legal fees or reparations if legal action is necessary. What this means for taxes is that the sole proprietor, or the owner, usually files their business taxes along with their personal taxes. There is no need to file separately, in most cases.

This structure can change, however, if the sole proprietorship begins to bring in a large amount of income. However, if that is the case, if your sole proprietorship yields high profits it may affect how you file your taxes, it is highly suggested that you change the structure of your business. Unfortunately, this amount of money is not the same every time. It depends on what kind of business you have, and how often you have a high-profit year. If you have one high-profit year while the other years are considerably lower, then the government may not ask for you to change your business structure. Or if your earnings are consistently high, then you may be able to still keep your sole proprietorship, however, you have to pay taxes quarterly instead of annually.

No matter, you will always be notified if your earnings require you to either change your business structure or change how your taxes are filed.

Partnership

The biggest difference between a sole proprietorship and a partnership is that in a partnership there is at least one more person owning the company in business. Partners do not necessarily have to own equal shares of the business; that is the business does not have to be divided 50/50 between two partners, or 25% each for four partners. The business can be divided any way you wish based on the business contract in place.

The income and the profits earned by the business are divided appropriately as well. Usually, owners with a higher share earn more money than those with a lower share, but again this is decided when the business is created. When you create a partnership and you register your business assets, you have to formally dictate how much of the business each person receives and how much of the proceeds the person will receive.

When it comes to liability and responsibility, this does not have to necessarily be formally divided, however, the responsibility is shared among the partners. Again usually the partner with the higher ownership share takes on the largest amount of responsibility and liability. Lastly for taxes, each partner files their own taxes individually based on their income earned by the business. In most cases, there is no need to file together as a singular business. However, this can change based on how much income and how profitable the business becomes.

Corporation (Limited Liability Corporation)

A corporation is probably the most complicated business structure in this choice of three. It usually entails that the ownership of the business is divided amongst shareholders rather than actual owners of the company. As far as payment goes, any profit that the business makes, once the employees are paid, are paid out to the shareholders as dividends.

For liability and responsibility, this is a little bit more tricky. The shareholders are usually not directly responsible or liable for anything that happens within the company. However, depending on the severity of the legal action or the issue, the shareholders can be affected greatly. Within a corporation, there is usually a ladder structure of responsibility where different severities of issues are dealt with by different employees of the business.

Since there are more people involved in a corporation, there are more people involved in the decision-making of the incorporated business. Many times there is a board of directors where the shareholders themselves or representatives of the shareholders meeting to discuss improvements for the business.

Come tax time, the corporation is seen as a singular person, and therefore any shareholder of that corporation is included in the filing of taxes for the business.

There are many benefits to incorporating your company, and they all revolve around insurance. In a corporation, there are more insurance benefits for the business owners than there are in a sole proprietorship. Therefore, many sole proprietorships that find themselves making large amounts of money, or that deal with risky situations, register their business as a corporation.

When it comes to your freight broker business, you may want to consider a corporation if you are able to afford the registration. In some states, it requires a fee. This is because you are going to be dealing with other people's cargo, in addition to negotiating contracts with many different individuals for one singular shipment. This is not to say that we are expecting you to be sued or face legal action, but in a business that just freight brokerages there is a higher risk.

Registering You Freight Broker Business

Once you have chosen the structure of your business, you then have to register your business as a freight broker business. Registering your business as a freight broker business is different from registering for authority which is a totally different stop in the process of becoming a freight broker. Registering your brokerage is considered the first step to applying for your Broker Authority. It is an act that says you are interested in creating this business for this purpose and that you are fully aware of the legal requirements of the job. Moreover, this registration is what determines your active or inactive status as a freight broker.

Applying for your brokerage Authority is what allows you to become a freight broker, registering your freight broker business is what tells the government, and shipping companies, that you are an active broker. You have to register your freight broker business with the Unified Carrier Registration service. The Unified Carrier Registration is the body that regulates the rules of the freight brokers nationwide. There is usually a fee of a couple of hundred dollars for your initial registration. However, for every year that your freight broker business is active—in other words for every year that your freight brokerage is licensed, bonded, and working—you have to re-register. This annual registration is usually no more than $100 and is on average $70 per year.

At this point of registration, you will also have to choose a name for your business. Perhaps the step that is the most fun.

Note On The Process

It is important to note that although we have organized this book as steps, the progression of creating and establishing your freight broker business is not necessarily linear.

Depending on your home state or country, if you already had experience in the transportation industry and a variety of other factors, you may need to change the order of how you complete this stuff and some of the following steps.

For example, some experienced freight brokers claim that you should only register for your business after you have received your bond, have set up your process agents, and have been approved for Broker Authority. On the other hand, other brokers have said that their Authority has been denied or delayed because they had not registered for their business yet.

A general rule of thumb, and a good piece of advice to follow then, would be to dedicate a few days and fill out all of the necessary paperwork together. This way when you apply for your Broker Authority the Federal Motor Carrier Safety Administration can see that the processes of the other necessary requirements have been started.

Another piece of advice we would like to offer before continuing with the following steps is that the registration end application process can be overwhelming. In fact, it is almost purposefully so to weed out any of those who are not dedicated to the position. However, try not to get overwhelmed by the stress of applying. It is rare that individuals are denied outright their registration, or flat-out denied their authority, or bondage.

Usually what happens when a denial is given is that it is followed up by specific steps you can take to be approved with your following application. In other words, the denial is always conditional upon certain things. The Federal Motor Carrier Safety Administration and the Unified Carrier Registration understand that aspect of human error and are usually understanding if a common error arises during the application process.

It is best to simply be as thorough as possible, take your time to apply, and make sure you have all of the necessary applications in process. Another helpful tip that we will discuss later on is hiring a third-party company to help you with all of your applications.

With these last words of warning and preparation, let's move on to the next step: applying for Broker Authority.

Step 3: Apply For Brokerage Authority

T he next step in the process is to apply for a brokerage authority. Again just like many parts of creating and building your own freight broker business, applying for a brokerage authority is not necessarily a difficult task to complete. Being said, there are a number of different aspects of the stuff that you have to understand to the best of your ability to truly ensure that the application goes smoothly.

What is the Freight Broker Authority?

Freight broker authority is the government-issued permission to work as a freight broker. It can only be granted by the Federal Motor Carrier Safety Administration which acts as a division of the United States Department of Transportation. You can either submit your application directly to the Federal Motor Carrier Safety Administration, or you can seek out the help of a third-party business to do so.

Many groups and companies that offer insurance to freight brokers, or freight broker training schools, also offer to help you with your freight broker authority application.

Usually, you only have to apply and be issued a freight broker authority one time. Unless your license is revoked, you are denied your initial authority, withdraw your application, and stop registering your freight broker business, you only have to apply for it once.

The standard form to apply for freight broker authority is labeled OP-1 and is readily available through the Federal Motor Carrier Safety Administration website, and other third-party websites that can help you with this application.

Benefits of Using a Third Party Company for Freight Broker Authority

The application for brokerage authority is not necessarily difficult or tricky, but it is easy to make a mistake. This is because the freight broker authority is your first step and application in the necessary licenses and registrations you have to do to become a freight broker.

It is easy to forget a part of the application end or other required document. As a result, you can be denied your authority simply due to poor paperwork. This is where it is beneficial to use a third-party company. There are many third-party companies out there that offer help for your brokerage authority. Their help ranges from simply helping you fill out your application, to actually completing and sending in applications for you. Of course, depending on how much help you would like, the cost of your application will increase.

That said, many of these third-party companies have packages for the freight broker authority. This means that along with your application for authority, you also receive items like your USDOT number, setting up your process agents, and even help with your surety bond and other kinds of insurance, and freight broker training school. In other words for an increased price, you can get help with your entire freight broker application profile not just your freight Broker Authority.

How Much Does a Freight Broker Authority Cost?

To apply for your freight Broker Authority it usually costs about $300. This is just for the freight Broker Authority and is a fee for processing the application.

If You choose to go through a third party to help you apply, the price can increase significantly. Depending on if you are just getting help with the authority application, you can pay an additional hundred or $200. If you are using the company for your entire freight broker application and registration, you can be paying over $1,000. On the other hand, if you choose to register for a freight broker certification school, you can pay a couple of thousand dollars.

Paying more money at this point is not a bad idea, but you have to take into consideration what exactly you need. If you already have freight broker training and experience, or if you have an insurance company set up for your surety bond and other sorts of insurance, then you need only to pay for your freight broker at the sorority and apply through the FMCSA directly.

But if you are a little inexperienced, and want to make sure that everything is applied correctly then you may want to pay a little bit more to make sure that happens.

Just be aware of what certifications and licenses you actually need as a freight broker. It is also important to remember that if you are an asset-based freight broker you are going to need certifications that allow you to transport and actually possess the goods in question.

The best way is to research a few different companies that offer freight Broker Authority assistance and look at the packages they offer and compare them to what exactly you need to become a freight broker.

What Is The Process Of Applying For A Brokerage Authority?

Whether you are submitting for a brokerage authority on your own or through a third party, it is important to understand the process to ensure that everything is happening correctly.

The first step is to submit your OP-1 how you form.

This form will allow you to get a grant letter and an MC number. Your MC number stands for your motor carrier number and it is a permission that is required for any business or person delivering and commuting goods between states. You can select to receive your Grant letter and MC number through the mail or over your email. If you choose to receive it through the mail it can take up to a few weeks but if you choose to receive it through your email you can get it within an hour or two. This motor carrier number is the beginning of being issued by the brokerage authority. But it does not mean that you are safe and legally allowed to become a freight broker just yet.

The OP-1 Form is merely an application stating your details of the business. The Forum will include lines where you need to share your company ties, your company's name and address, and the type of operating authority you are applying for. The type of operating Authority you will be applying for will be dependent on the goods you expect to ship. You will either be shipping household goods—in which case you will write down the broker of household goods—or you will be Shipping on household goods or raw materials—in which case you will write down the broker of property. If you expect to be shipping both you will have to apply for each type of operating authority individually.

Once you have applied and submitted your OP-1 form there is a 21-day vetting period. During this time you should be submitting and applying for the other parts necessary for your freight brokerage license and authority to go through.

For individuals who are looking to apply for their freight Broker Authority for the first time, they have to apply for the authority, and submit the OP-1 form, through the unified registration system. By applying to the FMCSA through the unified registration system you are telling the government that you are doing so for the first time and they will assign you a USDOT number. The USDOT number is the United States Department of Transportation number. Ultimately it is an identification and registration number that the government tracks you through.

If you already have a USDOT number then you can apply for your freight Broker Authority directly through the FMCSA.

What Happens If I Get Denied?

Though it is rare, it is possible for you to be denied your freight brokerage authority. This can happen for a variety of reasons.

Some of the more popular and common reasons for denial include, but are not limited to; Not filing correctly, not filing your subsequent forms correctly, not meeting financial requirements, and not being a citizen of your country.

Although it is rare for you to be denied, it is even rarer that you be denied outright without the possibility of applying again or improving your application. If you are denied usually the Federal Motor Carrier Safety Administration will provide you with a reason as to why. They will also likely give you ways in which you can improve your application and apply again.

When you apply again you will have to pay the filing fee once more, and most likely work to submit all other subsequent forms again as well. However, if you are determined to become a freight broker, the application process is a mere step in your larger goal.

Applying for your free Broker Authority is a necessary step in becoming a freight broker. In its simplest form, your freight Broker Authority is a mere application and submission of the OP-1 form. However, acceptance and issuance of your freight Broker Authority application is contingent on the successful submissions and applications of some other documents. Specifically the naming and listing of your process agents, and the acquisition of your surety bond.

Step 4: Select A Process Agent For Your Company

N ow that you have registered your freight broker business and have applied for your brokerage authority, you must begin to select and list process agents.

The Federal Motor Carrier Safety Association defines a process agent as an individual to which court and legal papers are served anytime a lawsuit or legal action is placed against a freight broker, a freight forwarder, or a motor carrier. Of course in your case, it would be if any client or individual were to sue you as a freight broker.

According to FMCSA legislation 49 CFR 366, every freight broker that is licensed must choose and name a process agent in each and every state they wish to work. This means that every state you plan on working from or have contracts with must have a process agent. Essentially your process agents are representing you and your business in other states. Therefore if legal papers have to be served they do not have to mail them to your home state office; therein potentially making you wait for important legal papers. Having process agents in every state allows you to receive legal papers the moment they are served and follow up with them in a timely and appropriate manner.

Each process agent has to live in the state for which they are a process agent. Thankfully you, as the owner of your freight broker business, can act as a process agent for your home state.

You can begin designating your process agents the moment you receive your MC number and have begun the process of being issued a brokerage authority.

How Do You Designate Process Agents?

The moment you receive your motor carrier (MC) number you can begin to list your process agents. There are a few different ways to choose your process agents. You can name them individually or as a blanket coverage agent. You have to wait for your motor carrier (MC) and your United States Department Of Transportation (USDOT) number because you have to include it on the process Agent form. Again it is these numbers that are used by the government and the Federal Motor Carrier Safety Administration to identify you. You can begin filling out the process agent form and begin the process of designating your agents, but you cannot file the form until your MC or USDOT numbers are received.

Individual Process Agents

To assign individual process agents you need only to choose people or businesses to represent you. Other than having to live in the states for which they represent, there are no other strict guidelines to select your process agents. That being said it is highly suggested that your process agents have an email address, a mailing address, and a telephone number. This is so you, and appropriate legal authorities are able to contact them.

Blanket Coverage Agents

Rather than assigning individual process agents to each individual state in and through which you conduct your business, many freight brokers opt for blanket coverage agents. Blanket coverage agents are process agents that come from a specific company. These allow for one person to act as a process agent in multiple and several states rather than having an individual in each state. This is allowed because the individual in question is backed by and vetted by an insurance and legal company. The home base of the process agent company does not have to be in your home state nor in any state that you work through. Instead, they just need to have offices in the states where you work.

No matter the method that you choose and appoint your process agents, the same form has to be completed and submitted to the Federal Motor Carrier Safety Administration. The form is called a BOC-3 Designation of Process Agents Form; in fact to speak in the terminology of the transportation industry and of freight brokers, many individuals do not use the term process agents. Rather they simply refer to the form name. For example, they say the next step would be to list and file your BOC-3's.

Although it is a freight broker's responsibility to assign and designate the process agent, it is the process agents themselves, or the process agent company themselves, that must file the BOC-3 form. This form lists all of the states where a progress agent is designated for a specific freight broker business, and the location and naming details of these progress agents. Once the form is filed, a copy is kept with a freight broker, with the progress agent, and one file with the Federal Motor Carrier Safety Administration.

The BOC-3 Designation of Process Agent Form

The designation of process Agent form is not difficult to fill out but it can be tedious. At the top, you will find space to fill out your USDOT number and space to specify when this number was designated.

After a portion of legal jargon, there is a place for you to specify Your freight broker business information. This includes your name, the name of your business, And the location. Then the potentially tedious part begins. The rest of the form is a listing of all 52 states. Beside that, there is a place to select this state and to write down your process agent number. Your job is to comb through each state and select which state your process agents are in.

Finally, at the end of the multi-page form, there is a designation for blanket coverage agents, where you would simply include the contents information of your process agent.

Again it is not a difficult form to fill out. However, if it is filled out incorrectly it can lead to legal issues down the roadshow me the or a delay in beginning your freight broker business.

Once the form is complete it must be submitted either through mail or online to the Federal Motor Carrier Safety Administration. Experts in the field say that submitting it online is preferred and your best option.

To be clear, the requirement to select and designate process agents is not because we are anticipating legal trouble for you and your freight broker business. Moreover, the Federal Motor Carrier safety administration does not require process agents because freight brokers face a significant amount of legal trouble. In fact, if you do your job correctly, work with reliable carriers, and have been thorough in your selection of insurance, you will likely face little to no legal troubles in your business.

Instead, process agents are only in place to help ease legal procedures if any are needed. After all, if there is a legal action against you or your business the timing of your response is crucial. You do not want to be delayed in your response as it can lead to further complications or lawsuits. If you only have your home office to receive legal documents, then such documents can be lost in the mail, take weeks to get to you, or be shipped to the correct addresses. Process agents in every state you are working allow for shorter distances and more direct handling of legal documents. Ensuring that you are able to handle them in an appropriate and timely manner.

Step 5: Acquire A Surety Bond

T he next step to becoming a freight broker is to acquire your freight broker bond. The freight broker bond is also known as a surety bond or by-the-coast BMC -84. This is the step that is typically the most difficult to complete. Not because the process or idea behind this step is complex, rather it's because the surety bond, and freight broker bonds, are in complex and confusing financial jargon. Essentially it is a special kind of insurance that you must get to become a freight broker.

In general, what it means to be bonded or bondable, is to be a reliable worker, and you have no intention of being fraudulent or a high-risk individual for crime. The surety bond, or the freight broker bond, is essentially the same thing but it puts a monetary value on it.

As a freight broker, you need a $75,000 broker Bond. Essentially what this means is that you have the security to be able to pay and remain faithful to the contract if some unexpected circumstances arise.

Bonds in general are more difficult to obtain than other kinds of insurance because it is based on the individual's background rather than the benefit of the company. This means that if you have defaulted on loans in the past, have an unforgivable criminal record, have been fraudulent on your taxes, or something else that the industry deems unfavorable, you will not be able to get a surety bond for your freight brokerage and therefore not be able to work as such. What's more, is that freight broker bonds are more difficult to obtain than any other kind of bond required in any other industry. This is because there is a higher level of risk related to the freight broker industry. To put it simply, too many things can go wrong when shipping Goods from one destination to another. This is why you need specific insurance and bonding for it.

Freight Broker Bond Terminology

The contract of a freight broker bond is quite simple and straightforward. It is merely marred with financial jargon which makes it confusing. Let's clear up some of the jargon here. First, to apply for a freight broker bond there is the principal. The principal is he who conducts business in such a way that it is compliant with all legal regulations and legislation. In this case, the principal would be you, the freight broker following the legal requirements of working as one.

There is also the obligee. The obligee party of a freight broker bond agreement is he who would be claiming against the bond and be paid out by the bond if the freight broker is unable to pay. In this case, the obligee could be your motor carrier, your shipping client, your employees, or anyone else that you would have to pay and exchange money with throughout your day-to-day business as a freight broker. To be clear if you have to pay out of your freight broker bond, not everyone related or associated with your business will receive money. Only those who make a claim towards it will be eligible to receive money. And even so, not everyone who makes the claim towards the bond will actually receive money. It is on a case-by-case basis. The third and final party of the freight broker bond agreement is the surety. The surety Is the company or party that issues the bond after a premium has been paid by the principal. This means that the surety is the company or insurance company that supplies and issues the bond to you. Essentially this party guarantees that the bonds will be issued and paid out if payment is defaulted by the freight broker. However, a surety is not like a cosigner on a loan or a guarantor on a contract or lease. The surety does not have to pay any money themselves if the freight broker in question defaults on payments to them of their bond. In other words, this party is not responsible for any money of the phrase broker. This third party is also the reason why the freight broker bond is also known as the surety bond.

As the principal, you are required to pay a percentage of the total amount of $75,000 to the surety party. This guarantees that the appropriate amount of money will be paid out to the obligee if a claim is ever made. You will have to continuously pay into and pay the principal for this bond. If a claim is made against the bond and the money is paid out and issued, then your continued principal payments will make up the difference of what was paid from the $75,000 amount.

You are also able to pay a full $75,000 amount upfront for your bond, relieving you of this monthly principal payment. However, if a claim is made against your bond and money is paid out, you will have to reimburse the surety for the amount lost or paid out.

Why Is It $75,000?

To put it simply, the bond amount is so high because of the amount of cargo that is dealt with on a daily basis by a freight broker. If wages are lost or contracts are broken, you are potentially dealing with payment amounts that are in the thousands. Therefore if for some reason you default on a payment, your bond has to be enough to cover it or you will have to pay out-of-pocket in a lump sum.

Before the summer of 2012, you only needed a bond amount of $10,000. However, in the fall of the same here, the Moving Ahead of Progress in the 21st century Act increases the required bond amount to $75,000 for freight brokers. This is to ensure that motor carriers and any other individual involved will not suffer too greatly if contracts are lost, and it, in turn, protects the freight broker from having to pay out-of-pocket for lost wages.

How Can I Apply for a Freight Broker Bond?

Step #1: Find and Choose Your Freight Broker Bond Company.

There are a number of different freight broker bond companies that can act as a surety for your bond. You need only to seek out what is right for you. Here is a list of some of the most popular companies and why they are chosen over others.

- Surety Bonds Direct – This one is seen as the best overall. It has good pricing, thousands of bond types, covers every state in the United States, and has a user-friendly website.

- MG Surety Bonds – This one is seen as the best for construction workers, but can still be useful to a freight broker. Has expertise and knowledge of the construction world and is very respected in the shipping and construction industry.

- Bryant Surety Bonds – This is the best bond company on a contract by contract basis. They offer customizable bonds for each contract and a 100% money-back guarantee if the bond is not used over the duration that the contract is open.

- Gallagher – This is seen as the best from a commercial standpoint. They are a rather large company that can handle a larger number of bonds than most other companies.

- SuretyBonds.Com – They have the highest level of expertise in the bonding business—according to some. They deal in high-quality services and have a website that provides clear information.

- BondsExpress.Com – This is seen as the bonding company that has the best value. This company offers pre-approval for bonds and one-hour approval for your bond.

Step #2: Pay For the Bond

You will either pay the lump sum upfront, pay monthly, or pay annually for your bond. It is up to you and the representative of the bonding company to negotiate how you will pay.

Step #3: Get Confirmation of Your Bond

If you follow every step perfectly, you will likely be approved and confirmed for your bond anywhere between 48 hours to a few weeks after your application. It depends on the company, and how long their vetting process is. You will not be sent the $75,000, instead you will be sent a confirmation that the bond has been established and that you are free to begin conducting business. The bonding company will also likely send the confirmation to the Federal Motor Carrier Safety Administration on your behalf.

This confirmation information should be kept in a safe place.

How Can You Lower Your Monthly Freight Broker Bond Payment?

Again unless you have $75,000 to pay upfront to your surety, you will have to pay a monthly or annual premium rate towards your $75,000 bond. This monthly or annual rate is based on a variety of factors and can be anywhere from 2% to 12% of your total bond amount.

There is some advice we can give to making this monthly or annual payment more manageable.

Tip #1: Have A Perfect Credit Score

Having a good credit score is beneficial all around, but it is especially beneficial when securing your freight broker bond. It shows that you are less of a risk when it comes to your finances and that you are reliable with your money.

Tip #2: Show Your Experience and Knowledge

It's important to show how long you've been in the shipping and freight broker industry when you apply for your insurance. Include all of your relevant experience on your application. This will help you save money in the long run because it shows that you not only understand the business but you are a reliable and beneficial member of the industry.

Tip #3: Pay Your Dues

In this case, paying your dues doesn't necessarily mean putting in the grunt work at a lower level. Instead, it means paying all of your overdue fines. Pay the parking tickets, pay child support, pay off your credit cards, and any other outstanding debts that you have. Even if they aren't all paid off when you apply for your freight broker bond, showing that you have the intention of paying off your dues and debts shows that you have the intention of paying off the bond as well.

Tip #4: Know and List Your Assets

Knowing what your assets are and listing them on your freight broker bond application can help lower your payment because your surety will know what you have for collateral if you default on a payment to them. Moreover, if you have more assets it shows that you are savvy with your money and a lower risk to take on.

Tip #5: Choose The Right Surety Bond Company

One last way to help lower your payment of your freight broker bond, is to choose the right bond company for you. Look over where the company has coverage, if they supply coverage for freight brokers, and what situations need to arrive in order for the bond to be paid out. You don't want a company that is incredibly strict with who is eligible to be paid out because that means you will have to pay more out-of-pocket if a claim or suit is filed against you. On the other hand, you don't want a company that pays out for every little thing because you will have to pay into your bond more often.

We suggest doing your due diligence and researching the freight broker bond companies closest to you and those that we've listed above.

Applying for a freight broker bond is one of the more difficult steps in becoming a freight broker, but it will protect your company, yourself, and your clients; therefore making it a necessary good.

Step 6: Get Insurance

It is true that there are no additional insurance types needed if you did become a broker; that is other than your surety bond of $75,000. That being said it is wise and highly suggested that you do look into and get other types of insurance. For example, you are going to want to insure yourself against any sort of liability if the goods are damaged; you might also want to insure your office supplies if your office is out of your home; you may even want to insure your trucks if you are an asset paste freight broker.

On account of the fact that insurance is not a necessity, we have decided to not explain the kinds of insurance you can look into specifically. But what we have done for you is cultivated a list of do's and don'ts when it comes to ensuring your freight broker business.

Before we begin to list it is imperative that we mention any sort of change in your insurance coverage should be discussed with an insurance agent or broker. While we are able to suggest certain options for you, only our insurance agent will be able to advise and guide you to which changes are best suited for your specific freight broker business.

DO or DON'T #1: DO Consider The Following Coverage Options

There are some coverage types that you should be looking at and either select or choose to opt out of.

- **Property and General Liability Insurance:** If your office is in a location that is other than your home—whether you lease the office from a landlord or you own the property itself—you may want to look into property insurance for it. This means that, any sort of damage to the building or the property occurs then you do not have to pay out-of-pocket to repair it. For this, it depends on the insurance company you are dealing with and your location in your country. So again speak to your insurance agent to discover which coverage is available to you.

- **Vicarious Auto Liability:** Even if you do not own trucks and a non-asset freight broker, it is still wise to look into auto liability insurance. If you are subject in a lawsuit that involves a truck—whether you own that truck or not—you may be on the hook to pay quite a large sum. This is because you still contracted that carrier and trucking company. If for some reason you are found liable the voracious auto liability insurance will be able to act as your legal representative and even help pay for damages in some cases. You may also want to look into umbrella coverage; that is coverage that covers you entirely not just if you are found liable.

- **Workers' Compensation:** Workers' compensation is a type of insurance that helps you to pay the salary of your workers, or help to pay a fine, if the employee becomes harmed or injured in some way. Even if you are the only employee of your freight brokerage, it is still wise to look into workers' compensation so you do not have to take money out of the business if you yourself become injured on the job. What's more is that since you are contracting out other businesses, such as trucking businesses, you may be liable for some of their injuries if their injuries are caused by something you planned on the shipping route. In short, workers' compensation is worth an examination, but your insurance agent will be able to tell you if it is necessary or not for your business.

- **Contingent Cargo:** Contingent cargo insurance helps to protect you from damages to the cargo if you are unsure of the shipping company's insurance coverage. Usually, the shipping company has quite substantial insurance that covers their cargo. In some cases this insurance also covers damages to you and your business; but in other cases, it does not. Contingent cargo insurance is meant to fill in any gaps that may be found. It also helps to protect you from liability if anything happens to the cargo during shipment.

- **Errors and Omissions:** Errors and omissions insurance also known simply as E&O insurance, acts as kind of a catch-all insurance for anything that the previous insurance policy does not cover. This kind of insurance specifically covers any errors in information shared. For example, if you provide the wrong information to a carrier or to a shipping company, and something unfortunate happens during the shipment, you can be liable for damages or loss. Errors and omission insurance are meant to help protect you. It is important to mention that errors and omission insurance will not cover a range of different kinds of damages that include but are not limited to; bodily injury or harm, or property damage. Depending on your contingent cargo insurance policy and your property liability insurance policy, your errors and omissions policy may be included already.

DO or DON'T # 2: DON'T Bother to Spend Time Looking Into The Following Types of Insurance:

- **"Excess" Auto Liability Insurance:** While it is good to look into insurance that helps to bridge the gap between the shippers insurance and the carrier's Insurance, oftentimes it is unnecessary. Let's illuminate this with an example. Let's say that your shipping company wants a carrier that has two million dollars worth of liability insurance and you have a carrier that has only 1 million dollars in liability insurance, it is not your responsibility to cover that gap. Instead of buying insurance to cover the gap such as this, make sure you have a contract with carriers that have different levels of insurance. That way you can match a carrier with the shipping company that can meet the insurance level requirements. After all, matching and pairing insurance level requirements is part of the freight broker job.

- **Be Added as "Additional Insured" By Your Carrier:** Generally speaking there are four kinds of insurance that your carriers will likely have. They are auto liability insurance, general liability insurance, cargo insurance, and workers' compensation.

  - Auto liability insurance covers the truck for the carrier. It is not necessary to be added as an additional ensure to this policy by your carrier. For the most part, every auto liability insurance policy for the carrier will include covering the freight broker and the shipping company. Therefore you do not need to ask your carrier to be added to their policy.

  - Cargo insurance covers what the truck is carrying. Being added to your carrier's cargo insurance policy does nothing for you. This is because you never take possession of is it good that the carrier is transporting. Since you have no legal possession, anything that happens to the cargo will likely not be your responsibility.

○ Workers' compensation actually differs from state to state and from country to country. Moreover, every worker's compensation policy differs based on the number of employees they have, the number of responsibilities their employees have, and how much employees are paid. Since you are not an employee of your carrier then being added to the workers' compensation insurance policy of your carrier adds no value.

○ General liability insurance is a policy that covers, as the name would suggest, general claims of damage or injury. This is where you want to be added to your carrier's policy. It adds value and supplements your own insurance as a freight broker and helps to fill the gaps where your policy may be lacking.

For moving on it is important to note that while these above-mentioned insurance policies add no value to your business as a freight broker, they should still be discussed with your insurance agent. For example, if you are an asset-based freight broker, that is if you own your own trucks and do your own transportation of goods, then your insurance policies will differ slightly. For example in this case you will want to get cargo insurance and auto liability insurance. Therefore even though we have provided you with a general overview of which insurance types are suggested, it is still wise to discuss your insurance needs with your insurance agent.

To add more value to this chapter, there are also different insurance areas where you will want to do your own research and fulfill certain requirements. Depending on how large your freight broker business is, and where you are working from, some of the following insurance details may be useful and important to you.

Insurance Certificates

Once an individual is insured they are usually given a sort of confirmation certificate. This certificate usually includes the name of the insurance company, the type of insurance it is, when the insurance year expires Etc. depending on the kind of insurance your carrier and your shipping company do not have to be carrying the certificate with them at all times.

That said, you should feel free to ask your carriers to show you their certificate of insurance before you hire them or begin a contract with them. In fact, it is highly suggested that you do. You should even ask permission to be able to jot down the information given to you by the certificate if they do not have a copy available for you to own. Keeping track of your carrier's insurance certificate can help you not only match the appropriate carrier with the shipping company, but it can help you from a legal standpoint ensure that you are covered.

You can either do this by keeping photocopies and physical copies in a filing cabinet. However, with the development of such technologies, such files and records can be kept electronically. In some cases, you can even contact the insurance company damn self and they will email you copies of your carrier's insurance certificate with the appropriate permissions.

- **Looking Into FMCSA For Information:** The Federal Motor Carrier Safety Association is the entity that state which insurances you need, which are highly suggested, and which are waste of time. Keeping up with the standards set by the FMCSA Is the best way to make sure that you understand and are up-to-date with your insurance certificates.

An added bonus of disassociation is that you can verify and double-check the insurance status of a chosen motor carrier. This is because carriers have to be registered with the Federal Motor Carrier Safety Association just like you do as a broker. For their own protection, insurance companies who register end cover carriers will volunteer their information to the FMCSA. If you want a complete picture of insurance you can go to the FMCSA Insurance monitoring service called Carrierwatch.

- **Be Wary of Incomplete Qualifications**: When it comes to insurance, and specifically the insurance of your carriers, you want your information to be complete. You want to know who their insurance company is, how much their insurance covers when their insurance expires, how often they have to renew it, and what kind of policy it is and that is really just the beginning. The more you know, and the more you are able to know about your carrier's Insurance qualifications the better.

The best way to make sure that your profile on your carriers is complete is to create a sort of procedure. If you are at a loss for how to organize and collect the information from your carriers you can look at the TIA framework. The Transportation Intermediaries Association, or TIA, is a group that provides brokers and others in the transportation industry with procedures and methods of how to collect the necessary information from your contract holders and carriers. Becoming a member of the TIA helps increase your knowledge of what to look for in a good carrier and what information to make sure you have in their profile.

Once you have developed your system, whether it be through the Transportation Intermediaries Association or otherwise, it is incredibly important to keep your records. Keep all of your records, especially your insurance records up-to-date and organized. If any part of the shipping process is compromised you are going to need these Insurance records to help determine who is liable and who was at fault.

Again none of these additional insurance coverage policies are necessary to have a successful freight brokerage. The only insurance that you need to be able to work is your surety bond. However, it is highly suggested to look into these other kinds of insurance policies. Since you are working and organizing a number of individuals, and organizing a route for products that you most likely will never have possession of, it is incredibly important to make sure that every step of the way is insured. That way if anything goes wrong it is easier to decide legal action, responsibility, and liability.

Deciding which additional insurance coverage policies are best for your specific freight broker business should be done through a comprehensive discussion with your insurance agency.

Step 7: Create Your Business Plan

Your business plan is simply a strategic outline of what you hope your business will turn out to be, your ideal way of how your business will function, and certain methods and strategies in place that will help you bring about this ideal.

It should set targets for profit and revenue in addition to specific milestones and growth percentages you wish to reach in a specific year's time. It will discuss budgets, expected expenses, marketing and advertising strategies, in addition to a plan for how to finance and pay back specific financing loans. It is important to remember to keep your business plan idealistic but manageable.

Essentially it is your master plan for your business. It can be as detailed or as simple as you like it to be although more detailed tends to be more useful. You can either create the business plan all on your own or you can use a business advisor for assistance. This latter option is your best bet to create a comprehensive and realistic business plan.

Generally a business plan does not have to be official or formal in any way. Usually it is only individuals associated with the business that look at the business plan. That being said The more detailed and organized the business plan is, the more likely you are to succeed because your plan makes sense. What's more is that if you seek out financial aid or investors, you will need to present them with your business plan. In this case you will want to formalize the plan in a way to attract your investors.

Each business plan will be different in the specific details. However, there are some comment steps and aspects to a business plan that will make it be more successful.

Ten Steps Of the Business Plan

Executive Summary

Usually one page or less, the executive summary is the beginning of your business plan. Interestingly, although it is presented as the beginning of your business plan it is usually done at the last step when creating the business plan.

This is because it summarizes everything that is to follow within the document. It acts as a sort of introduction to your business and lists what your company does, who owns the company, how your company makes money, and how your company is different from its competitors. All of this information is presented in a concise manner so as to not be redundant to the more expository parts that follow.

Because it acts as a sort of summary and introduction, it usually is written last to make sure that no information is missing or redundant.

The following is a very basic template of an executive summary:

- Our product/service is for [target customers]

- Who are dissatisfied or who are having an issue with [Name problem]]

- Our [products and/or service] solves [the customer problems] by doing [x]

- We are unlike [competing product or company], because we have [differentiating key features].

You can add a little bit more information to this, but this is the base structure of an executive summary.

Company Description

Your company description is a detailed account of what your company does. It usually contains three specific elements: a mission statement, company history, and company objectives. Let's look at each individually.

Mission Statement

The mission statement is a short paragraph—usually only a sentence or two—that states the reason that your company exists. This means it usually includes the problem that your company solves and how your company solves it. It can appeal to the emotional side of humans, or the practical and utilitarian side.

Company History

Your company history details everything that has brought you to the point of your company existing. If your mission statement is considered to be the president of your company, the company history is seen as the past.

You will want to include items in your company history like the date your company was founded, major milestones at your company has achieved, location and mailing addresses, and the key players in your company and changes in these roles that have happened over time.

You will also want to include the inspiration behind the creation of the company. What happened in your life that made you realize that something was a problem and that inspired you to solve that problem with your product or service.

Company Objectives

Your company objectives are the future of your company. These answer what your company wants to achieve while it exists, and the impact you want it to make on the world.

Your objectives should be very but have a similar thread that links them together. You also want your company objectives to be able to be measured, to be achievable, to be realistic, and to have an end date.

First, you want to be able to measure your objectives, otherwise, you will not know if your company is progressing the way you want it to. A measurable objective can include an ideal amount of profits that you want to reach or a specific number of contracts that you want to have. Secondly, you want your goals to be achievable and realistic: there's nothing worse than continuously working for a goal that you will never reach. Last, you want your goal to have an end date. This way you will be able to know if you hit the goal or not. Your aunt 8 can be anything. It can be 5 years, it can be 10 years, it can even be one year. As long as you have a date at which you will measure if your objectives have been reached.

Market Research

The market research portion of your business plan will include the research you've done that proves that there is a need for your product.

It will state we're in the world the problem you wish to solve is most prevalent. It will determine if there is a specific gender or age group that experiences the problem more than any other. It will also list how this problem came about and if anyone else is trying to solve it.

Essentially what your market research is going to tell you and anyone else who reads your business plan is the details of the problem you wish to solve and your target market to whom you're trying to sell your product and services.

You want to make sure that the problem you are trying to solve with your product is one that affects a significant amount of people, otherwise, investors won't consider your solution to be useful. On the other hand, you don't want to try and solve a problem that is too varied because the solution may be too difficult to come about.

Essentially your market research should provide you with a specific but general enough market and customer base that needs your product specifically to solve a problem.

Conduct Analysis Of Competitors

During your market research, you will likely come across other companies that are trying to solve the same problem. These people and companies are your competitors: they are who you are going to need to compete against in order to get your product purchased by the customers instead of theirs.

To increase your chances of your product being chosen, you should do an analysis of your competitors. This includes listing the competitors by name, providing a summary of their business model, and analyzing their product and marketing strategies. You should try to determine where, if anywhere, their product fails to truly satisfy the customer. It is in this gap that you can focus your product. For example, if you are building a freight broker business, and the main complaint of your competitor is that they do not reply to messages quickly, then you can employ a 24-hour message return guarantee. This will set you apart from your competitor as you are not only providing a necessary service to your customers, but you are also solving a problem they had with your competitors.

The analysis should be as thorough as possible and should include as many competitors as possible. The more you know about your competitors the more successful you can be in creating a product that is superior.

However, such an analysis does not have to be for making a better product, you can learn quite a bit from what your competitors do and have done. You can look at their marketing strategies to see which of them work and which of them don't. You can look to see what has made them successful in the past and what has perhaps hurt the freight broker industry.

Product or Service Description

At this point in your business plan, you should describe your product or service. What does your company do?

This description should include again what problem is solved, and how it solves it. It should include a detailed description of everything your product does or everything your service provides. It should also include any copyright or intellectual property laws that were required in order for your product and service to exist.

This description can also detail any previous prototypes of your product and how these prototypes failed and how the problems were rectified.

Marketing and Sales Strategy

Marketing and sales strategies are those methods that help you to get your company known by your consumer, and build interest in your customer base towards your product or service. You should reiterate what your target market is, and some of your goals towards your sales for your product.

After this summary, you should describe what different marketing strategies you're going to employ to achieve these goals. For example, are you going to focus on digital marketing campaigns through social media, or will you go through conventional methods like radio and television? You will need to describe why you chose each method and the different marketing campaigns you will use.

You will also need to include in this section, how much these marketing methods will cost you, and any potential downfalls that each method presents.

Business Financials

If you are just a start-up, then you may not have concrete business financials as of yet. However, you still need to include a section for it in your business plan. These can include simple projections of what you hope to accomplish financially speaking.

However, it can also include a summary of any financing or debt you've accumulated during your business startup. If you have incurred some debt then this part of your business plan is a good place to include a plan and strategy of how you're going to pay back that debt.

It should list how much you are going to sell your products for, how much revenue you expect to receive, and how you will be repaying any debt.

Once your business gets moving, then you can adjust this part of your business plan to reflect the projections and predictions you've made.

Organization and Management Description

Now that you've gone over the financial, the product, and the real meat and potatoes of the business plan, it's time to get into the administrative side. The organization and management description of your business plan will describe how your business is structured. For example, do you have a CEO? Do you have a CFO? Do you have any employees? and if so how are they structured: is there a manager or different supervisors for different departments?

In this section, you may also want to include the official business structure. For example, is your business a sole proprietorship or is it incorporated, or is it somewhere in between.

This will help anyone who reads your business plan to better understand who is in charge of what part of the business. It will also tell investors where they stand in the business structure, and who they will be dealing with to receive dividends of their investments.

Although it is not necessary you can also include specific hiring practices that you want to employ, notable employees that you want to make sure are mentioned and given credit and the expected responsibilities that go along with each role and job within the company.

Funding Requests

This part of the business plan does not necessarily have to be included if you don't have any funding requests. These parts are really reserved when the business plan is being presented to a potential investor or a loan service.

However, if you are included there are some things to keep in mind. For example, you have explained why you're asking for the funding or the loan, and where the money is going to go—that is what it is going to be used for. You should also include your repayment or distributions of dividends plan.

You have to list how your investors are going to be receiving their money back, and if any additional money will be given to them. You should include a best-case scenario and a worst-case scenario so the client knows the range of what can happen.

Your investor or potential funding associate should not have to guess when it comes to their money. You should give them as much detail as you possibly can about why their money is needed, where their money will be going, and how they will be getting their money back.

Again if your business plan is simply to make sure that you stay on track, this section is not needed.

List of Official Documents

The last part of your business plan should be a compilation of documents. This will include any licenses that you need to operate as a business and sell your product or service. It will include any loan documents that you have already acquired, any insurance information, and any financial information that is needed.

If you are providing this business plan to a potential investor, then you will want to include any piece of information that can make you look more favorable in their eyes and that will help them better understand your business. If you are keeping this business plan for your own information, then you should include every single document that was created in order for your business to be created in the first place.

Keep in mind that these should only be copies of the official documents. The official documents should be kept safely and separately.

Keep in mind that your business plan is just a plan. And plans change. You can be as thorough and as comprehensive as you like in your business plan, but the reality may be different than what you're expecting. Therefore it's important that you continuously revise and update your business plan so as to reflect what is going on.

Each update and revision should result in a new business plan. You should always have a copy of any previous business plan that you've made so you are able to contrast and compare where you may have gone wrong, and where you may have gone right. It is wise for you to set a standard revision date. Perhaps you revise your business plan every year. This may be overkill but it'll help you keep your business goals on track.

Step 8: Find Broker Contracts

T he next step in becoming a successful freight broker is to find freight broker contracts. As we've mentioned, you will not be consistently given work as a freight broker. You have to seek out shipping companies and motor carrier companies to create business contracts. Each shipment will be an individual contract, and each contract will be completed once the shipment has been completed.

Before we go into discussing how you can find different freight broker contracts, let's discuss the 6 contracts that you need to know as a freight broker (as not all contracts are the same).

6 Contracts Freight Brokers Need To Know

Broker-Carrier Agreements

This contract is the agreement between the freight broker and the motor carrier. It includes the details of what is expected of the driver to transport the freight. This agreement and contract are created only once the motor carrier and driver have been selected for the specific transport. This is a legal agreement that should include the following information:

- Name of a carrier company, and incense numbers

- Name of driver and license number

- Date that the shipment will take place, and any details of the route

- Origination and destination points: Where the driver is going to pick up the freight and where the driver is going to bring the freight to

- Any work that the driver will have to do in addition to driving: For example will they have to unload or load the freight themselves?

- Rates and payment terms

- List of equipment needed

- Bills of lading

- Potential problems and how they will be solved

Load Confirmation Contracts

This is a contract that dictates the details of the load and the freight. This is a required contract to be signed by the motor carrier as they assume responsibility for the freight. It can include:

- the value of the freight

- what the cargo is

- how much it weighs in total

- if it requires any special handling

- if it can potentially be dangerous to the driver

Rate Confirmation

This is a contract, agreed upon by the broker, the shipping company, and the motor carrier. It details the financial agreement that underscores the service of freight brokering. It talks about how much each party will be paid, and how additional charges will be incurred if anything were to happen. This sort of agreement will also include the process details surrounding wage loss, when the bill will be, and essentially anything that has to do with the money surrounding the shipment.

Accessorial Charges

This contract details the process of how to go about charging for accessible charges if they are needed.

Accessorial charges may include but are limited to:

- Layover charges and details

- Reclassification or reweighing of the cargo

- notification of delivery

- Driver loading or unloading requirements

- After-hours deliveries

- Fees for oversized or over-length loads

- Additional stops

- Storage or holding fees

This contract that is agreed to by the freight broker, the motor carrier, and even the shipping company, includes when certain accessible fees will be charged, a max or minimum amount that will be charged for each potential fee, and how they will be included or deducted from the total payment amount.

It will also list the steps that any party would be required to take if there is any issue or lawsuit poised against the excess rule charges.

Bill of Lading

The bill of lading, also known by the acronym BOL, is a sort of receipt that is given for the successful delivery of the cargo and freight. It is issued by the motor carrier and is given to the shipping company, the receiving company, and a freight broker. It can be included with the invoice.

Usually, the bill of lading includes items such as:

- A description of the freight

- How many items or pallets of items

- The total weight

- NMFC class

- Any special handling that is required to make sure the freight and people stay safe; such as hazardous material

- The location, address, and names of everyone associated with the shipment.

Of-Choice Contracts

This is a contract that passes any additional requirements for a shipment. It can list any necessary or additional stipulations or benefits. For example, if a motor carrier wants to ensure that they are insured to carry hazardous materials, then they may want to create an Of-Choice Contract to ensure their safety and compensation if anything were to happen. This kind of contract is named as such because it is created on the choice and at the discretion of those involved in the shipment.

Knowing the different kinds of contracts for a freight broker is not enough. You need to know how to acquire and build a network of clients so as to create these contracts. After much research, we have accumulated a list of 9 methods and ways in which a freight broker can build and create clients and contracts.

9 Ways Freight Brokers Can Find Contracts

Look at Current Clients

One way to build your client base is still a current client. Try to figure out if they have stores or warehouses in other parts of the world or your state. If so then you can become the freight broker for their entire company, not just for their local warehouse.

Make Cold Calls

Although it is never fun, cold calls can help build your client base immensely. Cold calls refer to the practice of calling companies and offering your services even though they have shown no interest in them as of yet.

The worst they can do is say no, or you get hung up on. You may also waste a little bit of time, but if you earn 1 new client out of cold calls then it is deemed a success. Many people don't realize they are in need of freight broker services. You can be the person who shows them this need.

To do so successfully you will want to craft a clear and concise message that you say the moment someone picks up the phone. This way you give them as much information as possible before they are able to hang up on you or change their minds.

Look For Referrals

Referrals are when one of your clients suggests your services to a friend of theirs or another company.

Referrals can work wonders in building your client base and increasing your carrier contract. Unfortunately, referrals often don't happen on their own and have to be asked for. Therefore, if you have finished a contract with a client, ask if they are satisfied with their experience. If they are, see if they are willing to refer you to their friends.

Again the worst they can say is no and you move on. However, if they say yes then you have another potential client on the way.

Make Warm Calls

A warm call is when you call a potential client who has already shown interest in your product or service, or who has received a referral from someone else.

Warm calls are an integral part of building your client base because it shows the potential customer that you are interested and care about their needs.

Warm calls, when done properly, usually end in a new client for you. Then if you ask them for a referral, you will have another warm call to make, and your business will grow continuously.

Add Your Name to Reserve Lists

Many times when you try to connect with a shipping company or a motor carrier company, you may hear that they are already working with a freight broker. This is totally fine. All you need to do is ask if you can be added to the list of reserve freight brokers if something happens with their current brokerage. Tell them about your services and how you can help them with their shipping needs.

What this can do is give you an incredible amount of potential customers or leads. Then If something were to happen with their current freight broker, then you are first on their list.

Contact Customers of Customers

Shipping companies in motor carriers always have a range of customers that they deal with. If you don't seem to be getting anywhere by asking your current shipping and motor carrier clients, then you can go directly to their customers. For example, if a company uses a specific business to acquire their raw materials to build their products, you can go to that business and ask to be the freight broker of their raw materials.

Create Loyalty Programs

One way to ensure that you have consistent business is to make sure that you have consistent clients. One way to do this is to borrow a method used by many coffee chains. Loyalty programs. Restaurants and coffee shops use loyalty programs to ensure that people come back. For example, every ten coffees that an individual buys they get a free one. The same sort of philosophy can be applied to your freight broker business. To be clear we are not saying that you should offer free freight brokerage to shipping companies: that is an incredible amount of potential income loss that you may not be able to afford.

However, you can offer different perks to your repeat clients. Maybe you can offer discounts, or additional services. You may even want to give gifts to your repeat clients or give cash prizes if a referral from a client gives your results in a new business. Any way to show that you are appreciative of clients' loyalty and repeat business will ensure that you continually get their business.

Use Mail

If calling potential clients is not really what you're into, you can also use mail to get the name of your business out there. You can send out emails to potential clients, or you can even send out physical mail.

Although the world may seem to have turned digital, the impact that mail has can still not be forgotten.

You can set up scheduled emails to potential clients to follow up on warm leads. You can also use mail to "cold call" clients. You can put flyers into every mailbox you see and on public and community boards. You never know who is going to see the flier and realize that they have shipping needs.

Use Shippers Lists and Databases

Another way that you can gain clients is to add your name to shipping lists and databases. This is similar to adding your name to the list of freight brokers for a specific business, but instead, it adds your name to a list of potential freight brokers in a specific area. Then if a company is in need of a freight broker, they can reference this list and choose their own.

MacRAE's Blue Book is one such database. Even if you do not gain clients through the use of these databases, it is a helpful tool to see who your competitors are and how they are doing in the freight broker industry.

———————◆◯◆———————

No matter how you put it, you will have to put in some legwork when it comes to getting consistent contracts and clients as a freight broker. It is rare to naturally and automatically be given consistent work in the field. However, the harder you work at the beginning, the easier it will be in the later years if your reputation is a positive one. Clients will seek you out specifically for their shipment needs and be willing to refer you to their friends.

Step 9: Set Up Financing

E ven though the number of freight brokers working in North America has increased exponentially over the last few years, the price of becoming a freight broker has not decreased.

There are Licensing, and Registration Costs

We have already gone over the different kinds of licensing and registration that are needed to become a freight broker. But again to summarize, the registration with the Federal Motor Carrier safety administration is $300. This is paid online when you submit your application to register and it is a non-refundable fee. This means that if for some reason you get denied registration or denied anywhere, throughout the line and you have to start the process over again, you will have to pay the $300 again. In addition to this initial $300 application processing fee, there is also the annual fee to continue and maintain your registration for your business.

There are also business licenses that are oftentimes required. Depending on the state you live in, and what you did before beginning your freight broker business, you may have to register and purchase a business license allowing you to own and run a business in your state. The cost of a usual business license can be between $75 to $150 depending on where you live. On the other hand in some states, the business license is free or not necessary at all. Furthermore, in some states, the business license can be close to $1,000. It's important that you check with the business association requirements for your specific State. These can be found through the Federal Motor Carrier safety administration website, your local state government administration office, or you can ask a financial or business advisor for help. Not double-checking the business license requirements for your state can bring forth some severe legal issues for you in the future.

Freight Broker School, Training, and Certification

Although it is not necessary there is also the cost of freight broker school and freight broker certification. As was discussed previously the cost of freight broker school and training can run from a couple hundred dollars to a couple thousand dollars.

Again it all depends on your level of experience before you begin your business endeavor. Remember that although some freight broker training is encouraged, not everything can be taught through school. Evaluate the courses and the curriculums to see if they offer exactly what you need and purchase the appropriate training package.

Freight Brokerage Authority

Applying for your freight Broker Authority will also cost money. This will cost a minimum of $300 per type of authority that you apply for. Remember if you are a household goods broker or a property broker you will have to apply for two different kinds of authority.

Moreover, if you file your freight brokerage Authority with another company it can cost you much more.

Surety Bond Expenses

The next expense is your Surety Bond expense. Again the freight broker bond is a kind of contract and agreement between a bonding and surety company and the freight broker. It acts as a fail-safe and protection to provide financial support in case contracts cannot be paid.

The bond has to be at least $75,000. You do not have to pay this upfront but you do have to pay a portion of the $75,000 upfront. This upfront cost can be between 1 to 15% of the total bond amount, making it between 700 to $10,000. This upfront cost will be based on your credit history, the company you go with, your payment history, and a range of other factors. After this initial upfront cost you will have to pay a monthly fee for your bond. Again your monthly fee amount will be based on a variety of factors. See the previous chapter about Surety bonds to see how you can lessen and have better control over your surety bond payments.

Business Equipment and Office Expenses

Working as a freight broker can be done from your home or from an office. This makes the cost of business equipment a little bit more reasonable.

If you choose to run your business from a different building, then you will need to pay rent increasing your business equipment and office expenses. On the other hand, if you choose to operate from your home the list of equipment gets significantly shorter. For example, you need only a computer or a laptop, and a phone that has access to the internet. You may also want to look into getting a fax machine, a printer, and a photocopier. This is of course in addition to filing cabinets and office supplies to fill the office and expenses to maintain your office.

If you work from home these costs can be around $5,000. Of course, they will significantly increase if you have to pay rental fees on a property. Thankfully if you work from home you can claim some of your utility expenses through your business.

The fees to run a freight broker business do not all have to be paid upfront. Depending on where you purchase your computer and other supplies from you may be able to pay monthly or finance certain equipment.

Business Insurance Expenses

Although additional insurance is not necessary you may want to look into it. There are different kinds of business insurance policies that range in coverage and liability. Generally speaking the more coverage you want the more expensive the policy will be. However, if you bundle your business insurance with other kinds of insurance you may be able to catch a break with the price. Depending on what you wish to additionally ensure this can cost you anywhere between $400 to an additional $3000 per year.

Marketing and Advertising Expenses

One more cost associated with freight brokerage is of course marketing and advertising. You should not just depend on word of mouth to get your freight brokerage noticed. You have to market and advertise your business to get the attention of potential shippers and carriers to work with. This of course will cost money.

Thankfully there are a range of new developments in technology that allow for marketing and advertising to be done very inexpensively or completely free.

Using social media platforms can help boost your business completely without any cost or relatively inexpensively. You may perhaps want to hire or consult with marketing and advertising experts to develop a strategy for your advertisement that stays within your budget.

When it comes to your marketing, however, it is important to remember that the more you pay does not necessarily mean you will get more clients. It is strategic marketing that is more important than volume.

Miscellaneous Costs for Freight Broker Businesses

In addition to all of the expenses that we have mentioned, there are some miscellaneous costs that you should know about. Some of them are associated with freight brokerage specifically and others are simply miscellaneous costs for small businesses. For example, you may want to hire a bookkeeper, or a secretary to help field a plethora of calls you will be receiving. This will increase your monthly and annual costs but add different value.

There are also additional costs depending on what kind of freight brokerage you decide to be. For example, depending on the kinds of goods you decide to ship and freight, it will also depend on whether you choose to be an asset base or an on asset freight broker. If you decide to have your own trucks for shipping your startup costs and your monthly and annual cost will increase as well.

Clearly, starting a business takes a considerable amount of money to do. It is rare that individuals already have this money set aside to afford their start-up. Fortunately, however, even if you don't have the capital it doesn't mean that you cannot speak in your business. Instead, it simply means that you may have to seek out some financing options.

Personal Investment and Capital

The first way to finance a business start-up is with your own money. Whether you've gained it through years of saving, through investments, or through selling off assets, using your own personal investment or capital is perhaps the easiest way to finance a startup.

It has its benefits of course. You do not have to pay back investors, which means that you can start making profits right away. Moreover, if you ever need a loan or investors down the road, showing that you started your business through your own personal investment gives you a little bit of an edge because it shows our investors that you not only are personally invested in the company but that you do have some money knowledge; as you did have the money to begin.

One downfall of this is that if your startup fails, then you run the risk of bankrupting yourself.

Love Money

Love money is considered to be a loan or an investment from someone who is personally close to you. For example a spouse, a family member, or a friend. In financial terms, this is also known as patient capital. It means that there is no financial institution that is backing below nor the investment.

There are a number of benefits from receiving love money or money from a family member or friend. For example, you will likely be able to set terms of their repayment. In some very fortunate cases, you may not even need to pay back the money that you borrow. What's more, is that you are afforded more forgiveness if you miss a payment.

Unfortunately, many individuals who are unable to afford to start at money themselves, rarely have family members or friends who do have such capital. Another potential downfall is that lending and borrowing money between friends and family can hurt the relationship. For many, it is best to borrow money from a third party or someone you do not have a personal relationship with.

Venture Capital Money

Venture capitalists are people who are rather wealthy and who are willing to invest in up-and-coming startup companies and businesses. One catch when it comes to venture capitalists is that they usually want an equity position in the company. This means that they don't simply want to invest money, they want to have some control of the company as well. Usually, this is because they want control of the money, but it can also be out of genuine interest and care for the business itself.

What you need to decide, as the business owner, is how much of the company you are willing to give back to the venture capitalist, and the specific terms of the agreement for the investment itself. For instance, will they have control over the company only insofar as their investment is being paid back, then their ownership share dissolves once their investment is paid back in full? Do they receive dividends on their investment, in addition to it being paid back? Does their ownership share increase or decrease for any reason?

The contract you drop between yourself and the venture capitalists can be whatever you want it to be. As long as the two of you agree to it, and the details themselves are legal, then there is no specific template or format that you have to use. That being said, once both of you sign off on the agreement it is a legally binding contract and any rule-breaking of this contract can result in legal action.

Just summarize, one of the benefits of getting venture capitalist money is that you can acquire incredibly large loans and investments. Alternatively, you do have to give up a portion of your company. What's more, is you may have to pay back all of the investment money whether your startup is successful or not. These are the largest pitfalls of this financing strategy.

Angel Investors

There are a few different types of angel investors. First and foremost there is the general conception of an angel investor which is a wealthy individual who invests money directly into your business. They do not ask for any sort of ownership or equity in the business, but they may want to receive updates on how your business is doing.

From this basic definition, we can get two different kinds of angel investors. The first is the investor that wants their money returned to them and paid back in full.

The second kind of angel investor is the individual who doesn't want their money paid back in full or at all. Instead, they just want to be named and given credit as an investor in the business. It should be noted that the second kind of angel investor is incredibly rare but does exist.

The benefit of angel investors is that you don't have to deal with the corporation nor do you have to give up a portion of your company in order to receive the money. However, there may be other details of your investment agreement that act as the pitfalls and downsides. Not to mention that angel investors are rather difficult to find.

Government Grants, Subsidies, and Scholarships

You might also want to look at government grants and subsidies when you are looking for money for your startup. Depending on whether it is your first business, if it is a business that you are creating based directly on your post-secondary degree, your level of education if your business will help to directly enrich the economy, or your own personal history, you may be eligible for financial help from the government.

Depending on a variety of factors you can receive a loan that you would have to pay back, a grant that you do not have to pay back, or subsidies which means that a portion of your start-up cost can be deducted.

One benefit of going to the government for financing your startup is that as a sign that your startup will do well. Governments don't usually take risks on startups that will not directly improve the state of their Nation. What's more, is that you might be given more options for your loan and you might be given more money in general.

The downside is that it is more difficult to get financing from the government. There are lengthy applications that you have to fill out, and you may be more limited and where you put the money. What's more, is that there will be less leniency and forgiveness if payments for repayment of the loan are missed.

Bank Loans

Receiving a loan from the bank is one of the most common ways of funding your small business startup. This is because banks are in the business of providing loans.

There are a number of reasons why bank loans are preferred. One of the largest is that they can be personalized based on your individual financial needs. Generally speaking, the process of receiving a bank loan is you go to your chosen institution, and meet with a loan officer. There you discuss your financial needs, your vision for your business, and your personal financial situation. Then together you will discuss which loan is best for you.

One of the benefits of getting a loan from the bank is that they are used to people loaning money from them. Therefore there are more options for the loan itself and more options for loan repayment.

However, perhaps the largest potential pitfall for getting a bank loan is that it is a legal agreement. Therefore any defaults on the loan, or any missed payments, can result in legal action and negatively affect your personal credit and financial situation.

The above list of financing options is not exhaustive. There are a variety of ways in which you can get money to build your startup. However, the above-mentioned are simply the most common. Keep in mind that financing usually involves a sort of loan that you do have to pay back. What's more, is that you're going to have to convince your investor that you are a good choice for their money. This is where your business plan comes in. The stronger the business plan the more likely you will be to get a loan and the more likely you will be to pay off the loan as you have already taken it into consideration and the creation of your business plan.

Step 10: Conduct Business

N ow that you've gone through all of the necessary steps of setting up your freight broker business startup, you have to conduct freight broker business.

How To Pair Shipping Companies With Motor Carriers

First and foremost your job as a freight broker is to pair the ideal motor carrier with the appropriate shipper. There are a range of different ways in which you can make and evaluate this pairing.

Place

One way in which you can match a motor carrier to a shipping company is location. If your shipping company is in one state and wishes for their goods to be shipped within that state, your best bet is to hire a motor company that is within that state. You do not want to charge the client extra money to use a motor carrier from further away.

If you or a shipping company wants to ship their goods across the country, you want to make sure that your motor carrier is available and able to drive and carry the goods as far as the shipping company wants them to.

Transportation Kind

You also have to consider what kind of transportation will be needed. Will you be able to Simply use trucks, or will you have to negotiate a change of carrier at some point in your travels?

Certain areas are only accessible through railroad or waterway access. This has to be taken into consideration because you do not want to match a shipping company with a carrier that cannot access the town to which the goods are meant to be transported to.

Cargo

When it comes to motor carriers there are different kinds of certification needed depending on the kind of cargo the motor carrier wants to transport. The motor carrier company you use has to have a truck or transportation type able to carry the goods.

If a shipping company wants to ship raw materials such as would, your motor carrier company has to be able to do so. If the shipping company wants to ship a raw material that is a liquid, your motor carrier has to be able to do so.

Environment

You also have to consider the environment and time of year. Some parts of the United States experienced all four seasons, while others only experienced one or two. Your motor carrier company has to be able to withstand whatever environmental season is thrown at it. If you are shipping your goods across the country where they experience the winter months, you have to choose a motor carrier that has transports that are able to drive on snowy and icy roads.

Experience

Some cargo can be more difficult to transport than others. For this reason, you may want to look at the experience of your motor carrier. For one of your more high-end and VIP clients, you may not want to choose a motor carrier that is just starting out. You want to choose one that has a lot of experience transporting goods to make sure that your client is happy.

Of course, as a freight broker, you are more than able to help Motor Carrier Companies expand their business. But you have to be incredibly selective when you choose a less-experienced motor company and a more experienced Motor Carrier Company.

Keep in mind that the level of experience a motor carrier has may affect the price.

Price

You also have to consider the price. When negotiating the contract with your shipping company they will likely give you a budget or a price within which they are willing to pay. Go to that price you will receive your own fee, and you will have to designate a portion of that payment to your motor carrier.

Other times the shipping company will pay you separately and outside of the motor carrier payments. You have to take into consideration how much you are going to be paid and how much you are charging versus how much your motor carrier company is charging. It is important to not choose a motor-carrying company that is beyond the budgeting point of your shipping client.

Another aspect of price that you need to consider is a contingency fund. Many times when a shipping company proposes a budget, it is at the maximum end. Therefore not only do you have to consider your own fee, the feet of the motor carrier, but you also have to leave some of that budget aside for emergencies.

In the end, you can essentially charge whatever you want as a freight broker, keep in mind if you charge too low, you will not be making a profit, and shipping companies may take advantage of your low price. Alternatively, if you charge too high you may be losing out on business because shipping companies cannot afford your services.

Shipping Company Requirements

One last aspect you have to consider when matching a shipping company with a potential motor carrier company is what the shipping company wants. The shipping company may request a specific level of insurance from the motor carrying company, they may request a specific budget, a specific kind of motor carrying company, and the list of requirements can really go on.

Completely ignoring your client's specific requirements is a big No-No in the freight broker world. You want to carefully consider each and every requirement asked by your shipping company and try to fulfill them to the best of your ability. That being said if there is something within your client's requirement list that is completely unreasonable you have to delicately negotiate for a different contract.

That said, be sure to carefully consider and go over your client's shipping requirements before negotiations.

Responsibilities For Day-to-Day Business

Indeed to conduct business as a freight broker, in the general sense, you will be pairing shipping companies with their ideal motor carrier company. But what are you going to be doing every day? What else are you going to be doing other than pairing shipping companies and motor carriers? While the specifics of these responsibilities will change from day-to-day, and from business to business, the general was responsible it will remain the same.

- Generating Leads

You will need to consistently look for new projects and new contracts. Even if you are working on brokering freight in one contract, you should always set aside time during the day to follow up on warm leads or create new leads.

- Identifying and selecting reputable carriers

Just as you will want to consistently look for a new contract, you will always want to be evaluating the freight carriers that you have. You should update your list every so often to ensure that the motor carriers that you are working with are the best in the business.

What's more, is that you should be consistently looking for motor carriers that do different things than the ones you already have on your payroll. For example, if you don't have a motor carrier that goes to a specific state, you may want to look for one that does. In doing so you will be expanding your business.

- Negotiating contracts with carriers

You will likely have multiple open carrier contracts at one time that are all at different steps in the process.

Therefore you will always want to set aside time each day to negotiate and look over these carrier contracts to make sure that they are in line with your business goals and ethics.

- Providing clients with updates

You will also need to connect with your clients on a daily basis as well. Whether it's providing them with shipping quotes, giving them an update about where their shipment is, or simply checking in. You want to make sure the communication between you and your client is often and clear.

- Tracking Weather and Construction

You will also want to set up notifications for construction and weather. This will help you better plan the routes that your motor carriers take. You should track and record these updates as you get them and set aside time during the day to ensure that the routes you have developed or changed and adapted accordingly.

- Tracking shipment status

You will need to also check on your shipments daily. This means any shipments that are in the process of being delivered, need to be checked in on and you should communicate with the driver. This information is then recorded and shared back with the shipping company.

- Follow up with government regulations, banking policies, etc. of the shipping process

You always want to make sure that you are operating under government regulations and the law. A failure to do so can result in legal action, the dissolution of your business, or debt.

- Invoice and Pay Expenses

While you may not be invoiced or pay your bills every day, you should always set aside time to double-check that every invoice is in progress, or that every expense has been paid. Falling behind on your company's bills can lead to your business's downfall.

A Day In The Life

Let's look at the skills and the day-to-day operations in the form of a randomly-generated day in the life of a freight broker.

To be clear the following is a made-up day for a freight broker. Let's say the freight broker works from 7 in the morning to 7 at night, and they work out of an office that is not in their home. Let's see what their day may look like.

7am-9am

- Arrive at the office

- Turn on all necessary devices and appliances

- Send out update messages to all active motor carriers through email and leave messages on mobile devices

- Listen to all phone messages left overnight and open any mail. Record messages and rank responses by importance and urgency

9am-12 noon

- Answer calls from shippers requesting motor carriers

- Call motor carriers based on their specifications and match them with the shipping company

- Develop and create a specific route for the shipment and hammer out details of the root itself

- Receive updates from motor carriers

- Communicate with shipping companies about updates on their freight

- Follow up on leads if there is time

12 noon-1pm

This could be where the freight broker takes their lunch and a short break

1pm-5pm

- Answer calls from shippers requesting motor carriers

- Call motor carriers based on their specifications and match them with the shipping company

- Develop and create a specific route for the shipment and hammer out details of the root itself

- Receive updates from motor carriers

- Communicate with shipping companies about updates on their freight

- Follow up on leads if there is time

5pm-7pm

- Closeout contracts and create invoices

- Invoice shipping companies

- Pay bills

- Make calls and leave word to motor carriers asking for updates

Tasks To be Done Throughout the Day

- Answer the telephone, reply to emails, record and track notifications about weather and construction

---

As you can see, the day of the freight broker is rather repetitive and requires an incredible amount of multitasking. Some days you will be incredibly busy organizing freight routes and communicating with shipping companies and motor carriers. Others it will be a lot of waiting to hear back from motor carriers and to receive jobs from shipping companies.

Staying calm and organizing his key and making sure that you got everything done you need to drain the day.

How To Get Paid As A Freight Broker

N ow that we have gone over what you need to become a freight broker, we have one more aspect to go over; how to calculate the charge for your services.

As we have mentioned throughout the book, you are going to need to bid on jobs and contracts, while also negotiating how much to charge the shipping company. Remember it is the shipping company that is paying for your administrative and brokering services. Moreover, you are paying the carrier that you use. So the money that you make and charge the shipping company, a portion of it is going to the carrier. You are not getting the full amount. Therefore you have to strategically create your invoice to make sure that you're charging enough to cover your expenses and make a profit for yourself.

To bid on projects means that you simply have to offer your services to the shipping company, offer them a price, and show that you are better for the job than your competitors. The shipper will then choose which broker they use. Perhaps the most influential factor in your bid will be the price of the contract; that is how much you are charging.

What To Think About When Calculating The Fee

There are a few different ways in which you can calculate and decide how much to charge your clients. You can set flat rates, or you can change your charging amount per client. Both methods have their merits. If you charge set in flat rates then you run the risk of not taking home enough profit if the job is larger than your flat rate; on the other hand if you change your invoice amount per contract and client then you have to be sure that you follow a strict framework of how to come up with an invoice amount.

This latter option is suggested, albeit slightly more difficult to do because you have to re-evaluate your calculations with every contract. For the second option, there are a few aspects that you should consider when you calculate your invoice amount.

The Distance of the Shipment

The distance of the shipment is perhaps an obvious aspect to consider. However, it's important that it is remembered. The distance of the shipment is calculated from where the product is picked up to where it needs to be delivered. It also includes any side trips or stops that the carrier makes along the way.

The further the distance, the more gas your carrier will need therein increasing the expenses, the further the distance, the more likely your carrier will need to take breaks, and may even need to spend the night somewhere, there in increasing the days it takes to deliver the product, and increasing the expenses.

In short, the distance of the shipment can increase or decrease the expenses. No matter the distance you have to take it into consideration when creating your invoice.

The Weight And Size of the Shipment

The size and weight of the shipment also have an effect on your invoice. The weight of the shipment can make the gas of the carrier be used up faster. Heavier weighted cars tend to use their fuel up faster. Therefore even if you calculate how much gas will be used over the distance of the journey, you may need to budget for more if the product is heavier.

The size and weight also mean that you will need to use a larger truck. Again larger trucks tend to use more gas, but additionally, they require more training on the part of the driver. Drivers that have more training generally ask for higher payments; again increasing the expenses.

One last way that the weight and size of the shipment can affect and increase the cost of the trip is that some roads and borders require more payments if the car is heavier. The infrastructure of some roadways and highways are not ideal for heavier trucks and therefore the municipality that owns the roadways charges heavier trucks for passage.

The Density of the Shipment

The density of the shipment also plays a role. Density is usually calculated by dividing the weight of the object or product by its volume. This means that a smaller heavier item, one that is denser, can incur a larger charge than a larger lighter item.

The density of the shipment is most important when the carrier you are using is a water carrier, as the density of the shipment can affect the buoyancy of the ship.

The Freight Classification

Free classification is important to keep in mind because different sorts of cargo require different fees and rates. The National Motor Freight Traffic Association has two classifications of frayed. A less than truckload or an LTL and a full truckload or an FTL. Under these two general classifications, there are 18 subclassifications. Each of these 18 subclasses include their own classifications which can range from 50 to 500 and number. Depending on the freight classification—Which is determined by the value of the cargo, how it's handled, how it can be stowed away, and any liability factors associated—the amount you charge the shipping client can increase. Essentially the more difficult and a higher classification the more expensive the invoice will be.

Base Rates and Minimums

Of course, merely taking these aspects into consideration is not enough. You need to have some sort of base right or starting point upon which you build your invoice. There are a few different ways that you can go about creating a base rate.

Flat Starting Rate

The first way is to have a flat starting rate. This flat starting rate is the bare minimum that you will charge any client no matter how small the cargo is or how short the delivery is. If you choose to go this way there are some aspects you have to consider when creating your flat starting rate. First, you should calculate how much it would cost—and essentially how much you would charge—for the shortest route or shipment that you are willing to do. How much gas would it use? What tools would you need to pay for on the shortest route? What is the minimum payout you would give to your carrier? Whatever this sum and price are would be your base rate.

In addition to this shortest route amount, you should also add in a small surplus for possible damage and loss, or paperwork that is needed for the shipment.

From this base rate, you can then increase or decrease based on the differentiating factors and detail of the specific shipment or contract. Keep in mind that if you choose to create your base rate this way you will almost always be charging your client more.

Competitive Pricing

One way to help you calculate your flat rate or base rate is to use load boards. Load boards are a reading tool that helps freight brokers decide what the best base rate is by comparing and providing the average base rate of shipments in their area. In other words, these are small companies that do some comparative work for you and provide you with suggestions of your base rate based on what your competitors and already established freight brokers are charging.

This method of creating a base rate is quite useful because it takes the work out of your hands. That being said it can be a little tricky because it is averaging the cost of freight broker contracts in your area. This means that in some contracts you will be charging last while some you will be charging more.

Freight Broker Software

One last way that you can create your base price and rate is through freight broker software. Freight broker software is designed to analyze and explore a variety of different aspects of shipping goods in order to create an average and base price that way.

The benefit of freight broker software is that it can be continuously running and generate a base price and rate for you with every new contract based on the subtle and up-to-date changes in the economy. For example, it will take into account changes in fuel prices, weather, and discrepancies in the industry in general automatically. This takes even more work off your plate because you will not have to keep such a close eye on fuel price changes or industry changes. That being said, it can be an expensive addition to your freight broker business.

Accessorial Charges

The last aspect that you should consider when creating your invoice is accessible charges. Excess real charges are those fees that cannot necessarily be determined before the shipments take place. For instance, the first group of aspects we discussed are all able to be estimated and predicted before the shipment happens. Similarly, your base price and rate are established before you actually get a contract. Excess real charges are those that are charged in addition to the agreed-upon shipment price. It's important to remember that these accessories charges can either be charged by the truck driver, by the shipping company, or by the freight broker. However, no matter who charges the Seas, it will affect your invoice, and therefore is important to know them.

There are six common accessorial charges:

Detention

This is a fee that is charged when the cargo takes longer to be loaded or offloaded by the shipper or by the receiver. Usually, there is a 2-hour grace period for any sort of loading or unloading delay. However, after this 2-hour grace period, truck drivers will charge a large sum per hour that it takes for the cargo to be unloaded or loaded.

Typical practice is for the truck driver to charge anywhere between 25 to $100 per additional hour it takes for the cargo to be unloaded or loaded. What is important for you, the freight broker to do is to negotiate this detention rate with your motor carrier before you hire them. After all, the more they charge in detention the less profit you are likely to make because your motor carrier will be charging you the fee because you are the one who is paying them.

One last important note about this detention fee is that you may be able to get the money back from the receiving party or the shipping party depending on where the delay was. However, that process can take a long time, and the request can be denied depending on the type of delay.

Reconsignment

Reconsignment is the fee charged to the shipping company by the freight broker when the destination or receiving party of the shipment is changed after the freight and cargo have been picked up. Note that it is okay to charge the shipping company between 50 and $75 for the route change, and it is common practice to increase your mileage costs accordingly.

All of this change in the invoice will be charged under what is called the recon-signment fee. Therefore on your invoice, you will have your initial agreement, then under the reconsignment heading, you will have all of the additional costs it took you to deliver their cargo due to the destination change.

Stop-Off Charge

The stop-off charge fee is an additional charge when there is Another load or cargo added to the initial shipment. Again when you create your contract with your shipping company you will discuss how much cargo is being brought from destination A to destination B. The fee is incurred because of the added time, gas, and labor that goes into loading the additional cargo and needed to go get the additional cargo. The typical stop-off charge will range from $50 to $100 dollars.

It is up to you, as the freight broker, to decide if you will be charging your client a stop-off charge or if you will commission an entirely new shipment for the additional cargo. You have to consider how much profit you will make with either option. Remember you will have to pay your motor carrier the additional income as well.

This should be negotiated with the shipping client. Keep in mind that while you need to make sure you make a profit, you also have to keep the shipping company and motor carrier happy. It is a balancing act.

Lumper Fee

The lumper fee is added to the bill when a driver or motor carrier company needs to hire additional help to handle the product. Usually, this is when help is needed to offload the product at the destination but it can be charged for any kind of help anywhere along the trip.

These fees can be rather small like 25-50$, or they can be rather significant and over $600 dollars. It will be your duty to pay your motor company and driver the additional fee, then speak with your client to discuss getting it back in your invoice.

Layover

This fee is incurred when your carrier is unable to load or unload the product at the destination at the scheduled date and time. Whatever the reason for the delay your carrier will likely charge this fee. However, it depends on why the delay happened for who pays. If it is the shipping company then it is usually paid by that company; if it is a scheduling error then you may have to pay it; if it was due to the weather then the pay can be negotiated. Layover fees are charged in the range of $200 to $500 dollars which can be a significant loss in your profits.

Truck Order Not Used

Also known as TONU, Truck Order Not Used fees are charged when the carrier chosen and hired to haul the products is canceled before the carrier can leave with the cargo. It is important here to know that his fee is only charged when the contract has already been signed and the truck is canceled the day of the loading. Usually, this fee is not charged if there is a cancellation the day before pickup. There are a number of reasons why shipments can be canceled including the product not being ready or the company not having the necessary border crossing permits. But if it happened on the day of scheduled pick up then the motor carrier company is paid the TONU fee. It is usually $150 to $250.

When it comes to invoicing, you as the freight broker invoice the shipping company that hires you to handle their shipment and product. The process usually is as follows.

First, you bid on a shipment or a contract and offer the shipping company an estimated price for the job. This estimated price is your base price calculated and changed with the specifics of the shipping company's specific journey.

Then once you are hired you hire an appropriate motor carrier company to fulfill this shipment; and offer them a certain amount of money to do so. This money will come out of the invoice and the amount charged to the shipping company. Whatever money is left over is yours to keep as profit. The driver of the motor carrier company that is assigned to your shipment will keep track of all of the expenses, delays, or other unexpected costs and issues with the shipment that may have not been in the original contract agreement.

These additional expenses and delays are then examined by you as a freight broker, you pee out your motor carrier company and you invoice the shipping company.

Your invoice will include the base price of the job in addition to the specifics of the shipment that were estimated. Following this, you will include any of the excess or all charges below which will increase the invoice amount. If none of the charges are contested or disputed you have been paid by the shipping company. That being said, you need to give the shipping company 30 days to contest any charges that they see as unnecessary or unfair. Similarly, however, you also have 30 days to contest any of the charges with the motor carrier company.

As long as you keep track of all expenses for each shipment, invoicing should not be difficult. However, it would be wise to hire an accountant, bookkeeper, or financial secretary to ensure that you are following any legal requirements for your invoicing. However, if you are doing everything legally and by the book, there shouldn't be any issues.

Freight And Its Many Kinds

Traditionally speaking the difference between cargo and freight depends on how the goods are being transported. If the goods are being transported by aircraft or by an ocean or sea vessel, it is not freight, it is cargo. On the other hand, trains that are transporting goods are considered freight trains. If the goods are being transported by car or truck it is also considered freight.

To simplify this even more, if the goods are being transported on land it is freight, if the goods are being transformed by air or see it is cargo. However, this distinction is only made when it is a commercially valued item. If it is a letter that is being mailed it is always considered cargo no matter the form of transportation.

Therefore, there is a difference between freight and cargo, which is interesting and good to know, but it does not necessarily have any weight or impact on you as a freight broker. If you want to be sure that you use the proper terminology then that is fine. However, you will likely not have compromised or hurt the entire transportation or shipment by using the incorrect term.

What Kinds of Freight Classification Are There?

There are a number of different kinds of classification and manners in which freight can be transported all over the world. While as a freight broker you may not be dealing with all of these kinds of freight, it is important for you to know the difference and the language associated with the different kinds of freight.

Less Than A Truckload

Also known by the acronym of LTL, less than a truckload freight is perhaps the most popular form of freight. This is because it is usually more cost-effective and reliable, not to mention it is easier to transport smaller truckloads of freight than larger ones. Essentially less than a truckload of freight means that the freight does not take up the entire capacity of the truck.

A Full Truckload

Also known by the acronym FTL, A full truckload freight takes up the entire capacity of space that is available in the designated motor carrier truck. This designation of freight is best when it is one kind of freight if it is coming from one shipping company and going to 1 isolated destination.

Intermodal Rail Freight

This is the freight that is loaded onto a train and transported by way of a railroad. This is a favorite kind of freight when hazardous materials are included in the shipment. The benefit of rail transport is that it can transport multiple different kinds of freight to multiple different destinations. In some cases, it is faster than using truckloads or motor carriers as there is little to no traffic on the railway.

Air Freight

As the name would suggest this is freight that is shipped and transported through the air. This is reserved for freight that needs to be at its destination urgently or in a timely manner. It can be transported by airplane, helicopter, or even jet. In an unofficial sense, you can also use hot air balloons, drones, or blimps. Usually, air freight is the most expensive kind of freight transportation.

Ocean Freight

Ocean freight is the classification of freight transportation that is used over waterways. Oftentimes this method of transportation is chosen when there is international trade at play. Just like truckload freight, ocean freight can be classified as full container load (FCL) or less than full container load (LCL). This distinction is similar to the full truckload and less than full truckload.

Expedited Freight

This kind of freight transportation is when the different types of freight are transported at incredibly high speeds. This is when there is an incredibly urgent need to deliver the freight at a specific time or day.

As a freight broker, you will be dealing most often with either full truckload or less than full truckload freight. However, depending on the size of your freight brokerage, and depending on where your shipping company's products are coming from, you may need to use or interact with other kinds of freight.

Marketing And Other General Business Start-Up Tips

E ven with all of the information we've given so far about starting your own freight broker business, we have yet to provide you with some general business. Although the freight broker business is specialized, it is still a business. This means that it can benefit from some general business start-up suggestions.

While there is a variety of advice out there, we've narrowed it to 5 key points that will deliver you to success.

Narrow your Market Focus

One of the problems that individuals who are wanting to start businesses face, is that they want to do too much. We touched on it in the previous chapter that you want to start out slow before you widen your next two clients. The same philosophy goes for your business in general. Larger and more established freight broker companies do more than just broker freight. That is to say, they can actually have motor carriers under their broker name, they may even ship the cargo or store it themselves.

In doing so these larger companies have a wider net of their client base and market. They can be used as a shipper, as a motor carrier, or as a freight broker. However, this is an ideal and future vision. For business start-ups, especially for freight broker business startups, you will want to narrow your market to one thing.

Be a freight broker for small shipping companies. Then you can expand after you've been established if you want to. By narrowing your market you will find it easier to market and advertise your business and get organized as a start-up. Then, depending on your success and interest, you can expand to a wider market or stay with this more narrow clientele.

Think About Your Future and Plan Accordingly

A business startup is never going to look like an established business. What's more, is that your business startup will likely not look like your ideal business. This is because an established business doesn't look like a business startup. An established business has structure, routine, consistent revenue, and profit, among many other factors. Alternatively, a startup, as the name would suggest, is the starting of a more successful business.

However, you have to keep your future business vision in mind for your startup. Think of your startup business as a sort of hint end first step to what your business could be. Then let that vision guide you.

For example, if you want a freight broker business that also handles the cargo and works as a motor carrier, then your startup will look different than someone who just wants to be afraid for their business. For instance, a freight broker business that eventually wants to become larger and deal with exports out of its own country will be networking differently than a freight broker business that wants to stay within its own state.

You have to think about what you want in the future and plan accordingly to bring it about.

Understand the Money

At its most basic, money is easy to understand. To be a successful business you have to make more money than you spend. However, when starting a business your finances can be a little complicated.

For instance, starting a business requires a large amount of capital and investment before you can start making money. You have to buy materials and supplies; not to mention having to potentially pay employees. This initial funding of your company can be done through a variety of financial loans. What makes money complicated in this first phase of a business startup is that you have to balance making a profit with paying off these loans. It is highly suggested that you don't use all of your profits to pay off your loans, because then you will have no money to spend on further expenses or to pay yourself and your employees.

To make matters more difficult, many businesses opted to invest in the stock market or in other businesses to help make their profits earn more money. As a result, you are at the mercy of the ever-fluctuating stock market. Alternatively, you have to keep your investors happy and make sure that they are receiving their dividends appropriately.

Essentially all of this is to say that you have to understand where your money is going, what your money is being spent on, where your money is coming from, and ensure that your payment and expenses schedule line up with each other so as to always be able to pay off any bill.

Not understanding money is one of the largest end critical mistakes any small business can make in the start-up phase.

Use Every Moment

Perhaps the biggest piece of advice that goes unshared when it comes to business startups is that you should learn to use every moment to your advantage. By this, we do not mean to be working 24 hours a day 7 days a week. You do not have to use every moment to work for your business. Rather it's to make sure that every moment is being used productively.

Make sure that during work times you get as much done as possible. However, at the same time, it's important that you use scheduled breaks to give yourself that time to pause and rest in order to maintain motivation towards your business goal.

There are a number of different ways that you can "use every moment". You can create a to-do list every day that includes all items that will help improve your business. You can also do a daily routine to make sure that everything that needs to get done is getting done.

When you're creating your business every moment matters. You cannot afford to let opportunities and time pass you by. Make sure that you are being productive whenever you can, while at the same time using the moments given to you for rest and recovery to make sure that you stay motivated to your goal.

Learn How To Solve Problems

Critical thinking and problem-solving skills are abilities that will benefit you in nearly every area of your life. However, when you are building a business and a start-up, learning how to solve the problems is one way to set yourself up for success.

Be sure you have methods in place to help you solve the different issues that can arise. During the planning stages of your business, you should familiarize yourself with some of the common issues that are specifically related to your field.

As a result, you will be able to better prepare for them before they happen. For example an individual opening a restaurant will want to familiarize themselves with issues surrounding food safety, quality, and cleanliness of the kitchen. It is out of these three areas that most problems stem from during restaurant service and serving food to clients.

For your freight broker business, You should familiarize yourself with some common problems of the shipping industry. For example what causes late shipment, what causes delays, and what causes customer satisfaction. All of these potential issues can be solved before they even happen by the implementation of fail-safe procedures.

Another key to success is marketing. To get your name out there you need to market and advertise your business to not only reach the masses but to show them that you are the company they need. There are a variety of different marketing methods, just as there is a variety of marketing tips and tricks. What we've done for you is collected the most useful marketing suggestions for different categories.

Category #1: Marketing Advice Through Marketing Strategies

The first category is marketing strategies. Currently, there are two marketing strategies that are proving to be incredibly successful; social responsibility and inbound marketing.

Social Responsibility

Social responsibility is the idea that a company takes up important issues and social problems. Usually, businesses have a larger platform to speak from to bring attention to problems in our world and society.

Lately, thanks to a general shift toward a critical social consciousness, a brand and company's social responsibility plays an important factor in getting their company noticed. This is because people tend to favor companies that take up and try to resolve a social issue.

If you market your company to stand behind a special problem your marketing can reach more people and increase your clientele. Of course, don't let your social responsibility take over your business—rather allow it to add to your identity as a business.

Inbound Marketing

Inbound marketing is the strategy where you gear your message towards your specific clientele. This differs from the conventional method of marketing where you force your general message down the throats of all consumers.

Inbound marketing takes a little bit more work but yields much greater results. The work mentioned involves tailoring your message toward your clients; this means you have to know what your client wants. It also involves reaching your client in a method and manner they are already familiar with. If your ideal client has a large social media presence then you should make advertisements for different social media platforms.

Although, inbound marketing is more work you will not be wasting your time advertising to clients that will never need or want your services.

Category #2: Advice from Modern Day Marketing Experts

Other than employing presently popular marketing strategies, you can also look at what other marketing experts of our day are suggesting.

Delightful Products and Smart Marketing

The first thing you need, according to marketing experts, is a product that is actually useful and valuable to people. If your product does not actually add any value to the lives of your clients, you're going to have a harder time not only selling it but coming up with an effective marketing campaign.

Once you have a delightful product, all you need is smart marketing. Contrary to traditional beliefs, effective marketing and advertisement is not a campaign that bombards your client. Your advertisements don't have to reach every single person, they just have to be effective to the people they do reach.

Therefore in order to be successful in marketing, you need to have a good product and a smart marketing campaign.

Turn Your Brand Into a Spectacle

What you want to sell, when you're selling in advertising your product, is not necessarily the product itself, but the experience the product will give the client. For example, when you are advertising for a shoe, you don't strictly talk about the shoe itself. Instead, you will talk about how this shoe is going to change the lives of your client.

When it comes to your freight broker business, you don't necessarily want to simply list the services you offer, how fast you are at shipping goods, or how much cheaper you are than your competition.

Instead, you're going to want to focus on the experience your customer will have while using you as a freight broker. Will their shipping needs be met unquestionably? Will their shipping experience be free from stress?

Focussing on the spectacle or the experience that your product is going to give your client, will make your marketing campaign more effective.

Know the Customer is Smart

One thing you have to remember when you are setting up a marketing campaign for your business is that your customer is smart, and you must treat them as such.

Consumers know when they are being talked down to and belittled by an advertisement. Understanding your client and what they need, can help you to make sure that your message is coming across clearly, and not in a patronizing way.

Don't waste your client's time by sharing information that they either already know, or that they do not need to know in the advertisement. For example, you don't have to detail every single use or purpose of a freight broker. Most of those people who are in need of a freight broker know what it is. Focus instead on how your freight brokerage is different and better than the others.

Focus on The Results and What Works

In our world, there is a lot of focus placed on what doesn't work and the negative. This is a general observation of all of our society in general. However, in focussing on what doesn't work and on the negative, you can become unmotivated.

For instance, if you create a marketing campaign with three different advertising styles, and two of them fail you may think that the marketing campaign was a failure itself. That isn't necessarily the case. Instead, focus on the one marketing and advertising style that didn't fail. Examine what was good about it and try to replicate those results through another marketing campaign that is based upon it.

By focusing on the results and focusing on what works, you will find that your marketing campaigns are yielding more positive results.

Category #3: Advice for Small Businesses

Not every marketing strategy and piece of advice work for every kind of business. In fact, there are specific pieces of marketing advice that are meant to help small businesses—like freight broker start-ups—thrive.

Work With Influencers

Influencers are individuals on social media platforms that have become famous due to their lifestyles. Many companies, especially small startups, are starting to partner and work with these influencers to help get their name out and further their reach.

Working with influencers is arguably rather easy. You need only to find one that complements your product, reach out to them and offer them as a deal. It could be that the influence receives some sort of dividend or commission when they advertise our product, or that they can use your product to help get them more followers. No matter the contract or agreement you create, partnering with an influencer is usually a sort of given take agreement.

For freight brokerages, you may work with influencers and social media personas that focus on marketing or shipping goods. You can even partner with influencers that have their own merchandise: and offer to freight their goods for them in exchange for advertising about your freight brokerage.

Focus on Getting Attention

There is an incredible amount of external stimuli coming at us from every direction at every moment in the day. What's important for marketing and advertisements in our modern-day is that it captures our attention.

Capturing the attention of your customer doesn't have to include flashing lights or colors. Focus on providing an advertising experience that is different than anything else that's out there.

Don't Fight Virality or Trends

However, you also don't want to be too different. Structuring some of your advertisements to parallel and mirror some of the trends found in marketing, can help your company thrive as it provides a familiar image to your consumer.

Using a specific filter, or specific audio clip to back your advertisement can relate to your consumer in a way that makes them feel comfortable with your product.

You don't necessarily want to do the same thing as everyone else, but you shouldn't fight being viral or some of the trends on social media simply for the sake of being unique. Trends happen for a reason, and they reach millions of people. So if you find that one of your advertisements fits well with the current advertising trends, feel free to use it!

Category #4: Classic Marketing Advice

In addition to making sure that your marketing strategies are current with the times, and fit the small business structure, you can always lean on classic marketing advice. These pieces of advice are timeless and have proven to be effective no matter the marketing strategy, business structure, or current trend.

Make Magical Memories

What's going to help sell your product is the memory that you give your client after they use it. If they remember your product being difficult to use, I made them feel bad while using it, then you will likely not have a repeat customer. However, if your product helps them, makes them feel good about themselves, and overall adds value to their life, then you will likely have a loyal client base.

These so-called magical memories begin with your advertising. If your advertising and marketing strategies make the clients feel positive in some way, then they will likely look favorably on your product and use your product. Or at the very least be willing to suggest and recommend your product to other people. For example, if your commercial makes them laugh, or smile, then they will most likely have the same opinion about your product initially.

In sum, you want to do your best to create magical and positive memories surrounding your product at every turn. This begins with your marketing campaign.

Anticipate The Needs

When it comes to marketing and advertising, your customer and client, and their needs, is really all that matters. Although feeling a current need is important, what is most important is anticipating a future need.

If you solve a problem that your clients don't even know they're going to have, it shows that you are not only knowledgeable about your area of business, but that you care about your customer enough to anticipate their problems for them. It will also make your business more useful and favorable when individuals are looking for their problems to be solved.

Have Fun

There is something to say about making sure your clients know that you are taking them and your product seriously. However, this doesn't mean you need to abandon amusement, entertainment, and having fun altogether.

Showing your clients that you are not only taking your product seriously but that you can have fun with your product shows a deeper understanding and appreciation for your line of work.

Instead of simply focussing on sharing your message with your client, try to also inject some amusement into it. Add humor to your marketing. Make jokes with your customers through your marketing and advertising campaigns. In this way you are creating a sort of inside joke between yourself and your clients, further strengthening the bond between you and your customer base.

Knowing what makes a freight broker business successful specifically can help further your chances of creating an established freight brokerage. However, it's important to remember that a freight broker business is still a business. Therefore understanding general marketing techniques, and business strategies can act as supplemental information to further help you in your business goals.

Myths And Misconceptions

J ust as with many other occupations, there are some myths and misconceptions related to the job. Let's clear some of those misconceptions relating to freight broker businesses, and discuss how they apply to you as a new and budding freight broker.

Myth #1: A Freight Broker's Services is More Expensive

Many people hesitate to get into the freight broker business because I feel like there is no need for brokers. This believe comes from the fact that freight brokers are expensive and therefore shippers do not use them; therefore making the job redundant and not a good career choice.

This is a misconception of the job. Indeed freight brokers make their money by finding and pairing shippers with motor carriers and are then paid by the shippers to do so. And while the fees of hiring a freight broker can be high, it is worth it in many cases. Not only will a freight broker match a shipper and carrier, but they will also seek out ideal prices for shipments and journeys. In other words, freight brokers can help save shipping companies money and other areas.

What's more, is that freight brokers provide a service that helps the shipping companies and alleviate some of the stress of transporting goods between states and across the country. This is a service that many shipping companies opted to hire. Therefore, making the freight broker business one of the most demanded jobs.

Myth #2: Freight Brokers Are Unreliable

Unfortunately for freight brokers, there is the belief that they are unreliable. While this may have been true many years ago, the freight brokers of our present-day have become a staple in the shipping industry. Thanks in part to the many advances in technology and communication, it is much easier for freight brokers to stay on top of their shipments, and stay on time with their deliveries.

What has also helped the freight broker industry become more reliable is the increase of the freight broker surety bond to $75,000. This high cost of surety bond has made only serious freight brokers enter the business. As we have mentioned previously in the book, The surety bond is to reimburse the shipper if the freight broker defaults on their contracted agreements. This high surety bond has discouraged anyone who simply wants to make a quick buck to enter into the freight broker business.

Another development in the field of shipping that has made freight brokers more reliable is the requirement of a license. While you do not have to go through formal schooling you do have to apply for a brokerage authority and get your brokerage license. These many steps, however tedious, are not difficult and have made sure only serious freight brokers enter the business.

By starting your own freight brokerage you have the chance to further bust this mess of unreliable freight brokers and solidify the truth as a middleman who is reliable.

Myth #3: Freight Brokers Add No Value To The Shipping Experience

This again is false. The freight broker does more than simply pair a shipper with a potential carrier. They oversee the shipment from point A to point B, they plan out the route and look ahead for potential stops. They take into consideration and look into possible construction, weather patterns, or other environmental factors that can damage or interfere with the shipment.

The essential redo all of the organizational and administrative work that goes into shipping something from one state to another. This adds value to the shipping experience because it takes that responsibility and stress away from the shippers and the carriers. Therein allowing these two parties to simply focus on their job at hand. The carriers can now focus on simply getting the merchandise and commodities from point A to point B. And the shippers simply focus on creating and manufacturing their product.

Freight brokers are expert networkers and communicators. Therefore they can even lower the cost of some shipments if they have good relationships with the carriers, with the destination, or with certain stops along the way.

Freight brokers also cover carriers over a range of different modes of transportation. They deal with trucks, ships, trains, and even aircraft to carry merchandise across the country. Ultimately freight brokers add value to the shipping experience because they take over much of the administrative burden that goes with moving commodities and maintaining a strong supply and demand chain.

Myth #4: Freight Brokers Take the Cheapest Path And Do Not Care About Quality

On the contrary, freight brokers are quite selective with the carriers they deal with. Their job first and foremost is to pair the appropriate carrier with the appropriate shipper. If they do not make the correct match then their job is not being done properly.

In this way, free brokers are obliged and made to care about the quality of carrier they use. But they also have a financial reason to care as well. While the freight broker is focused on saving the shipping company money, this does not mean that they will use the cheapest and fastest way of delivering the product. They want the goods to be delivered safely because if the goods are damaged they are the ones that are at fault and have to deal with the repercussions. Not the shipping company.

Therefore free brokers have to carefully walk the line between choosing an incredibly expensive carrier and a cheap carrier while taking into consideration the safety of the merchandise, the length of the journey, and any perceived obstacles that can make the journey difficult such as weather or construction.

Therefore you, as a freight broker should not have cost and saving money for the shipping company at the forefront of your mind. What you should focus on is making sure you choose the right carrier and the right shipping experience for the company. After all, if you exceed the expectations of your clients they are going to be willing to pay whatever the cost. Do not cheap out on the experience. Make it worth it, for you and your client.

Myth #5: Freight Brokers Who Do Not Own Their Own Trucks Are A Waste of Time

There is a common misconception that freight brokers who do not own their own trucks to fulfill the shipping requirements are a waste of time. This is of course false. The primary job of the freight broker is to pair the shipper with the motor carrier or other sort of carrier. There is no necessity for the freight broker to own trucks of their own and carry out the shipment themselves.

Indeed some of the larger freight broker businesses do own fleets of trucks or other carriers. There is a benefit in owning your own fleet because you will be earning more money; you will not need to pay a carrier to fulfill the shipment, you can do it yourself. But again it is not a necessity. In fact, if you are just starting out as a freight broker it is highly suggested that you stick with the primary job of the freight broker and not expand into the trucking or carrier markets.

Freight brokers that do not own their own fleet are known as non-asset freight brokers because they do not own any assets. But these non-asset freight brokers have value just as asset freight brokers do. Non-asset freight brokers are usually less expensive to use than the alternative because they don't charge to ship the products.

For you who are just breaking into the freight broker industry do not feel pressured, or give in to the pressure, of owning your own fleet of trucks. Freight brokers who own trucks are usually much larger in size and have more employees they are responsible for and require more licenses and higher insurance coverage. It can be a goal for you later on, but if you are just starting out being a non-asset freight broker is ideal. Don't forget you will still be forging and cultivating relationships with carriers. If these relationships are nurtured then you may even be able to enter into a partnership with a specific carrier. When you are just starting out, start small.

Myth # 6: Freight Brokers Are The Same Thing as Freight Forwarders and Freight Broker Agents

As we have mentioned multiple times throughout this book, freight brokers are not the same as freight forwarders or freight broker agents. The job of the freight broker is to create a matching or a link between the shipping client and the carrier that moves the merchandise. The broker never actually handles or comes into possession of the merchandise itself. That is the job of the freight forwarder. The forwarder is actually given and entrusted with the merchandise. Lastly, freight broker agents work in a similar way to freight brokers but do not have the same sort of standing, responsibilities, or licenses that freight brokers do. They were under and assisted the freight brokers.

Myth #7: You Can Learn Everything You Need to Know About How To Be A Freight Broker Online

This myth is an interesting one because it is technically and partially true, and there are a few different ways to begin tackling this myth. Bear with us while we tackle it in a sort of roundabout way.

First, there is no formal or necessary schooling required to be a freight broker. However, there are online certifications to help better prepare you for the job instead of making you simply jump in without any preparation at all. These courses can be found and completed online; In fact, many of them are online. Stop being said depending on your region there may be some freight broker preparation courses taught at your local community center. These in-person sessions allow for a little bit more hands-on experience. In this way yes everything you need to know can be found online; through this lens the myth is correct.

But here is where the myth is false. Like with any job, experience is what truly helps you learn and understand the position in the industry. Contents and information you learned through a course is really only the theory of that job; to really understand and know any job real-life experience is the way to go. Therefore, while you can learn all the theories you need to know online, in order to learn everything you need to know you should enter into the industry end work. We suggest finding an apprenticeship or a low-level job in the shipping and trucking industry. In doing so you will learn about certain things that you could never learn online and through a course.

Lastly, what makes this myth false is the use of the word "everything." To claim that you can learn everything about the freight broker business online is a misconception. The freight broker business, alongside the shipping and trucking industries, and the trade market in general, continuously change. Therefore it is fair to say that you will never be able to learn everything about the business. All you can do is continue to learn as you go.

Therefore to debunk this myth simply, yes you can learn enough about the freight broker business online for you to begin your business. But that information is not enough for you to become a successful freight broker.

Myth #8: The Only Way To Become a Freight Broker and Get A License Is To Pay $75,000 Up Front

While there are some high costs associated with becoming a freight broker, there is nothing that says you have to pay the total amounts upfront. In fact, many companies offer emerging freight brokers lines of credit or payment options in order to receive the full amount.

When the $75,000 surety bond is concerned there are two different options that you can choose from so as to not have to pay the total amount. Of course, you can pay the $75,000 upfront or through a line of credit. The other option is to file a BMC-84. This is an agreement where you pay a premium that's $75,000. This premium is a portion or a fraction of this larger amount. The amount is based on the finances of both you as an individual and your business. This way in paying this monthly premium you will slowly reach this $75,000 bond and financial necessity without having to pay the lump sum.

Myth # 9: You Cannot Be A Freight Broker Or Get Bonded As Such If You Have Bad Credit

In fact, having bad credit does not necessarily affect your ability to become a freight broker as much as you may think. Depending on the reason as to why you have bad credit, the bond will still be granted. It may simply change how you pay for the bond. For example, if you choose the method of payment where you pay a monthly premium, your monthly premium may be a little bit higher.

What's important to remember is that it is incredibly rare for anyone to be denied outright. A denial or rejection will always be followed with a list of ways that you can actually be accepted. For example, getting a cosigner, taking time to improve your credit, offering to pay more money, or putting up an asset as collateral, are all ways that you can help yourself get bonded. These messages usually take time and more effort on your part, but they are worth it if becoming a freight broker is your goal.

Myth #10: You Do Not Need A License To Become A Freight Broker

Although you do not need any formal schooling or training to become a freight broker, you do need a license. The license is called property broker registration. And it has to be applied for through the Federal Motor Carrier Safety Association. Again the FMCSA Is a division of the United States transportation department.

Without this license, and the necessary registration, bonds, and paperwork, you cannot be a legal freight broker.

Myth # 11: Freight Brokers Take Possession of the Commodities They Help to Ship

This myth stems from a misconception and a misunderstanding of what a freight broker does. Again the primary job and role of the freight broker is to pair a shipping company with the carrier and organize the shipping route. A lot of this work is administrative. As a result, most freight brokers are never actually in the same room as the merchandise or products themselves. In fact, freight brokers don't even have to be in the same state as the shipping company or even look at the cargo.

That being said, this does not mean that freight brokers are not allowed to hold on to the cargo. Depending on the services you offer you may be offered to hold onto the merchandise and loaded onto the carrier. Or in the case of asset-based brokers—those freight brokers that own their own trucks and carriers—the cargo is usually in the possession of the freight broker for a short amount of time.

But even with all of these different scenarios, it is not common practice for a freight broker to hold on to the merchandise or product at all. The freight broker does not take, become owner of, or possess the cargo. The job is primarily organizational.

Myth #12: If You File Your Authority With An Expert Or Company It Will Be Faster

When you file for your authority there is a 21-day waiting period from the day Federal Motor Carrier Safety Administration received your application to when you are either granted or denied authority. This 21-day waiting period is meant as a vetting period. This means that within these 21 days the FMCSA will look into your application and will look over your surety bond registration, your process agent requirements, and a number of other areas to ensure that you are qualified and properly licensed to work as a freight broker.

Hiring the services of an expert or a company to help you file your authority, and your other necessary requirements does not speed up this 21-day waiting. It can ease the process for you and make the act of filling out the applications less stressful, but it does not make the process faster.

Myth # 13: There Are Different Types And Levels Of Freight Broker Certification

There are different levels of jobs within the realm of freight brokerage, but there is only one level of a freight broker. The official and formal name for a freight broker is a property broker. As a property broker, you need to be registered, have your authority, have your process agents, and have your surety bond. Individuals may think that completing courses that offer certificates make you a higher-level freight broker. This is incorrect. As we've said multiple times there is no school needed. All you need is your license—and the following necessary paperwork.

Don't let anyone tell you that because you didn't take a specific course you are not a high-level freight broker. As long as you have followed the steps we've given to you in the book, and you will follow them successfully and legally, you are a freight broker. The only way to set yourself apart in value is to be the best freight broker and have the best freight broker business you can. Focus on customer satisfaction, and doing a good job, instead of certifications. They can help but they do not add actual and measurable value.

Frequently Asked Questions

W e have covered quite a bit of information in this book so far. Perhaps too much. What we have decided to do with this last chapter is summarize the information—and add to it—by way of some frequently asked questions about the freight broker business. Hopefully, these questions will help you answer some of your remaining questions and summarize some of the information we have already covered.

Question #1: What is a Freight Broker?

Answer: A freight broker is a sort of middleman when it comes to the world of shipping and goods distribution. The shipper hires and pays the freight broker to organize and set up the shipment of their goods. Following the freight broker hires and pays the carrier to carry out their shipment plan. The freight broker keeps a specific and agreed-upon portion of their payment from the shipper; that is their profit.

Legally speaking a freight broker is a kind of property broker. A property broker is an umbrella term used to describe any sort of broker or agent in the world of shipping and goods distribution. In terms of the Federal Motor Carrier Safety Administration, a property broker—and through consequence, a freight broker—is a licensed person or company that eases the shipping process.

The freight broker organizes routes, plans stops, schedules shipment in transportation, in addition to hiring in choosing different carriers to carry the goods. Freight brokers can also double as a loading dock where the shipments are actually loaded at their freight brokerage office and sent out from there.

Question #2: What Is the Difference Between a Freight Broker and a Freight Broker Agent?

Answer: A freight broker differs from a freight broker agent first and foremost because the freight broker owns their own business. A freight broker agent, on the other hand, works under the broker.

The freight broker is required by law to meet specific standards and requirements in order to run their business. These requirements include authority and insurance, surety bonds, etc. The broker is the one that assumes all responsibilities for any legal or financial business the brokerage does. They must follow the guidelines as set by the FMCSA for how to conduct their business and ship their cargo.

A freight broker agent is an independent contractor that works on commission. They usually work with a freight broker.

Question #3: Are Freight Brokers a Needed Position in the Industry?

Answer: Agricultural and manufacturing industries all over the world, but specifically in the United States, are growing at an alarming rate each and every year. This in turn creates a large demand for goods to be sent all around the world. In fact, experts guess that there are nearly 1 million shipping companies. This means that there are 1 million different companies that want their goods to be shipped nationwide. In order to organize all of these shipments, freight brokers are needed. About 30% of all shipped goods are transported using third-party freight brokerages. And 30% of 1 million is still quite a bit. The goal of a shipping company is to get their product around the world. And they have other things to worry about than the shipping details. This is why the need for freight brokerages is so high.

Question #4: How Can I Find the Carriers and Shippers for My Business?

Answer: You can find carriers and shippers in a variety of areas. There are actually industry databases that many freight brokerages use that list a number of different shippers and carriers nationwide. These databases usually charge a membership fee or purchase fee to use. However, the help they provide is priceless and can really help you jumpstart your freight brokerage.

Another way of finding carriers and shippers is forming co-broker agreements with other freight brokerages. This is when you partner with other firms to share clients and resources. This can help you with your business because if your partner freight broker is overloaded with work then they will send you the work that they cannot do, and vice versa.

You can also attend conferences and legislative sessions about the shipping industry. There you can network with shipping companies, legal representatives, and other important individuals in the shipping world that can help bring in more clients for you.

However, be prepared to be trying to contact shipping companies quite often. In fact, this will be your primary job in the business.

Question #5: How Much Money Will I Make as a Freight Broker?

Answer: Generally speaking, the income you make as a freight broker will be based on the amount of work you get. As you will be paid on a case-to-case—or shipment-to-shipment—basis, the more work you get the more money you will make. If you are determined to succeed and make your freight brokerage one of the best then you can make quite a large profit annually.

As a dedicated full-time freight broker, you can easily make $50,000 annually as a minimum. In fact, many freight brokers have said that they make well over six figures, and well into the hundreds of thousands of dollars every year. Some well-known freight brokerages eventually turn into multimillion-dollar businesses. Of course, when you are just starting out it is wise to keep your income expectations realistic.

Keep in mind that although money will be streaming in as a freight broker, it is hard work and you make what you put in.

One benefit of the freight broker business is that it is recession-proof. Even in the worst of economic situations and recessions, the shipment of goods will always be necessary. Therefore as long as you take advantage of the opportunities provided to you, you can make your freight brokerage into a $100,000 a year business.

Question #6: What is a BOC-3?

Answer: A BOC-3 is another name for a process agent. A process agent is a person who represents your freight broker business in every state where you do business. They are the person who will receive any court or legal documents if legal action is necessary against your company or clients.

Question #7: How Much Does a Surety Bond Cost?

Answer: The base price for a surety bond was only $10,000 dollars. But in recent years the FMCSA has raised the minimum amount to $75,000 dollars. You may have to pay more based on the bond type you select, how large your company is, how far you ship, which insurance and bonding company you work with, etc.

Question #8: How Much Does Applying for Your Authority Cost?

Answer: The Federal Motor Carrier Safety Administration traditionally charges $300.00 to apply for your operating authority. This is the authority that covers any motor carrier—both property and passenger—freight forwarders and freight brokers. The required application is 4 pages long, but you can fill it out on paper and send it in by mail, or fill it out online and email your application. You should note that any changes to the document may also require you to pay a fee. For example, changing your name on the form will incur a $14 dollar fee.

You can also get companies to help file your authority application for you, but they will likely charge you a hefty fee. For example, Transport Training International can file your operating authority form for you but they charge $150 dollars for the service.

Question #9: What Are the Legal Requirements to Work as a Freight Broker?

Answer: While there is no school that you legally have to complete to be a freight broker, there are some requirements.

You must:

1. Apply for authority from the Federal Motor Carrier Safety Administration

2. Post a surety bond in the amount of $75,000 dollars

3. File your BOC-3—or your process agent

4. Complete annual registration for Unified Carrier

Other than that there are no legal requirements. However, there are some highly suggested requirements—that we have covered in this book—that will make you a more successful broker.

Question #10: How long is the course to become a Freight Broker?

Answer: If you do choose to complete the course to become a freight broker, you can find them online. Since there is no actual school for the job most of the courses are self-paced. This means that once you begin your course of study you can take as long as you want to complete it.

At the end of these courses, there are usually quizzes, tests, and a sort of graduation exam that provides you with a certificate of completion. But remember these courses are not mandatory to be a freight broker by the Federal Motor Carrier Safety Administration.

Question #11: Can I work from home?

Answer: Yes you can work from home as a freight broker. In fact, working from home can help you to keep your costs low when you are first starting out. All you need when first starting out is a good internet connection, reliable communication methods, and good organizational skills.

Work from home as long as you can then expand to an office when you have more capital to do so.

Question #12: How much can I earn as a Freight Broker and how soon can I start earning?

Answer: As we have mentioned above, you can make anywhere between $50,000—$100,00 dollars per year as a freight broker. And you can begin earning as soon as you get your first contract. But you will have to be patient for the first year or so. You will need to accumulate more clients to make a steady income.

Question #13: Can I apply for a Freight Brokers License if I have a felony on my record?

Answer: Yes you can. Having a felony on your record does not automatically disqualify you from getting a freight broker license or getting approved for all of your registrations. You need to be a valid resident and citizen of the country that you want to work in. Also, it is wise to disclose any felonies on your registration forms when asked. Not filling out your forms properly can lead to more issues than actually having a felony on your record will cause.

Question #14: Is Freight Broker Training School required?

Answer: Freight Broker Training School is not required to become a freight broker; in fact, a formal freight broker training school doesn't actually exist. To receive your broker authority all you need is properly fill out your forms and pay the fee.

That being said, the failure is high among freight brokers who have zero knowledge, training, or experience in the industry. This means that although formal freight broker school does not exist you should still seek out some training or working experiences that can help give you an inside perspective of the shipping and freight broker industry.

If you are having trouble finding some courses and work placements, you can look into transport training services.

In short, freight broker school is not required but some sort of training is highly—*highly*—recommended.

Question #15: Is there a way to get into the Freight Broker industry without having to get a bond and license?

Answer: Yes you can, although you will not be a freight broker. Instead, you will be a freight broker agent. You will not have the same responsibilities or the same legal requirements as a freight broker.

Your job will be to work with and assist a freight broker. You will likely not make as much money as the broker but you will be able to do much of the same work without having to register for any authorities, bonds, etc.

Question #16: What equipment will I need to get started?

Answer: To begin your business, as far as equipment goes, you really only need a computer and a high-speed internet connection. You may also want to invest in a reliable phone and a fax machine. Printer, copiers, and standard smaller office supplies are a must as well.

When you are first starting out you don't need anything else that you probably don't already have at your home already. You won't need anything that you can't buy at a reasonable price at your local office supply store.

Question #17: How long will it take for my business to become profitable?

Answer: You won't start making money until you get a contract. This means that it will take some time before you start making real money. You have to first build your customer and client base and solidify some contracts before you can start making money. Most new freight broker businesses don't start making money until six months of hard dedicated and consistent work. That being said, try to stay patient as you may not begin making money until the first year is over. But don't fret, your hard work will pay off in spades!

One way to help keep your mind off of the question "what am I going to make money" is to focus on your clients. The satisfaction of your clients and your relationship with them is what is going to make you the money. Happy clients mean consistent work, consistent work means more money.

Question #18: How do I find customers?

Answer: The best way to get customers for your freight brokerage is to begin with people you know. Being small with smaller and local shipping companies. You can also begin by offering your services to local shops that need their products shipped around the country.

You can also pay attention to the companies you see in your everyday routine that advertise that they are shipping companies and contact them. You will want to begin small to really get a handle on the business and iron out any kinks before tackling large-scale clients and shipments.

Once you get into a good groove you can ask your clients for repeat work and referrals to other clients. You can also then, once you have made a little bit of money, pay for the memberships to national databases of shipping and carrier companies whose contracts you can bid for.

Question #19: How long does the process take after applying with the FMCSA?

Answer: The Federal Motor Carrier Safety Association will activate your freight broker authority as soon as your application is approved, and you prove that you have secured your surety bond and fulfill your BOC-3 and process agent requirements.

Generally, there is a 21-day waiting period where you will be vetted and your application will be looked over. These 21-days begin when you get your US-DOT or your confirmation notice that your application was received. During this time you should set up your Surety bond and your process agents, and send those confirmations to the FMCSA.

Once you receive a business status of "active authority" then you can legally begin working as a freight broker.

Question #20: Why do you need a $75,000 Freight Broker Bond?

Answer: The Federal Motor Carrier Safety Association makes the minimum bond $75,000 because it will be enough money to act as a financial cover in case anything happens. It has increased in price because the cost of living has increased.

If you do not pay your carrier they can file against your bond and get paid that way.

Question #21: What are the benefits of using a third party to fulfill the FMCSA's surety requirement?

Answer: Third-party companies like PFA—Power of Freight Broker Authority—can help you get broker sureties. They will handle the investigation, versifications, paperwork, and other steps of the application process. Therein, lessening the stress on you and decreases the chances of your filing improperly.

While their fees can be high, their expertise can help you in ways that you perhaps did not realize.

Question #22: Do you have to pay $75,000 outright to get a Freight Broker Bond?

Answer: No. You either file a BMC-84 or a BMC-85.

BMC-84 Surety Bond – This is given out through an insurance company that specializes in surety bonds. The premium that you pay to get your bond is based on the worthiness of your credit.

BMC-85 Trust Fund Agreement – This is given out through any certified financial institution. While the FMCSA does ask that the $75,000 be paid in cash or a letter of credit, you do not have to pay for that in one invoice or payment. You can go through your financial institution. they will provide you with payment options to make it more affordable for you.

Question #23: Do I need to apply for a business loan?

Answer: You do not have to apply for a loan but you will likely have to. Unless you have enough money and capital saved up, you will need a large sum of money to help get you started. There will be costs to begin your business such as fees for registration, your bond payment, and costs for office supplies. A business loan is the best way to get started. Contact your local bank to set one up!

Question #24: Are there any other insurance products that Freight Brokers are required to obtain?

Answer: There are no additional insurance requirements other than your surety bond that you need to be a freight broker. However, it is wise to set up some other insurances just to cover your bases. You may want insurance to cover the cargo that is under your watch during the shipment; you will want insurance to cover the contracts you create with your clients. You may even want to insure some of your machines and office supplies depending on how much they cost and where you work from.

Conclusion - Freight Broker Business Startup 2023

The world economy relies on not only the concept of supply and demand, but on the industries of trade, shipping, and transportation. However, there are many moving parts when it comes to shipping goods from one place to another. The role and job of organizing these moving parts have been placed upon the freight broker.

As a result, the freight broker has become one of the most in-demand and lucrative jobs. In fact, over the past decade, the number of freight brokers working has increased exponentially. Not only can you begin being a freight broker without any lengthy education, but you can work from home and have a business with just yourself.

If being an integral part of the world's shipping and transportation industry is something that you're interested in while making a significant amount of income and working from home, then creating a freight broker business is the right choice for you. This book has given you everything you need to know to begin your business. So what are you waiting for? Begin your journey to a lucrative and successful career today.

www.ingramcontent.com/pod-product-compliance
Lightning Source LLC
Chambersburg PA
CBHW071329210326
41597CB00015B/1386